Critical Educational Psychology

Critical Educational Psychology

STEPHEN VASSALLO

American University, Washington, DC

Johns Hopkins University Press

Baltimore

Johns Hopkins University Press
2715 North Charles Street
Baltimore, Maryland 21218-4363
www.press.jhu.edu

Library of Congress Cataloging-in-Publication Data

Names: Vassallo, Stephen, 1976- author.
Title: Critical educational psychology / Stephen Vassallo.
Description: Baltimore, Maryland : Johns Hopkins University Press, [2017] | Includes
    bibliographical references and index.
Identifiers: LCCN 2016040206 | ISBN 9781421422633 (pbk. : alk. paper)
    | ISBN 9781421422640 (electronic : alk. paper) | ISBN 1421422638 (pbk. : alk. paper)
    | ISBN 1421422646 (electronic : alk. paper)
Subjects: LCSH: Educational psychology.
Classification: LCC LB1051 .V347 2017 | DDC 370.15—dc23
LC record available at https://lccn.loc.gov/2016040206

A catalog record for this book is available from the British Library.

*Special discounts are available for bulk purchases of this book. For more information,
please contact Special Sales at 410-516-6936 or specialsales@press.jhu.edu.*

*To my children, as well as
the loving memory of my sister
Debbie and my father, Charles*

CONTENTS

ACKNOWLEDGMENTS

This work would not have been possible if not for the amazing people around me. First, I would like to acknowledge the support of Tim Corcoran. He is a committed pioneer for critical educational psychology. Tim's scholarship and friendship inspire me to continue work in this field. My participation in his projects has been instrumental for developing the ideas in this book. I will always remain indebted to Jeff Sugarman. Regardless of how busy he was with family and research, Jeff was always responsive to questions and concerns about this book. I will always remain indebted to Jack Martin. I first met Jack in 2007. Since that time, he has always been supportive of my work. This book would not be possible without the friendship and camaraderie of Tim, Jeff, and Jack. They have paved the way for me to situate educational psychology in power, politics, ideology, and culture. I am truly standing on the shoulders of these amazing intellectuals. Much of how I frame, approach, and conduct analysis can be attributed to Lynn Fendler, a brilliant philosopher and researcher whose impact on me has been enduring. Her scholarship was instrumental for building critical arguments within psychology. I would also like to thank Greg Goodman. Greg believed in me early in my career and provided me with the momentum and inspiration to bring critical perspectives to educational psychology. Greg is a great friend and mentor.

I would like to thank the editorial team at Johns Hopkins University Press. I want to thank Greg Britton for believing in this book and patiently waiting for the manuscript. Greg saw the importance of this book, giving me the motivation to complete it. Catherine Goldstead was patient, supportive, and responded rapidly to my inquiries. I want to thank the entire editorial team who put great effort into the aesthetic and conceptual quality of the book. Among this team was David Coen, who took great care in providing editorial suggestions.

There are many people to thank from American University. Stacey Snelling was instrumental for helping me maintain the right balance between service, teaching, and scholarship in order to complete this project. Sarah Irvine

Belson was always in my corner, ensuring that I stayed the course. She strongly supports my scholarship and is a dear friend and an amazing colleague. My department comprises a diverse group of thoughtful colleagues. Many formal and informal conversations with them helped me develop and evaluate the arguments in this book. Although each of my colleagues has been influential in his or her own ways, and I am grateful for all their support, I would like to give particular acknowledgment to Vivian Vasquez, Jennifer Steele, Lauren McGrath, Charlie Tesconi, and Marilyn Goldhammer. Charlie read parts of the book and always had his door open for me to share my thinking with him. He carefully considered the broad goal of the book as well as what I was trying to do in each chapter in order to give suggestions to make the book better. (Of course, any shortcomings in the work are my own.) I did not always agree with Jennifer, Lauren, and Marilyn, but our conversations helped me articulate and account for various dimensions of numerous controversies. Vivian has always been a strong supporter of my work. This book would not have been possible if not for the support of Peter Star and Scott Bass, who work hard to help faculty balance university responsibilities. They make it possible for faculty to develop their scholarship without compromising teaching and service.

The graduate and undergraduate students I worked with at American University were amazing. My students thoughtfully engaged with many of the ideas in this book. Integrating the underpinnings of this book into my classes was instrumental for developing the arguments. I am grateful that students were passionate about this work and were eager to understand and engage with them. Aside from those in my classes, my student research assistants worked hard on this book. I want to give a special thanks to Kimberly Oden, Kirsten Hagen, and Rebekah Frank. Kimberly had incredible passion for the work and conducted research that helped me to develop my arguments. Kirsten focused on the grunt work of the book. Rebekah, with her editorial prowess and her knowledge of educational debates, was an amazing resource.

This book would not have been possible without the support of family and friends. I want to first thank my wife, Frances, who encouraged me to persist when I was deflated, to write when I was tired, and to believe in the book when my confidence was shaken. My children, Anthony and Lily, are always in my corner and always bring a smile to my face after a long, exhausting day of writing. Their love was and continues to be inspirational. During one of the last round of edits, Lily, who at that time was seven years old, listened to me as I read parts of the book aloud to her, in exchange that I listen to her short story. Anthony has grown up to be an amazing person;

this inspires me everyday. I want to give special thanks to Brian Smith, who although he had little background in my field, read parts of the book and provided thoughtful conceptual and editorial feedback. I want to give special thanks to Mike Baker and his wife Elizabeth. Their enduring and deep friendship enabled me to get through the many challenges of writing this book. In addition, Mike was always eager and willing to talk about various parts of the book. He was always there to offer a laugh or workout to help unwind from a day of writing. Although she herself has five children, all of whom always checked on my book progress, Elizabeth frequently watched my children so I could spend more time on the book. Although my parents and siblings live a couple of hundred miles away, their love and support for my work are resounding. Thank you to my mother and to my father, who passed away during the time I was writing the book. The pride my mother shows in my work is a strong motivational force. Thank you to my siblings Vicky, Charlie, Billy, and Eddie. I want to thank my aunt Sara. I also want to thank all my nieces and nephews. Having a truly strong family foundation has made this work and anything I do possible.

Critical Educational Psychology

Introduction

DEFINING WHAT TEACHERS need to be, do, and know in order to teach well has been and continues to be the subject of debate. Some researchers and policy makers emphasize the mastery of content knowledge, while others point to the importance of teachers' embodying certain character traits, such as care, empathy, leadership, and respectfulness (Noddings, 2006; Bondy, Ross, Gallingane, & Hambacher, 2007). Others emphasize the importance of pedagogical knowledge, which involves both knowing how to present information and structure classrooms in order to produce the desired learning outcome (Ball, Thames, & Phelps, 2008). Critical theorists tend to emphasize the need for teachers to understand the politics and ideology of schooling in order to mediate policy mandates for the pursuit of social justice (Giroux & McLaren, 1986; McLaren & Farahmandpur, 2001; Smyth, 2001). Although all these characteristics are not necessarily incompatible, conversations persist about the required knowledge and qualities for good teaching.

For several decades, educational psychology, or the study of human learning, thinking, and behavior in formal and informal educational contexts, has also been part of this conversation. Although it was not always historically the case, knowledge of psychology has become a key feature of a teacher's knowledge (Woolfolk-Hoy, 2000; Emmer & Stough, 2001). The field of educational psychology comprises a broad range of populations and topics. Research and theory include studies of learning and development across the life span in a number of settings, including home, work, and school. Although broad in scope, scholarship tends to center on areas associated with students' learning and development in pre-K through 12 settings. The topics that are typically studied in these contexts include:

classroom management, higher order thinking, human development, assessment, intelligence, identity, memory, cognitive processes, and motivation.

In formal school settings, educational psychologists endeavor to map students' psychology, connect their psychology to achievement outcomes, and explain the conditions under which students act. They are committed to (1) understanding mental and behavioral phenomena, (2) establishing a scientific basis for claims, (3) producing generalizable principles, and (4) predicting and controlling thoughts and behaviors. The assumption is that knowing how students think, what they are likely to do under certain conditions, and how and why they respond in the ways they do are necessary for teaching well (Smith, 2013). The belief is that if teachers are equipped with educational psychology knowledge, they will have the tools to deliberate over how to shape their interactions with students and alter classrooms to produce an intended effect: achieving curricular goals while fostering student well-being. For this reason, educational psychology tends to be treated as indispensable and invaluable for teaching.

Educational psychology is a relatively modern construction; it has been formed only over the past two centuries. Both the formation of psychology as a science, and the acceptance that education could be studied scientifically were significant for the formation and relevance of the field (Berliner, 1993). Educational psychology is informed by general psychology and its subfields, such as developmental psychology, social psychology, and cognitive psychology. Other disciplinary infusions include evolution, philosophy, sociology, anthropology, and biology. Given this interdisciplinary nature, the field of educational psychology is replete with philosophical, ethical, conceptual, and methodological debates. It is also far from monolithic, incorporating competing theories and ideas, academic factions, and ideological battles related to what it means to know, assumptions about persons, theories of learning, and models for teaching.

Educational Psychology's Value for Teaching

Although the field is diverse, educational psychology tends to be represented to teachers in neatly packaged theories, models, and perspectives, which are intended to bring some basis and certainty to pedagogical decision-making. Teachers are promised that if they know and apply certain educational psychology ideas then they can create desirable effects within their classrooms. Educational psychologists, policy makers, and researchers have all agreed that teaching effectively requires knowledge of educational psychology. For this reason, teacher preparation programs (both university-based and alternative) have educational psychology components. Policy documents about teacher quality and professional development seminars often draw heavily on research from educational psychology (e.g., see Council of Chief State School Officers [CCSSO], 2011; and National Board of Professional Teaching Standards [NBPTS], 2012). Furthermore, teachers must demonstrate knowledge of foundational theorists, perspectives, and theories for their certification examinations and advanced certification (see NBPTS, 2012). Even the five-week summer institute for Teach for America includes educational psychology content.

Still, when it is not formally present in preparation programs, policy, or pedagogical decision making, educational psychology is present in everyday reasoning and practices that involve (1) evaluations of students' self-esteem, confidence, and emotions; (2) administration of reinforcement and punishment; (3) reflections on motivation; (4) evaluations of intelligence; and (5) assessments and measurements of learning. Hardcastle (1998) argued that even the most mundane observations and assessments of students are grounded in some type of psychological theory. Therefore, psychological tools, instruments, and concepts are used to interpret the meaning of behaviors, verbal language, performance indicators, and body language in everyday interactions in the classroom.

Although ensconced in teacher education, educational psychology was not always accepted as a foundation to teaching (Berliner, 1993; Woolfolk-Hoy, 2000). From its inception to contemporary debates, theorists have questioned the value, use, and efficacy of educational psychology for teaching (Berliner, 1993; Gallagher, 2003; Fendler, 2013). In response, educational psychologists have worked to align with the gold standards of science in order to demonstrate the field's legitimacy (Berliner, 1993; Fendler, 2013). The goal was to create generalizable models, theories, and practices that can be applied in any situation to produce a particular effect. The achievement of this alignment no doubt will increase the field's legitimacy in a climate that lauds the value of scientifically and evidence-based practice (Fendler, 2013). And the more that is learned from scientific analyses in educational psychology, the more such knowledge will contribute to teachers' efficacy and efficiency for achieving classroom goals.

Educational psychology's place in teaching is part of a larger contemporary cultural trend to turn to psychology to solve problems, address challenges, and manage troublesome situations (Rose, 1999; Martin & McLellan, 2013; Smeyers & Depaepe, 2013). This willingness is informed by the perception that psychology is a science, not unlike the physical sciences, that can be used to prevent and solve problems by changing people in some way. This can be done either through preemptive interventions or the reformation of those who are problems to institutional orders. Schools are often conceptualized as in a state of crisis, such as lagging international testing comparisons, disparities in achievement across populations within the United States, and challenges with preparing individuals for a twenty-first-century economy. The cultural impetus to turn to psychology to improve schooling outcomes and address a wide range of social, economic, and global problems is understandable.

A Critical Pause

Although it is assumed to be a necessary component of a teacher's knowledge base, some critical theorists have raised concerns about the value of educational psychology (Fendler, 2013; Martin & McLellan, 2013; Smeyers & Depaepe, 2013; Corcoran, 2014). These concerns have led to an outright rejection of the field to a need for rethinking its foundational commitments. On one end of the spectrum, Fendler (2013) has argued that there is no scientific basis for concluding that teachers need educational psychology in order to teach well. She suggests that teachers might better serve their students with studies in communication and culture. Fendler's resistance is grounded in critiques that psychology in general can be normalizing, pathologizing, unscientific, ideologically informed, and used as an instrument of institutional power. Although not as dismissive, other researchers and theorists are critical of the field. While they do not question the place of educational psychology in teaching and teacher preparation, they have expressed concern about the limitations and dangers of dominant concepts, views, theories, and methods (Billington, 2014; Claiborne, 2014; Corcoran, 2014; Goodman, 2014; Martin, 2014; Sugarman, 2014; Vassallo, 2014).

A major assumption underpinning educational psychology is that the discourse is neutral, value-free, ahistorical, and disassociated from politics and culture. However, a small group of researchers and theorists are committed to illustrating the contrary. They have worked diligently to show that certain ways of thinking about and applying psychology in the classroom can produce unintended consequences, endorse a particular ideology, align with a particular brand of politics, and propagate dominant cultural norms. Those who engage in this work can be categorized as critical educational psychologists. They are dedicated to advancing a critical educational psychology (CEP) perspective by examining widely accepted ideas, concepts, beliefs, and methods in educational psychology through different perspectives in order to consider ways that the field's discourse is implicated in politics, ideology, culture, governance, and institutional power.

CEP is about telling different narratives about the discourse that is used to construct and constitute students' psychological lives. These narratives (1) involve analyses of how psychological tools, concepts, models, and principles came to be; (2) ask why certain knowledge is accepted as truth; and (3) address the consequences of applying certain kinds of psychological knowledge. The narratives involve illuminating the conceptual insecurities, ideological battles, cultural contexts, political purposes, and academic alliances that surround the emergence, acceptance, and prevalence of educational psychology knowledge. CEP is critique from within that is not necessarily intended to endorse the abandonment of, rejection of, or resistance to educational psychology. Rather, for CEP, critique is about illuminating ethical, historical, and ideological dimensions of well-known and pervasive educational psychology ideas, concepts, and imperatives.

This critical orientation is informed by Foucault, who stated, "A critique is not a matter of saying that things are not right as they are. It is a matter of pointing out on what kinds of assumptions, what kinds of familiar, unchallenged, unconsidered modes of thought the practices that we accept rest. Criticism is a matter of flushing out that thought and trying to change it: to show that things are not as self-evident as one believed, to see that what is accepted as self-evident will no longer be accepted as such. Practicing criticism is a matter of making facile gestures difficult" (1988, p. 154). In the context of CEP, critique is intended to show that the educational psychology concepts, categories, imperatives, and assumptions that are represented in teacher education and in classroom applications are not self-evident, natural, and neutral and do not necessarily need to govern interactions with students and the constructions of their being. The application of educational psychology knowledge can be dangerous if one assumes that such knowledge objectively represents students and unequivocally supports teaching. The driving force behind critique of educational psychology knowledge is thus a commitment to invite reflection about such dangers while creating opportunities for rethinking students, learning, and teaching.

Analyses in Educational Psychology

The purpose of this book is not to make a case for the legitimacy or illegitimacy of educational psychology in teaching and teacher preparation. Rather, this volume is about the contexts that underpin many of the foundational educational psychology concepts, ideas, and imperatives that teachers are likely to encounter and apply. It is about supporting teachers in recognizing the ways psychology informs their teaching and to enable them to reflect on the possible dangers, limitations, and consequences of applying psychology in the classroom. The reader is introduced to broad topics in educational psychology as well as the many theories and concepts that are associated with those topics. Certain topics featured, such as knowing students, higher order thinking, classroom management, human development, attention, motivation, and assessment and measurement, are conventional in educational psychology texts. Approximately the first half of each chapter is dedicated to reviewing the dominant and current ways of thinking about the chapter's subject, and is then followed by critical examination.

AN ANALYTICAL FRAMEWORK

Although CEP tools are not prescriptive or homogeneous, certain commitments can guide critique. Consider three interrelated strands for critical inquiry informed by a review of the critical work in educational psychology and psychology: polyvocalism, emancipation, and sociohistoricism. While critical inquiry constructed using any single framework certainly has limitations, these three strands can nonetheless be useful as starting points for critical inquiry and can help frame the critiques in this book. The analyses in each chapter are not strictly dedicated to any particular strand of the framework. Although some analyses are aligned more closely than others, all strands are used to think critically about foundational topics, theories, and concepts in educational psychology.

Polyvocalism

The term *polyvocalism* means "many voices" and is associated with the literary critic and philosopher Mikhail Bakhtin, who used the term to suggest that any one utterance is a mixture of social voices, not a single authorial consciousness (Cresswell, 2011). When one utters a statement, a confluence of forces gives form and meaning to that utterance. In the context of CEP, polyvocalism has varying connotations but at its core is about many voices. When engaging critically with educational psychology, a commitment to polyvocalism involves asking the question, what perspectives and voices can be used to help understand the various ways psychological phenomena can be interpreted and understood? Polyvocalism means bringing as many perspectives as possible to bear on psychological knowledge, claims, concepts, and imperatives. As Bruner (1996) argued, including different perspectives and voices supports the understanding of concepts that might seem ambiguous or irrelevant.

To engage in polyvocalism one might draw on cross-cultural knowledge and research to consider the cultural norms that underpin the understanding and evaluation of psychological phenomena. One might also draw on different theories of psychology or look outside the field to philosophy, biology, anthropology, and sociology in order to form a different understanding of psychological phenomena. This theorizing is about diverse representations of concepts, and it's an important line of inquiry because of a common concern raised about psychology in general; that is, the argument that depictions of development, attention, motivation, intelligence, and selfhood are argued to reflect the norms, values, and representations of a narrow subset of the population (Kincheloe, 1999; Gallagher, 2003; Pino-Pasternak & Whitebread, 2010; Vassallo, 2013b). Relying on a psychological discourse that is culturally specific and normative to make sense of all students not only propagates certain values but can also lead to student marginalization, disengagement, and disempowerment for those who are not represented in the discourse.

Emancipation

Another strand of critical theorizing involves analyses of the way educational psychological ideas are implicated in emancipation. One assumption is that psychology is supposed to support the liberation from a number of constraints on thought, movement, possibilities, and potential. One such promise is that educational psychology can help support students' emancipation by contributing to the realization of their full potential. Knowing and applying educational psychology promises to support students' achievement of academic standards by motivating them and fostering positive self-perceptions. Monitoring, assessing, and measuring students' psychology can provide information used to intervene and to support success, which can be viewed as further means for emancipation from social, economic, and cultural restrictions. But in spite of educational psychology's strong association with emancipation, CEP has repeatedly pointed to ways that psychology discourse is constraining and can be used to render persons amenable to oppressive social structures and conditions (Ibáñez & Íñiguez, 1997; Parker, 1999; Gough, McFadden, & McDonald, 2013). The guiding question for this line of inquiry is, how can educational psychology be implicated in both constraint and liberation?

Sociohistoricism

Sociohistoricism is based on the idea that psychological terms, norms, and practices emerge within a particular time and place for particular reasons.

Given historical, political, social, cultural, and ideological conditions, certain truths can be formed about persons. Concepts, rules, authorities, procedures, and techniques make it possible to produce ways of speaking truths about the persons. In an example, Crary (2001) showed that the modern understanding of attention emerged in the 1800s in the context of industrialization, capitalism, technological changes, and a shifting philosophy of the mind. Lesko (2001) illuminated how the modern understanding of adolescence emerged in the 1880s and was driven by a sociopolitical imperative to shape a particular citizenry as well as maintain social hierarchy, racial supremacy, and masculine dominance. The idea behind sociohistoricism is that while certain ways of constructing persons' psychology have not always been available, such ways of understanding persons became possible because of historical context. The guiding question for these types of analyses is, what are the conditions that led to the emergence and acceptance of psychological truths?

CRITICAL NARRATIVES

The critical theory strands of polyvocalism, emancipation, and sociohistoricism inform the analytical tools used to tell different stories related to the educational psychology topics discussed in this book. The analyses in the chapters that follow are not, however, strictly dedicated to any particular strand of the framework described. Although some analyses are aligned more closely with one strand than others, all available tools were used to think critically about foundational topics, theories, and concepts in educational psychology.

To reiterate, the three guiding questions for this inquiry are:

1. How can different theories and perspectives be used to highlight different meanings of psychological phenomena, terms, and concepts?
2. How is educational psychology entangled in issues of emancipation and constraint?
3. What are the historical, philosophical, cultural, and ideological underpinnings of educational psychology knowledge?

These questions are reminders that the application of psychology in the classroom is not a neutral, value-free consequence of scientific objectivity and progress. However, values and contexts are not always recognized and included as part of the discourse in education. Typically, educational psychology texts are designed to introduce teachers to theories, models, principles, and concepts that they must master and apply in the classroom. Teachers are expected to develop a psychological tool kit for solving problems, planning instruction, and supporting students' success. The present volume, on the other hand, will move beyond such introductions to show the ways that the foundational educational psychology discourse is enmeshed in politics, cultural and institutional power, and ideology.

Neoliberalism

Although specific critiques are associated with each of the major topics in educational psychology discussed in this book, a recurring theme throughout is that neoliberal ideology can be implicated in the educational psychology discourse. An economic ideology lauding the notions of free-market practices, competition, and choice, neoliberalism is about aligning social, economic, and political orders with free-market principles (Harvey, 2007). The ideology assumes that laissez-faire capitalist economic policy is the best way to ensure prosperity and well-being for all. Neoliberal agendas place major emphasis on increasing choice and competition, ostensibly while limiting governmental regulation. Ultimately, these commitments are assumed to support economic prosperity, improve global competition, drive innovation, and increase efficiency. The neoliberal goal is to shape all institutions to operate like a free market and to serve an economic agenda.

Although rhetorically about governmental deregulation, neoliberal policies reorient the educational system to serve corporate interests and propagate values that serve those interests. Specifically, educational reforms such as privatization, choice, and competition embrace neoliberal philosophies, which add an intense pressure to measure and accumulate data under the guise of ensuring transparency and accountability (Giroux, 2009; Mathison, 2008). Other neoliberal-based reforms center on the production of particular types of persons, what is referred to here as the neoliberal self. In order for the free market to function properly, persons must be (re)defined in terms of value, marketability, and human capital. Accordingly, individuals are expected to experience themselves as acting rationally, autonomously, and in pursuit of maximizing their own self-interest. In this pursuit, the neoliberal self is productive, consumptive, and entrepreneurial. Rose (1998) wrote that the neoliberal self will "make an enterprise of its life, seek to maximize its own human capital, project itself a future, and seek to shape itself in order to become that which it wishes to be. The enterprising self is thus both an active self and a calculating self, a self that calculates about itself and that acts upon itself in order to better itself" (154). Within this neoliberal framing, the purpose of schooling is reconceptualized in such a way to ensure the production of human capital; the identity of a student is reduced to discrete characteristics thought to predict his or her trajectory for economic success. Human capital is the knowledge, skills, values, and dispositions that enable individuals to perform economic functions that raise their personal value (Becker, 1993).

The neoliberal self is inherently individualistic, efficient, productive, and able to regulate the achievement of educational and economic outcomes (Rose, 1998; Apple, 2006). It is organized around practices dedicated to maximizing autonomy and freedom of choice in the pursuit of happiness, success, and personal fulfillment as rationalized in terms of economic purposes and competition (Rose, 1998; Hilgers, 2013). Maximizing the efficiency and productivity of workers on all levels of economic strata is an essential feature of neoliberalism (Hursh, 2000; Agostinone-Wilson, 2006; Harvey, 2007). These goals are achieved if individuals embody neoliberal selfhood and conform to the neoliberal conceptualization of self-determinism and responsibility over their futures. Here, it becomes clear that neoliberal practices do not liberate the self from regulatory practices of institutions but instead represent a shifting rationality of responsibility from institutions to the individual.

The major takeaway from neoliberal educational policies and practices is the commitment to productivity and profit over the maintenance and development of democratic, communal, and collective processes and goods. The entanglement of educational and economic practices degrades the incentive to work toward democratic goals and public interests, given the emphasis on individual responsibility for one's economic outcomes (Giroux, 2009. Critical theorists have shown that psychology is tied to neoliberal ideology (Foucault, 1988; Rose, 1998; Parker, 2007; Martin & McLellan, 2013). This influence is problematic because neoliberal ideology contributes to the erosion of democracy, the exacerbation of economic inequality, dehumanization, radical individualism, and existential angst (Rose, 1998; Freire, 2000; Hursh, 2007; Giroux, 2009).

Knowing Students

The imperative for teachers to know their students is widely accepted as a sound and necessary pedagogical practice to which educational psychology has a great deal to contribute. The imperative seems intuitive and aligned with humanistic and democratic visions of schooling, and when considered within a binary including the choice to not know students, can be accepted without critical interrogation. There are several ways in which students can be known. Educational psychologists seek to form representations of students' cognitive, social, cultural, and emotional lives. The underlying assumption is that if these features of students are known, then teachers can use that knowledge to shape educational environments in ways that produce a particular outcome. Although CEP does not dispute the potential value of this pedagogical imperative, it does pose critical concerns. Critique here involves exploring the different ways of understanding identity, the role of power in constructing students' identity, and the function of student knowledge. As part of this analysis, neoliberal ideology is implicated in constructing students in specific ways.

Higher Order Thinking

The notion of higher order thinking (HOT) has gained a great deal of attention in recent decades, and not just among educational psychologists. Both policy makers and business leaders put a high premium on the imperative to cultivate HOT in schools. In educational psychology discourse, the notion typically includes creativity, self-regulation, problem-solving, metacognition, and critical thinking. Researchers and theorists who otherwise have diametrically opposing visions for schooling and the good student value HOT (Vassallo, 2014). HOT skills are attractive qualities for teachers to cultivate and for students to embody because they align with humanistic and democratic visions for schooling. However, as with the mandate to know students, the growing interest in HOT and efforts to institutionalize it can be connected to a neoliberal purpose of schooling. Furthermore, neoliberal pressures are shaping the meaning of each of the types of skills associated with HOT. As the discussion included in this book demonstrates, critical educational psychology's identification of the link between HOT and neoliberalism is not about the rejection of such thinking skills as pedagogical aims, but rather about awareness of the way ideology operates through the application and measurement of HOT.

Human Development

Human development theory is contested and controversial. Typically, differences are framed in terms of the theories of cognitive development associated with Jean Piaget and Lev Vygotsky. Although helpful for considering the complexity of development, critique must involve a consideration of the notion of development itself, what it means to construct students developmentally, why some theories are accepted over others, and the function of developmental theory. Depictions of developmental states are not reflections of natural or neutral features of persons that are observed and measured, but part of historical, ideological, cultural, and psychological narratives told about individuals. The analysis in the chapters to follow does not intend to pronounce human development theory as normal, natural, or contrived, but rather to illustrate that any invocation of the notion of development is underpinned by a certain understanding of change and a normal trajectory for that change.

Attention

Attention is a psychological capacity that is considered essential for teaching and learning. Aside from its importance for learning, the concept is conceptually and philosophically ambiguous, and is explored using three perspectives: information processing theory, statistical learning, and embodied cognition. Such exploration helps to highlight the conceptual murkiness of attention. The historical aspect is also important. The emergence of attention as a concept of study can be understood within the context of historical advances in industry, technological advancement, capitalism, philosophical shifts about subjectivity, and certain types of psychological measurement. The discourse of attention is thus situated within a matrix of institutional, cultural, political, historical, and economic circumstances.

Motivation

Motivation is a key area of interest for teachers. The central questions are, what compels individuals to perform activities that are aligned with institutional expectations; and what factors contribute to the sustainability and persistence of that activity? Educational psychologists have been formally studying these questions for decades. In much of contemporary discourse, perceptual factors, such as self-efficacy, learned helplessness, attributions, expectations, and values, are treated as instrumental in shaping students' motivation. One major objection to such discourse is that it identifies motivation as a product of perceptions. Thus, lack of motivation may result from students' readings (and ostensible misreadings) of tasks, teachers, and themselves. But as we will see, targeting students' perceptions can detract from considerations of instructional settings, asymmetrical power relationships, and curricular problems. Thus interventions to change students' perceptions can serve merely to render them amenable to problematic learning environments.

Classroom Management

Like motivation, classroom management (CM) is of high interest for teachers. There are several classroom management models, principles, and strategies. CM is ultimately about the question of how teachers can get students to behave in ways that are valued, acceptable, and conducive to achieving curricula goals. Some models are based on behaviorist principles of reinforcement and punishment. Others are based on what might be described as democratic and humanistic ideals. The critical conversation begins with illuminating the different ideas about the role of teachers, needs of students, and purpose of schooling that inform CM approaches, models, and orientations. It evolves by considering the ethics of the term *management*. Teachers may attribute problems in their classroom to insufficient knowledge of management strategies. However, a critical reading is that the metaphor of teaching as management, which emerged in a particular historical moment, might contribute to so-called management problems. Thinking about teaching as management can be implicated in teaching problems, rather than problems with creating school culture, projecting authority, and setting classroom rules.

Assessment and Measurement

Contemporary education discourse sensationalizes the need for more effective assessment and measurement (AM) tools. While there is something to be said for having an interest in measuring students' academic performance, the use of AM in educational policy and practice—efforts fueled by state and corporate interests alike—has been appropriated to satisfy a neoliberal agenda. The infiltration of AM into education research and policy represents a societal infatuation with the ability to accumulate data, devising means of evaluating those data, and constructing conclusions based on that information. Eventually, this data is presented in comprehensive, ostensibly objective reports on the state of education within the context of the global, competitive economy. In this, education practice and policy becomes entangled in ontological debates, further complicated by political and economic interests and scientific terminology, all in an effort to quell the national concerns raised by *A Nation at Risk* in 1983.

Engaging with the Analyses

As I have suggested, the purpose of this book is to show the ideological, cultural, political, and philosophical underpinnings of the educational psychology knowledge that teachers are likely to encounter and be encouraged to apply in the classroom. Analyses of these types tend to be absent from the education discourse, contributing to perceptions that educational psychology is objective, natural, logical, and common sense. The analyses in this book are intended to challenge these perceptions, to encourage teachers to accept that educational psychology no longer operates under the cloak of scientific objectivity, and to problematize the search for objective depictions of students' psychology.

The starting point from a CEP perspective is that all psychological knowledge is bound to specific contexts. The version of psychological reality that is truthfully accepted has become so not because of the progression of science to objectively represent the students but because of specific circumstances. Danziger (1990) argued that the acceptance of psychological narratives results from power alliances, ideological battles, and cultural hegemony. This understanding of educational psychology does not entirely preclude its usefulness for classroom application. However, exploring the underlying contexts of practices and policies that are informed by psychology provides a starting point for conceptualizing the ethics of those practices and policies. Such a conceptualization is necessary because, as noted, the application of psychology can be dangerous.

The analyses in this book are not intended to legislate or to prescribe teaching. A plethora of researchers and policy makers have tried to exercise this influence over what happens in the classroom. The trend to increase top-down control over all aspects of teaching is worrisome. The analyses in this book are, admittedly, legislative in the sense that they represent a call to treat and analyze psychology in a particular way, to recognize that there is more to educational psychology than what is focused on in teaching and teacher education. Telling critical narratives about key topics in educational psychology, as well as inviting a critical orientation toward all psychological ideas, is important for ensuring ethically aware teaching practice. This awareness can invite new possibilities for thinking about students and teaching. While the critical angles, as well as the psychological terms, practices, and instruments identified herein, are certainly not the only ones in need of analysis, this book is intended to serve as a starting point for teachers to explore a complex narrative of educational psychology.

CHAPTER ONE

Knowing Your Students

THE IMPERATIVE TO KNOW your students is a foundational component of good teaching, as well as the major goal of educational psychologists. There are arguably many benefits to knowing students. Powell and Kusama-Powell (2011) have explained that knowing students can support the creation of a psychologically safe environment for every learner, enable teachers to determine each student's readiness for learning, help teachers increase engagement and success by identifying multiple access points to the curriculum, and help teachers and students both to develop and demonstrate emotional intelligence in the classroom. Educational psychologists contribute to these aims by developing concepts, tools, instruments, and frameworks for constructing students' psychological profiles, which can be informed by developmental theory, cognitive science, social-emotional theory, intelligence, and learning styles. The expectation is that teachers use these categories to construct knowledge of students in order to guide pedagogical decision-making.

The imperative to know students is ostensibly beneficial, especially when considered in relation to its apparent binary which is to not know them. To commit to the latter is tantamount to teaching empty vessels and abstractions or ignoring students' knowledge and experiences. Not knowing students can lead educators to ignore ways that identity plays a role in schooling and can curtail efforts to recognize, respect, and account for cultural diversity in the classroom. Culturally responsive pedagogy is difficult without knowing students. Educational researchers and theorists who support equity and justice tend to support the imperative to know students (Ladson-Billings, 1995a; Freire, 1968/2000; Gay, 2002; Richards, Brown, & Forde, 2007). Such knowledge is important to realize Freire's (1968/2000) critical pedagogical philosophy to ensure that cultural knowledge and experience serve as the foundation to education. Furthermore, not knowing students goes against contemporary emphases on differentiated instruction. Knowing students is more appealing than the apparent binary.

Critical analysis of the idea of knowing students is, however, not an endorsement of the alternative. Nor should the dangers associated with not knowing students necessarily lead to the uncritical adoption of the imperative to know them. Endorsing an imperative because of its apparent binary can shroud critical concerns. The idea of knowing students is philosophically, ideologically, psychologically, and culturally complex. These complexities will be explored in this chapter by considering the following questions: (1) how are students composed; (2) is this composition objective, relativistic, or something else; (3) what role does power play in constructing student knowledge; (4) what is the purpose and function of such knowledge; and (5) what are some contemporary ways in which students are known? From this analysis, it is my hope that rather than adopting a commitment to not know students, teachers will engage with the imperative and practice of knowing students with a critical lens. That means being skeptical about the unequivocal construction of students (i.e., students may not be what one ascribes them to be), conducting analyses of the underpinnings of knowledge categories (i.e., ideological, philosophical, cultural, and political contexts shape possibilities for ways of thinking about students), and reflecting on the functions and purposes of knowing students (i.e., knowing students is tied to the achievement of institutional objectives).

The Composition of Students

If one is committed to knowing students, then a natural and seemingly simple question is what does it mean to know them? To "know," however, is far from simple. Philosophers, researchers, and theorists have debated the nature of knowing and knowledge for centuries. The complexity surrounding what it means to know is compounded by debates about the identity of that which is to be known. In the context of this imperative, teachers must ask, what are students composed of, and can that substance be known? The former question is a primary focus of this chapter. To begin to answer the question, consider the question of ontology, which is a major driver of the field of educational psychology.

ONTOLOGY

Ontology is a branch of philosophy related to the nature of being, becoming, existence, and reality. The imperative to know students involves an understanding of what they are and how they came to be that way. There are at least two ways of thinking about students' ontology. One way is to treat students as having natural psychological qualities that can be known through careful study, which requires valid psychological categories and reliable instruments. The idea is that there is something inherent to students that can be known; all that is needed are the tools to know them. On the other end of the ontological divide is the position that there are no real or objective psychological phenomena. Sugarman (2009) stated that those who endorse this view treat psychological phenomena as "arbitrary inventions, nothing more than figments of cultural and historical imagination" (7). On this side of the debate, the ways in which students are constructed are not representations of real, actual, essential, and universal natures.

The debate relating to attention deficit disorder (ADD) is a good example of these ways of thinking about students' ontology. Some believe that ADD is an objective psychological disorder that relates to brain chemistry. From this perspective, deficits in attention that are inherent to the individual merely require that we have the tools and instruments to measure the deficit. However, others argue that this disorder is a myth perpetuated by cultural norms, flawed measurements, pharmaceutical interests, and economic pressures. So ADD is contentious, and its objective existence is explicitly debated. Ontological debates focus on whether ADD is a "real" disorder or a cultural construction. This debate can be used for any number of psychological categories and descriptions. However, there is no ADD-style debate over whether constructs such as self, self-esteem, self-regulation, intelligence, developmental states, self-efficacy, and goal orientations are representation of students' psychological lives. Many educational psychology terms are taken for granted as representing what students are. Though this description oversimplifies the debate between real and imagined psychological constructs, consideration of these possibilities is a good starting point. However, as Sugarman (2009) argued, the conversation about knowing students must move beyond the binary between "real" versus socially constructed concepts.

HISTORICAL ONTOLOGY

As an alternative perspective to traditional ontological debates, Sugarman (2009) drew from post-structural theorists to advocate for historical ontology: "Historical ontology is premised on the assumption that everything that exists comes into being in its own distinctive historical process. Understood in this way, ontology is not abstracting ultimate principles of reality. Ontology informed by history attempts to reveal the historical conditions of possibility within which a particular object becomes intelligible and the styles of reasoning on which such intelligibility depends. It details how an object becomes conceived as something that can be identified, described, classified and, often, manipulated, measured, and put to practice" (Sugarman, 2009, p. 6). Rather than constructing persons as objective beings who can be understood through measurements or entirely fabricated from imagination, historical ontology is about the conditions that make it possible to construct, classify, and describe persons in particular ways. This view represents a challenge to relativistic and objectivist interpretations of persons. Rather, persons are actors who operate in a particular historical moment and in relation to historically specific styles of reasoning, which include criteria for making judgments, standards for objectivity, vocabulary, and instruments. In other words, any knowledge of selfhood is made possible because of historically specific actors and ways of categorizing, classifying, measuring, evaluating, and reasoning about those actors. Historical ontology is not about saying unequivocally and objectively what persons are but rather what makes it possible to construct, understand, and constitute persons as having certain qualities.

Some of the analyses in this book illuminate the historical conditions that make it possible to construct students in specific ways. Drawing from the work of theorists such as Crary (2001), Burman (2008), Sugarman (2009), and Martin and McLellan (2013), contemporary ideas about development, attention, and selfhood are situated within a historical moment, as well as within modern political and ideological contexts. Historical ontology helps to highlight a seemingly banal point; namely, that every psychological concept we have either did not exist at one point in time or changed significantly during a particular moment in time. Categories, concepts, and instruments emerged, for specific reasons, that contributed to our ability to constitute persons in specific ways. The emergences are connected to political, technological, cultural, and ideological contexts. Illuminating these contexts contributes to denaturalizing psychological descriptions and reasoning.

Conditions of Emergence

A significant contribution of historical ontology relates to the narrative surrounding the emergence of psychological categories and descriptions. This narrative includes the depiction of ideological, political, philosophical, and cultural battles that contribute to the emergence, acceptance, and rise to dominance psychological categories and reasoning about persons as psychological beings. Psychological concepts and reasoning are shrouded in debates and controversies, although certain truths emerge that become an accepted part of discourse. Once accepted, the contexts of emergence are forgotten, leading to assumptions that psychological descriptions are natural, objective, and universal representations of persons.

As Horkheimer and Adorno (2002) famously noted, "all reification is forgetting," which they argued is necessary for objectivity (191). When psychological categories and concepts are taken for granted as unequivocally representing a person, the political, historical, cultural, and ideological contexts that shaped the emergence and transformation of those ideas are forgotten. This forgetting is necessary for a science of psychology. If one forgets the context of the emergence of psychological concepts, which are used to construct students' psychological profiles, then representations of students might seem like objective depictions. The acceptance of those concepts might be explained in terms of better science for mapping students' psychological lives. Historical ontology is about remembering those contexts so that depictions of students are situated within historical, cultural, political, and ideological contexts.

The major assumption of historical ontology is that psychological concepts and styles of reasoning do not emerge or evolve arbitrarily but rather within a historical moment. Here lies a critical point about the imperative to know students. When psychological concepts and categories are evoked to know students, there is the danger of forgetting the historical, ideological, cultural, and political contexts that surround that knowledge. There are a host of terms by which students may be known as well as specific reasons why certain terms are used. Historical ontology is about recognizing the historically situated ways of reasoning and the accompanying vocabulary that are used to constitute knowledge of students. By recognizing the historical conditions that contribute to knowing students, the ontological certainty can be cast into doubt and students can potentially be constructed in different ways.

For example, as discussed in the chapter on development, the contemporary understanding of adolescence is rooted in nineteenth-century practices of classism, sexism, and racism (Lesko, 2001). The purpose of the evolution of the notion of adolescence was to produce a citizenry that was modeled off of the ideal person, who was Western, white, male, and middle-class. If knowing students means using this understanding of adolescence, then there is the danger of reifying normative and dangerous underpinnings of a so-called naturalized stage in development. Thus, to rely on certain psychological categories can evoke, affirm, and validate ways of constructing students that are rooted in dangerous contexts. Given the imperative to know students via constructing their psychological profiles, it is important that critical educational psychology includes a commitment to historical ontology.

Yet policy makers and researchers continue to endorse specific ways of knowing students and offer new ones as if they were ontological certainties. For example, in contemporary discourse, policy makers are turning their attention to a set of attitudes, dispositions, skills, and behaviors grouped under the term *noncognitive skills* (NCS). These skills are also referred to as social-emotional skills, soft skills, or character. They include curiosity, grit, self-control, gratitude, zest, optimism, and social intelligence. Because NCS are argued to predict academic success, emphasis on the teaching and evaluation of NCS has grown in the twenty-first century (Tangney, Baumeister, & Boone, 2004; Duckworth & Yeager, 2015). Policy makers and researchers are interested in institutionalizing NCS by developing measurements to evaluate students' learning of them, as well as teachers' effectiveness at cultivating them (Duckworth & Yeager, 2015). While efforts to measure NCS have been met with some skepticism, NCS has become a framework to make sense of students, to reason about who they are, and how those qualities shape their academic outcomes.

The emergence of NCS as a mapping of the variables that effect achievement is rooted in the persistent style of reasoning that students' psychology can be reduced to variables that are causally related to their achievement. This reasoning, which is not without its past and contemporary critics, is responsible for identifying any number of psychological variables that are responsible for academic success. At one point, intelligence was the predictor of achievement. Now, a number of cognitive skills have been identified as predictors. These include self-regulated learning, executive functioning, information processing abilities, and a number of perceptual variables (see the chapter on motivation). Constructs and ways of reasoning come in and out of fashion to explain psychological causes of success and failure. The new framework of NCS is now emerging and being peddled as a predictor of achievement. Thus, in contemporary discourse, success and failure tend to be attributed to character traits such as zeal, optimism, grit, and gratitude.

Solutions to address academic achievement problems involve measuring and if necessary reforming those variables that purportedly predict academic achievement. Therefore, the work of teachers is to use the NCS framework to construct profiles to identify students who do or do not have the kinds of NCS that are associated with success and to design the appropriate intervention. If, for example, students are deemed as not possessing grit, then teachers must design an intervention to try to foster grit. Grit becomes a measure and representation of students and a pedagogical target. Setting aside debates about whether or not NCS such as grit could or should be taught, this framework is nonetheless being advanced for specific ideological reasons. NCS can be connected to the growing influence of neoliberalism on schooling.

A curricular and pedagogical focus on NCS may be another way for authorities to communicate to students the message to "work hard, be grateful for your situation, be positive about your situation, know it can change with your perseverance, recognize your individual power to overcome obstacles, and control your destructive impulses. There are no direct oppressive regimes, it is only your character, perception, and work ethic that are responsible for your life outcomes." This message is not new and has always been part of a neoliberal ideology to produce responsibilized citizens and endorse an individualistic and meritocratic view of achievement. NCS has roots in historical narratives about school success that extend beyond the twenty-first century. However, modern ideological influences are implicated in the growing acceptance and value for the discourse of NCS that are used to make sense of and reason about students.

Concerns are that formalizing NCS in schools is a way of making up people that can align with meritocracy, endorse radical individualism, justify hierarchy, garner complicity to hierarchy, and encourage optimistic assessments of institutional structures. NCS can be tied to the rendering of subjects docile to institutional organizations, which increasingly reflect neoliberal arrangements. When formalized and taught within neoliberal educational structures, NCS can function to serve neoliberal ends. However, what may happen in the evolution of education discourse is that NCS will come to be considered an unproblematic representation of students and used as a normalizing framework to identify both those who have and are lacking the "right" qualities and quantities of NCS.

Making Up People

Recognizing the conditions that surround the emergence and evolution of psychological ideas is one aspect of historical ontology. However, there is another feature of this perspective. As Sugarman (2009) explained, the emergence and acceptance of psychological categories and descriptions are implicated in the formation of self. Categories and concepts used to know students contribute to their constitution. This understanding is vastly different from the position that students have an objective, essential, and core self that is merely known via tools, instruments, concepts, and categories.

The difference between these views can be understood in terms of making (or ascribing) and finding (or describing), respectively. Historical ontology supports an understanding of psychological categories as ascriptions, not descriptions. Rather than identifying psychological qualities that exist, it is critical to consider that the language and tools employed to students contributes to the making of them. From this perspective, the idea of knowing students is replaced by constructing students.

The difference between ascribing and describing persons has been the subject of philosophical and psychological debates about the composition of persons. These debates center on the notion of self. Some enduring questions include, is the self stable, malleable, compartmental, holistic, continuous, and plural? Is there a core self, one that provides the motivational and cognitive structures to coherently organize thoughts and behaviors? Where does the self come from? What features of self are inherent and which are learned? Can a self be known? Critical theorists do not assume that the self is a natural or inevitable quality of persons. As Mead (1934) argued, there is no inherent self that is transcendental, universal, or self-evident. Rather, the self is a cultural artifact made possible by social, experiential, historical, and linguistic markings that demarcate one physical being from another. The concept of self typically connotes that a physical being is separate from others and the world, has an interior life, is continuous and coherent, and has limitations, boundaries, and talents. This notion of self is a Western psychological and cultural construct used to mark individuality and humanness (Cushman, 1990; Sugarman, 2014).

The self, its ontology, and its intelligibility are subject to enduring debates. Coming out of these controversies is a litany of terms: saturated self, dialogical self, empty self, neoliberal self, democratic self, I-self, me-self, scientific self, expressive self, and communal self. Each of these terms has different meanings, conceptualizations, and philosophical underpinnings, but all incorporate the use of self. Those who are concerned with ontological certainty are committed to defining the qualities and ontology of the self. However, from a historical ontological perspective, the self is a notion that stands as a representation of persons. In other words, aside from what one might perceive qualities of the self to be, the self is itself a way of making sense of people. The notion of self connotes inevitability, objectivity, coherence, and disconnection from historical moment. However, critical theories have offered a view of self that is emergent, contingent, political, and cultural (Mead, 1934; Cushman, 1990; Gergen, 1992; Sugarman, 2009). The assumption that persons are selves with unique, enduring, and internal qualities is troubled in critical psychology. Within this tradition, the self is not denied. Rather, the self and its perceived qualities are made possible because of experiences that are interpreted as signifying a self. This understanding of self is a key feature of historical ontology.

Sugarman (2014) explained, "We experience ourselves as persons only because we do so under certain descriptions. Personhood consists in taking up and acting in terms of the descriptions made available to us. When persons become aware of how they are described and classified within their groups, societies, and cultures, they experience themselves in particular ways as a result of these classifications, and form and alter the kinds of persons they are" (53–54). According to Sugarman, classifications do not deterministically define persons but become the reference point for personal and interpersonal evaluations, assessments, and conclusions about the contents of self. The idea is that categories, assessments, and measurements do not determine the formation of self. Persons can self-interpret their alignment with categories and classifications as well as act in order to change them. Thus concepts and categories shape possibilities for constructing and understanding the self.

To illustrate, the notion of self-regulated learning (SRL) did not exist prior to the late 1970s. Although similar terms, such as *self-control* and *self-monitoring*, existed prior to this time, the emergence of SRL became a new and specific way to evaluate, judge, and reform students. Now that it is gaining attention, being formally studied, applied to schooling, and integrated into curricula, the notion of SRL can function to evaluate students' regulatory prowess and can inform interventions for those who are found lacking. SRL can be explicitly applied to students, who can use this notion to make sense of themselves and their academic engagement. Students can conclude that they are good or bad at self-regulating their learning. This marking of selfhood is possible because the term exists, SRL has an empirical basis, behaviors can be recognized as self-regulated, personal sources of academic achievement are sought, and there are instruments to measure SRL. Although some researchers have argued that SRL is a natural human disposition, others have suggested this way of mapping and marking the self is cultural, ideological, and political (Martin & McLellan, 2008; Vassallo, 2013a). From a historical ontological perspective, SRL is a marking of self that is neither natural nor self-evident.

As another example, the growing influence of neoliberal thinking in schooling, curricula, and pedagogy encourages the evaluation of students in terms of their flexibility, creativity, entrepreneurialism, and risk-taking.

These features of selfhood comprise the neoliberal self. With the integration of frameworks for neoliberal selfhood in curricula and policy discussions (e.g., see twenty-first-century competency frameworks), students can be evaluated in terms of their proximity to ideal representations of this self. In other words, neoliberal reasoning about the world, and the types of people needed for it gives rise to a particular conception of the ideal self, instruments for evaluating this self, and pedagogical interventions to foster that self. These notions can be used by teachers to evaluate students and by students to constitute themselves. Students can organize their perception of self around how well they embody the ideal neoliberal self.

If the imperative is to know students, then one must know of what they are comprised. Historical ontology is not about what is or is not real, but about the conditions that enable one to make truth claims about being. These truth claims are made possible by a particular style of reasoning about academic achievement and the taken-for-granted assumption that categories and descriptions are consequences of the objective nature of persons. A teacher can use psychological concepts and descriptions to create student profiles. However, it is important to recognize that these concepts and categories are rooted in historical moments, emerge for particular reasons, are not objective representations, serve particular ideological purposes, and contribute to the constitution of persons. Understanding psychological knowledge from a historical ontological perspective can help to orient inquiry to the purposes and consequences of using certain descriptions and categories to make sense of students.

IDENTITY POLITICS

From a historical ontological perspective, to know students is to constitute persons rather than to make a disinterested and objective evaluation. Teachers employ a style of reasoning to make sense of students. Evaluations are not necessarily deterministic, but can be given privileged status for marking selfhood. For this reason, knowing students is complicated by identity politics, which is a term that captures the political activity and theorizing about the injustices related to particular groups. The notion of identity politics captures neglected struggles of identity and self-determination between groups that tend to have more political power and groups that tend to have less. These struggles circulate around identity, experience, and injustice. Central questions are: Who gets to define whom? Whose representations of students are valid? What cultural norms underpin representations of students? And whose voices are heard when constructing knowledge of students?

Critical scholars have long been concerned with the cultural norms that underpin the construction of students as made possible by formal psychological assessments as well as teachers' perceptions. Often cited is the matter of the relative homogeneity in terms of race, class, and sex of the teaching demographic. Feistritzer (2011) reported that in 2011, 84 percent of teachers were white and 85 percent were female. Although the socioeconomic class background was not part of the demographic report, teachers are generally believed to come from middle-class backgrounds. This information is important insofar as one believes that unifying perceptions, dispositions, values, and personalities may be found across the range of individuals who share these identity categories. The homogeneity of the teaching demographic, the assumption about shared perspective among that demographic, and the authority afforded to teachers and schooling can lead one to question the norms and values underpinning knowing students.

What one believes he or she knows about students can be constructed through a particular lens in which class, race, sex, religion, and sexual orientation shape student profiles. A concern is that institutionally sanctioned knowledge of students can be assigned validity over other possible representations. Rather than focusing on the context around the emergence of psychological categories, the issue with identity politics and knowing students is about who gets to define students, what knowledge is valid, and whose voice is heard.

TECHNICAL RATIONALITY

Another concern with the imperative to know students has to do with assumptions about the predictability and controllability of persons. Psychology rests on the idea that through careful observations people can be known. From this knowledge, one may believe that it is possible to predict others' behaviors and potential outcomes. Since its beginnings, psychology has been underpinned by the general assumption that the scientific method was the way to attain this understanding. Philosophical, theological, and other metaphysical sources are not empirical and cannot provide valid and reliable knowledge. The foundational assumption is that knowledge claims about anything must be verified through observation, value-free description, and quantification (Johnson, 2015). This view is captured in a well-known quotation by the behaviorist John B. Watson (1924/2009): "Give me a dozen healthy infants, well-formed, and my own specified world to bring them up in and I'll guarantee to take any one at random and train him to become any type of specialist I might select—doctor, lawyer, artist, merchant-chief, and, yes, even beggarman and thief, regardless of his talents, penchants, tendencies, abilities, vocations, and race of his ancestors" (p. 82). Watson believed that in controlled environments using careful observations, any behavior, disposition, and skill could be crafted. This way of thinking is an example of technical rationality.

Technical rationality is represented in the following way: if W is known about student X, then pedagogical strategy Y can be implemented to produce outcome Z. This type of thinking reflects the gold standards of science to predict, control, and cause. Technical rationality informs educational psychology as well as general expectations for teachers. Schön (1987) wrote, "Technical rationality holds that practitioners are instrumental problem solvers. Who [sic] select technical means best suited to particular purposes. Rigorous professional practitioners solve well-formed instrumental problems by applying theory and technique derived from systematic preferably scientific knowledge" (pp. 3–4). According to Schön, technical rationality can be applied to different problems and different purposes. Different teachers may construct the same students in different ways in accordance with the specific conditions of a classroom. Notwithstanding, the type of thinking about knowledge, prediction, and causality remain intact. The assumption is that if students are known, then an intervention can be matched to that knowledge in order to produce a certain outcome.

Although this type of thinking can be rationalized to serve students' interest, there are a number of problems with technical rationality. Most broadly, there is the matter of applying science to map persons and to reliably discern causal relationships between psychological phenomena. Arguably, humans are complex and unpredictable, and consequently behavior is not subject to the same laws of natural phenomena as is science. Then there is the question of whether or not technical rationality can actually work to shape students. This question is not entertained in educational psychology discourse because it threatens the relevance and value of this discipline for teaching, especially in a climate centered on evidence-based practice. Educational psychologists endorse the idea that if students are known then teaching can be shaped in ways to produce particular outcomes.

Aside from practical and philosophical issues, there are ethical problems with this reasoning. Marcuse (1964/1991) argued that technical rationality is the commodification of humans based in the industrial revolution. Just as the technical and systematic conditions made the production of commodities efficient, Marcuse argued that technical rationality was supposed to support the engineering of persons to render them instrumental for whatever social, political, economic, or ideological need. Technical rationality requires a construction of the form of students (what they are) and locks them into instrumental thinking (what they are supposed to be and for what purpose). Whenever technical rationality is applied, there is an endpoint toward which the intervention is directed. For this reason, Martin and McLellan (2013) called technical rationality a "straight-forward and predictable instance of social engineering" (p. viii). The argument is that knowing students cannot be understood independent of conversations related to control. Even if students were knowable via the scientific method and such knowledge could be used to predict and cause outcomes, an ethical question remains about the role and function of this knowledge. Knowing students can serve to make them more amenable to institutional lessons.

The imperative to know students requires deliberation over concerns about the composition of students, objectivity and relativism of student knowledge, the effects of knowledge on forming subjectivity, authority in defining students, and the purpose of knowing them. These deliberations can be broad but also specifically tailored to specific ways of knowing students. As noted, NCS is gaining traction as a way to know students. Other new concepts and categories are also being peddled as knowledge. Not only for knowledge that is accepted and knowledge that is gaining traction, but for knowledge yet to emerge, deliberations about authority, purpose, and ontology are important components of the practice of critical educational psychology.

Ways of Knowing Students

Educational psychology is fundamentally about knowing students, which involves defining qualities and how those qualities impact learning. Some of the common ways of knowing students include understanding their motivational structures, developmental characteristics, quality of higher order thinking skills, needs, beliefs, desires, and cognitive processes. Critical concerns with these ways of knowing are highlighted throughout the book in order to make the point that knowing students is not merely to observe what they objectively are. Rather, knowing students is about using methods, concepts, and descriptions—psychological, cultural, political, and ideological—to render students knowable in particular ways. The analyses in this book can all be connected, in some way or another, to a critique of knowing students.

In addition to those featured in this book, other contemporary ways of knowing students are gaining traction. For example, although arguably not a specific way of knowing students, contemporary discourse on data-driven instruction has contributed to the transformation of students into data, and knowledge of them as having quantifiable characteristics. In response to the trend to reduce students to quantitative data points, researchers have suggested that educators teach the whole child, which is a concept that can guide the imperative to know students (Eisner, 2005; Noddings, 2005). And in response to overemphases on high-stakes assessment, which prioritizes academic qualities, researchers have again suggested that teachers need to teach the whole child. This call requires teachers to know students wholly. Although a seemingly more appealing option than knowing students partially, the concept of the whole child needs to be critically considered. Students as data and the whole child are merely two examples of the myriad ways to know students that are tied to specific purposes of schooling, philosophical beliefs about personhood, governance, and ideology. These analyses of ways of knowing students are but two illustrations among many that require critical interrogation.

STUDENTS AS DATA

Contemporary educational rhetoric is replete with calls for data-driven instruction. The foundation of this call is the imperative to know students. Principals and teachers are pressured to collect copious amounts of student data through many different forms, such as standardized tests, psychological tests, formative evaluations, informal interactions, and observations. Teachers are urged to keep detailed data notebooks on students. These notebooks are intended to map progress on well-defined, and oftentimes quantifiable, tasks. Data-driven instruction is the norm in contemporary education reform rhetoric. This acceptance is associated with emphasis on "value added" teaching.

The use of data is nothing new to teachers; they have always relied on formal and informal assessments of students to inform pedagogical structures and interventions. However, it was not until the last few decades that data collection became a top priority, leading to questions about how best to collect, monitor, manage, and use student data. Some view the goal to improve assessments and data management as the key to improving schools (Armstrong & Anthes, 2001; Lachat & Smith, 2005; Kerr, Marsh, Ikemoto, Darilek, & Barney, 2006). A less favorable interpretation is that treating students as data, teaching as data collection, and using success as value added are tied to neoliberal thinking (Hursh, 2007; Giroux & Saltman, 2009; Lipman, 2011).

In a climate of data-driven accountability, students are data, and knowing them means representing them in terms of data and data points. Thinking of students as sources of data can conflict with recognizing their humanity by reducing them to their quantifiable changes in academic performance. The emphasis on data can lead to the positioning of students as instrumental pawns used to achieve state-mandated curricula goals. Sir Ken Robinson (2013), who is well known for his support for creativity in classrooms, validated this concern when he stated that policy makers "treat education as an industrial process rather than as a human one. They are driven by a culture of testing and standardization that has narrowed the curriculum and sees students as data points and teachers as functionaries rather than as living breathing people" (paragraph 6). Robinson connected standardization and testing to the transformation of students as data and teachers as functionaries who use data to achieve institutional goals. Given the stakes associated with test performance, teachers are strongly encouraged to care only about features of students that support achievement and performance, as determined and dictated by curricula standards. Thus, only that which counts as valid data is connected to academic performance. In other words, the only important knowledge of students is that which is quantifiable and recognizable, and associated with the achievement of schooling goals.

Given that student data can come in several forms, teachers can collect qualitative and quantitative information about students. The broadening of the methods for accumulating knowledge of students can soften the concern with the transformation of students as data. However, even if histories, stories, and experiences are norms for what counts as student data, the labeling of this information as data is still objectifying, rendering life and experience scientifically knowable and manageable. When students are data, regardless of the type of instruments that are used, they are in danger of having only those features of themselves validated that can be associated with academic improvement. When teachers value only that which can be reasoned to add value, they are in danger of objectifying students and being concerned only with the economics of education. Thus, knowing students by representing them as data can be viewed as dehumanizing.

THE WHOLE CHILD

Today's educational climate is characterized by high-stakes assessments, global competition, competition among peers, and assignment of heightened value to particular content areas, which include science, technology, engineering, and math. The economic and political instrumentalism of schooling is clear. Schooling objectives are about the development of cognitive capacities for the purposes of preparing students for a particular representation of the twenty-first century. School funding, administrative control over schools, and teachers' employment all hang in the balance of students' test performance. Thus, teachers are under increasing pressure to maximize instructional time so that students can perform well on assessments that are intended to signify learning of the curriculum. As a consequence, every moment in the classroom must be strategically and coherently centered on progressively moving toward an explicit learning objective—one on which students will be tested. In today's academic climate, the pressure to maximize instruction to achieve predetermined curricular goals can invite an intense focus on students' cognitive capabilities at the expense of considering their social, emotional, and personal states.

The notion of the whole child runs counter to treating students as data and narrowing that data to cognitive ability. Educational theorists and researchers who operate from a humanistic philosophy endorse policy and practice that involves teaching the whole child (Eisner, 2005; Noddings, 2005). But, what is the whole child? A commitment to know and teach the whole child must be accompanied by an understanding of the entire composition of the child. Soder, Goodlad, and McMannon (2001) conceptualized the whole child as a one who is of sound character, social conscience, critically engaged, committed, and aware of global issues. Smith and Sobel (2010) argued that a commitment to teaching the whole child involves connections between classrooms and lived experience; building social, human, and cultural capital; building leaders; and reconnecting students to the natural world. The assumption is that the whole child is communal, social, goal-driven, fluid, and part of nature. The Association for Supervision and Curriculum Development (ASCD) gives a Whole Child Award to schools "that have gone beyond a vision for educating the whole child to actions that result in learners who are knowledgeable, emotionally and physically healthy, civically active, artistically engaged, prepared for economic self-sufficiency, and ready for the world beyond formal schooling." Common features in the contemporary conceptions of the whole child include character, morals, emotions, drives, needs, and reason. Teaching the whole child means recognizing, acknowledging, and developing all these parts not in isolation of each other but rather in concert.

Although the notion of the whole child is appealing in schooling contexts that overly emphasize cognitive abilities, it gives rise to some critical concerns. To entertain such concerns is not to endorse a narrow focus on isolated or specific parts of persons. Rather, critical analysis here involves a consideration of the underlying ideas about persons and the purposes of the notion of the whole child. The notion of the whole child signifies a specific idea about being, one in which persons are coherently organized around fragmented parts. Although whole, the child is fragmented into discrete parts that can be isolated and independent of each other. Teaching the whole child does not necessarily mean challenging such fragmentation, but rather ensuring that schooling is adequately attuned, in a concerted way, to those various parts. Problems arise when some parts of the child are ignored while others are targets of pedagogical structures.

Researchers and teachers are likely to agree that it is important to teach the whole child, and that various conceptualizations about the substance of that child share common themes. Notwithstanding, considerable debate, ambiguity, and critical concern have accompanied the discourse of the whole child. Some of the top philosophical and theoretical psychologists have recently taken up this debate (Amsel, 2015; Johnson, 2015; Martin, 2015). Although Martin (2015) argued that efforts to unify persons and teach them wholly are not in themselves a problem, he also argued that such efforts often involve the integration of competing theories and conceptions of the person. In other words, the whole child is a composite of the various parts of being—of course represented as a unified substance. However, Martin argued that there are different theories about that composition, the forces that influence it, and the ontology of those parts. The potential for contradictions saliently emerges when considering what counts as healthy, good character qualities, proper emotional development, good moral reasoning, and adaptive personality development.

Another philosophical concern with the notion of the whole child has to do with ontology. From a historical ontological perspective, the notion of the whole child is not an objective construction of persons that merely needs to be observed and measured. The notion of the whole child is a particular representation of persons, which is based on the assumptions that persons are fragmented, unified, and have internal compositions. Although the notion of the whole child is an attempt at the unification of persons, the idea that children can be dissected and understood in terms of their isolated parts is foundational. As Amsel (2015) argued, psychologists tend to fragment persons. It is not uncommon for psychologists to separate persons from their brains, emotions from rationality, behavior from personality, and cognitive from noncognitive skills. The notion of the whole child is based on this type of fragmentation but with the added theorizing about how parts work in concert for pedagogical activity. In this regard, the notion of the whole child is a kind of technical rationality. The logic is that persons are fragmented and that each part can be isolated and known in order to support pedagogical interventions that can contribute to the concerted development of those parts.

With the notion of the whole child, there is the simultaneous fragmentation and unification of personhood that can be known and controlled. Although researchers recognize parts as interacting, each component of the child stands as a distinct part. This fragmentation may not at all be how children experience themselves, but rather how they are constructed. The purpose of this fragmentation is to ensure that adults masterfully work on each component as independent or interrelated features. For this reason, Martin (2015) argued that such a conception of the whole child is underpinned by scientism and psychologism.

Psychologism is the idea that persons have internal features that serve as causal explanations for thoughts, behaviors, and outcomes. This commitment competes with historical ontology by assuming that persons are naturally composed of parts that make up their wholeness. Students are constructed as psychological beings who have inner, essential, and enduring characteristics such as learning style, emotional development, character, intelligence, temperament, needs, developmental stage, interests, strengths, weaknesses, self-esteem, self-efficacy, and cultural identity. In scientism, as Martin explained, psychologists attempt to apply the methods of the so-called natural sciences in order to develop laws of human psychology. Although Martin contended that psychologists have not been able to achieve this goal, they operate under the veil that they have or at least are making progress toward this goal. The laws of personhood are embodied in the conception of the whole child, who is dissectible, knowable, and controllable.

Scientific tools are supposed to enable researchers to understand the composite features of persons. As conceptions of the whole child change and expand, the assumption is that the whole child is better understood. Fendler (2001) captured this argument: "Educational programs that inscribe aspects of desire, fear, and pleasure as calculable 'objects of science' are generally based on the assumption that such research represents progress in scientific understanding; aspects of 'the inner self' that had been mysterious or vague can be brought to light and rationalized through scientific investigation" (p. 123). He referred to the notion of the whole child as an example of an educational program that inscribes desire, fear, and pleasure. The term *inscribe* is key for this quotation. Fendler does not say that educational programs measure desire, fear, and pleasure. This claim assumes objectivity and measurability of an already existing "inner self." Rather, aligned with a historical ontological perspective, the notion of inscribing connotes a style of reasoning about persons that in no way reflects objective and natural qualities of persons or the validity of the target of educational interventions.

Another point that Fendler (2001) made was that the discourse of the whole child renders students susceptible to scientific management. The notion of teaching the whole child suggests that no part of that child should be left untouched by schooling. If the imperative is to know students in terms of their composite parts, and the pedagogical goal is to ensure that if all parts are taken into account during schooling then no part of the child is supposed to be free from institutional lessons. Fendler stated, "The thrust of 'whole child' education is that the child's entire being—desire, attitudes, wishes—is caught up in the educative process. Educating the whole child means educating not only the cognitive, affective, and behavioral aspects, but also the child's innermost desires. There must be no residue of reluctance to learning; success for 'whole child' education means not only that the child learn, but the child desires to learn and is happy to learn. No aspect of the child must be left uneducated; education touches the spirit, soul, motivation, wishes, desires, dispositions, and attitudes of the child to be educated" (p. 121). Fendler did not implicitly validate the notion that there is a whole child and that knowing it renders children susceptible to management. She also did not give validity to the scientific construction of this type of personhood. Like Martin (2015) and other critical theorists, Fendler does not endorse a view of the whole child as a characterization about the nature of persons. Rather, she has merely pointed out that the discourse of the whole child is complicated by efforts to inscribe a particular type of subjectivity for the twenty-first century.

Aside from debates among educational philosophers and philosophers of psychology, there is also debate among researchers and theorists in education about notions of the whole child and what it means to teach to the whole child. For example, Perkins-Gough (2013) interviewed Angela Duckworth, a theorist often associated with the notion of grit. In this interview, Duckworth stated that she believed an emphasis on the cultivation of grit and other noncognitive skills, such as zest, character, optimism, and gratitude, signified attention to the whole child. Grit is defined as perseverance with a task in the face of challenges and difficulties (Duckworth & Yeager, 2015). This so-called NCS is generally considered a feature of one's character that is separate from but instrumental to the development of cognitive skills.

Although Duckworth has argued a concern for grit indicates movement toward a whole conception of students, Kohn (2014), who is an outspoken critic of grit, has argued the contrary. Kohn notes that a focus on grit is about pushing behavior without considering the satisfaction and moral direction of that behavior. For Kohn, the whole child must include this moral dimension as well as the relationship of gritty behaviors for psychological well-being, which he suggested is measured in terms of personal satisfaction. However, Kohn pointed out that proponents of grit are generally concerned with behaviors (e.g., spending time on a task, pursing a particular outcome, practicing, and being pertinacious) and the products that result from those behaviors. Kohn (2008) stated that "if we're interested in the whole child— if, for example, we'd like our students to be psychologically healthy—then it's not at all clear that self-discipline should enjoy a privileged status compared to other attributes" (p. 168). Although Duckworth believed she endorsed a multidimensional view of persons, Kohn contended that her perspective of the whole child narrowly conceptualized children by focusing on behavior that is intended for specific schooling goals.

Those who endorse grit from a neoliberal perspective support a narrative of personhood based on meritocracy, personal responsibility, and efficient production. Kohn (2014) operates from a liberal-democratic perspective that centers on the importance of individual choice, personal fulfillment, and expressing one's voice. Although there are issues with both theorists' assumptions about the whole child, this example illustrates the contradictory and competing nature of the notion of the whole child. In general, notions of the whole child are embedded in assumptions about the purpose of schooling, political commitments, the philosophy of personhood, and ideology.

Know Thyself

Knowing students has become an important component of teaching. This imperative is extended to include helping students know themselves. In liberal democracies and neoliberal economic structures, the importance of knowing oneself and self-discipline are paramount. Fendler (2001) made this point and implicated the discourse of the whole child in this commitment:

> The discourse of educational psychology has constructed desires, hopes, and fears as rationalizable attributes; significantly, however, as a condition of governance in a liberal democracy, the educated subject is self-disciplined. This means that the reinforcement or the motivation to "have a positive attitude" must be exercised *by* the self *on* the self. In order to be recognized—or recognize oneself—as "educated," the subject understands and reflexively disciplines desires, feelings, loves, wishes, and fears. The construction of the "whole child" is a relatively new configuration in educational discourse, and

inscribes a new target—or substance—for pedagogical technologies and self-discipline. (p. 124; emphases in original)

In this view the imperative to know students involves explicitly working with them to support their knowing of themselves. Regardless of who the source of knowing is, the underlying assumption is the same; knowledge of self is necessary to support academic achievement. Yet the emphasis on self-knowledge may be mistaken for autonomous engagement. The practices of formulating self-knowledge in schools require not only the use of particular instruments and concepts as well as training and guidance from experts. The idea that students are responsible for self-knowledge may just reflect a shifting of responsibility to students of what was previously an institutional function, in which case the pursuit and ostensible determination of self-knowledge does not represent freedom and liberation from the constraints of others a but merely transfer to the student of responsibility for constituting the self.

Conclusion

As we have seen, the imperative to know students seems intuitive and aligned with humanistic and democratic visions of schooling, especially when framed in terms of its binary opposite, to not know students. But as I have argued in this chapter, the notion poses a number of critical concerns. The purpose of this critique is to promote consideration of the ethical, ideological, and political underpinnings related to ways in which students are known. Categories, frameworks, concepts, and descriptions used to know students are not neutral and objective representations of their psychological composition. Yet, the imperative to know students implies that they have a substance that exists that must be measured and observed in order to teach them. In this line of thinking, knowing students implies that there are objective qualities to students' internal psychological and biophysical lives. Therefore, the key to teaching is to unlock that mystery.

However, as suggested, the imperative to know students is entangled in political, cultural, ideological, and historical contexts. Psychological profiles of students are not self-evident nor are they without consequences. These consequences relate to the possibility of endorsing problematic contexts through the specific marking of students' being. Knowing students is not simply a matter of defining who they are universally, essentially, and objectively. Rather, it is the process of taking their behaviors, thoughts, and dispositions and evaluating them in terms of the available language, statements, and reasoning. As psychological theories evolve in relation to cultural, ideological, and political shifts, acceptable ways to know students can shift. However, regardless of the ways in which students are constructed, it is important to endeavor to situate those ways of knowing in political, ideological, cultural, and historical contexts.

CHAPTER TWO

Principles of Motivation

WHAT COMPELS SOME STUDENTS to set challenging goals and commit to achieving them while others are quick to give up? Why do some students procrastinate while others plan ahead? Why do some students study for hours while others choose not to study at all? Why do some students need reinforcements to engage while others do so without prompting? For decades, psychologists have puzzled over these questions. They sought to understand human motivation by identifying what compels certain behaviors and thoughts, the goals toward which people strive, the purpose of goal pursuit, and the persistence at pursuing those goals. This area of study is of utmost importance to anyone responsible for directing others in ways to achieve specific outcomes. Business leaders take a keen interest in understanding how to energize workers to achieve optimal performance. Parents may want to know how to motivate their children to meet certain standards for school performance, develop social relationships, participate in extracurricular activities, and adopt certain eating habits. And, of course, teachers cite knowledge of human motivation as a major area of importance for achieving curricular mandates.

Educational psychologists believe that understanding student motivation is key for supporting the achievement of teaching goals and the realization of students' potential. This understanding is important because motivation is used to explain school success and failure: if students are motivated, the assumption is that they can achieve academic goals. Thus, research centers on understanding what motivates students and how teachers could use that knowledge to motivate them to achieve. However, academic achievement is not the only endpoint in research. Researchers strive to encourage positive experiences, character development, value in learning, and mastery of knowledge (Brophy, 1983; Bandura, 1997; Linnenbrink & Pintrich, 2002; Wentzel & Brophy, 2014). Achieving these dual aims is a major challenge for educators, one that highlights the point that not all student motivation is equally valued.

Brophy (1983), a prominent educational psychologist, made the distinction between "motivated to perform" and "motivated to learn." Students who are motivated to perform are described as committed to finishing tasks with minimal cognitive engagement and engaging in behaviors only for a reward or to avoid undesirable consequences. Educational psychologists refer to this type of motivation as extrinsic. On the other hand, motivation to learn is characterized as an intrinsic interest for mastery, persistence, and achievement. The difference between learning and performing can be understood as a desire for mastery versus pursing a grade independent of the conceptual understanding of the material, respectively.

Debates about the value of performance and learning have been discussed. For example, Pink (2011) argued that motivation to perform is a powerful and effective tool for rote tasks. However, he argued that being motivated to learn tends to be beneficial for tasks that require creativity, problem-solving, and self-regulation. For this reason, Pink argued that in order to help students function within twenty-first-century environments, which requires certain types of thinking skills and competencies, schooling must be committed to motivating students to learn rather than to perform. Although many educators and psychologist agree that motivation to learn is more beneficial than motivation to perform, classrooms tend to be aligned with a commitment to the latter. A major obstacle with motivating to learn is the persistent use of reinforcements and punishments (Deci, 1971; Harackiewicz, 1979; Brophy, 1983; Kohn, 1999; Pink, 2011).

Educational philosophers and theorists conceptualize students as having a natural drive to learn and pursue mastery (Montessori, 1946; Piaget & Inhelder, 1969; Dewey, 1910/1997; Ayres, 2010; Pink, 2011; Ryan, 2012). Yet, educators must go to great lengths to try to energize students to learn for mastery. Contemporary theorists used different metaphors to explain that the goal of motivation knowledge is to "unlock," "tap into," "harness," and "free" an internal energy for the pursuit of mastery. The connotation of these metaphors is that students have the natural desire to be motivated to learn but face the difficulty of accessing or the danger of suppressing this natural drive. Motivating students is thus about figuring out how to harness and access what is already a quality of students. Therefore, as Ryan (2012) contended, the problem that motivation researchers grapple with is not only trying to understand the mechanisms responsible for behavior but also the contexts that thwart this capability.

To understand the mechanisms and context responsible for students' motivation to learn, as well as the contexts that thwart this type of motivation, remain empirical and pedagogical goals. In modern discourse, the focus is on students' perceptions, which include self-efficacy, sense of belonging, values, goals, expectancy of success, control, and autonomy. Researchers depict students as likely to be motivated to learn in contexts in which they value tasks, expect to be successful, feel part of a community, are not too anxious, have choices, and perceive themselves as competent and autonomous (Bandura, 1996; Ryan & Deci, 2000; Pintrich, 2003; Seifert, 2004; Dweck, 2006). The assumption is that students with these particular perceptions are likely to pursue task mastery and challenging goals, sustain their commitment to their goals, and academically achieve, all while experiencing personal satisfaction. From this modern view, motivating students to learn involves fostering certain perceptions.

The following overview and part of the critique provided center on the targeting of this focus. In addition, analysis includes critical concerns with the overall framing of teaching problems as issues with students' motivation. The critique includes (1) the limitations of the metaphors of motivation; (2) the context in which perceptions are targeted; (3) the dangers with attributing motivation to perceptual variables; and (4) and the ethical function of motivation research. The main argument presented is that shaping students' perceptions to energize them to be motivated to learn is a way of targeting psychological conditions in order to render them amenable to institutional lessons. Knowledge of human motivation plays a key function in organizations and situations in which people need to be adapt to organizational structures. In this regard, motivation research is rhetorically framed as supporting students' potential and satisfaction with schooling when in fact it serves a governing role.

Background

Researchers and teachers have been unlikely to question the importance and value of understanding and applying knowledge of human motivation to schooling, especially if it is framed as supporting the manifestation of natural drives, realization of students' potential, satisfaction with learning, and mastery of content. Nonetheless, the literature on human motivation is vast and replete with debates, contentions, and diverse perspectives. Neither the forces that move students nor their origins are always agreed on. Also debated are the origination of drives (i.e., natural or learned) and degrees of control that individuals can exercise over those drives. Even if these debates were resolved to produce a homogeneous picture, pedagogical controversies have arisen about which classroom structures are optimal for motivating students (e.g., see Kohn, 1999).

Historically, the conceptualization of human motivation has reflected multiple trends. The formal study of motivation can be traced back to the early 1920s and has roots in psychoanalytic theorizing (Graham & Weiner, 1996). At that time, motivation was understood in terms of physiological impulses, appetites, aversions, defense mechanisms, and an external regulatory system (i.e., the superego). Since the time of this original formal study, motivation has been understood in different ways. Graham and Weiner (1996) have contended that up until the 1970s grand theories of human motivation prevailed. That is, dominant theories attempted to coherently explain motivation as universally applicable, despite the complexities of situations, history, and culture. However, in contemporary theorizing, as Graham and Weiner have described, motivation is understood by applying a broad range of principles and constructs that can be adapted and revised according to situations. The modern discourse is about applying a variety of principles in order to shape students' perceptions.

THE MECHANISTIC ERA, 1930–1960

Graham and Weiner (1996) have called early accounts of motivation mechanistic, meaning that human behavior could be explained in deterministic and physiological ways. These authors have contended that Freud's psychoanalytic theory exemplifies this view. Freud emphasized the power of physiological drives to shape thinking and behavior. From this view, motivation is largely outside willful control. Aligned with this view, Hull (1943), a prominent American motivational researcher, contended that instances of motivation were instigated by the body's detection of a physiological deficit. According to Hull, humans have four physiological needs: hunger, thirst, sex, and avoidance of pain. Deprivation of any of these needs causes disequilibrium. According to this theory, people are driven to act in ways to restore equilibrium—that is, to satisfy needs. Physiological deficits spur drives as the organism performs behaviors to mitigate deficits. Rewards and punishments, whether administered by adults or indirectly experienced from existing conditions, are an essential component to this theory. Those behaviors that lead to the mitigation of deficits have the potential to form into habit. Behaviors that were previously reinforced will be enacted again when physiological need arises. Motivation starts with a physiological deficit and manifests in a set of behaviors that depend on reinforcement history. This physiological deprivation theory is featured as the lowest, but in no way unimportant, level in Maslow's hierarchy of needs, to be discussed.

The mechanistic approach has roots in behaviorist thinking. Like Hull (1943), some behaviorists argued that physiological deficits are stimuli that instigate activity, or in other words, cause behavior. These underlying causes of behaviors are not learned but result from the shifting stasis of a biological organism. However, some behaviorists have emphasized the learning of motives that extended beyond the return of the body to equilibrium. That is, they were interested in how learning and drives interacted to produce behavior. For example, money is a piece of paper that has strong motivational qualities because it has been associated with satisfying hunger, warmth, and exercising power, which one might argue is another human drive. The value associated with money via the satisfying of physiological needs can lead to behaviors and thoughts that are geared toward capital accumulation beyond satisfying those needs. As Lewin (1946) contended, people develop a sense of need and goals that arises from their experience of reality. The perception of needs and goals causes an energizing force and tension in the person until they are satisfied and achieved. Although he is grouped with mechanistic theorists, by emphasizing goals and aspirations Lewin begins to depart from this view of motivation.

THE COGNITIVE ERA (1960–1970)

Gollwitzer and Oettingen (2001) described early theories of motivation as characterizing people as machinelike organisms who are compelled to act by internal and external forces that are outside of their control. This view of motivation began to shift during what Graham and Weiner (1996) termed the cognitive era of the 1960s. During this time, different theories emerged that highlighted persons' rationalistic ability to choose behaviors and goals to pursue. For example, the social learning theory of motivation, which still has remnants of a mechanistic approach, is based on the idea that people choose to engage in behaviors that they expect will lead to the most personally rewarding goals. Expectancies come from past reinforcement for a behavior or experiences of reinforcement. However, the emphasis on choice for behaviors informs this narrative of motivation. From this view, persons can believe that they are responsible for their behavior and the reinforcement they receive. Furthermore, this narrative brings in perceptions of external conditions. Persons can believe that other people or luck are responsible for their behavior and subsequent reinforcement. So now rational deliberation, choice, and perception are added to the motivation equation. Although attribution theory—to be discussed—had not emerged yet, theorists were accounting for individuals' perceptions regarding their behaviors and motivational tendencies.

With the introduction of cognition, people were now considered interpreters of rewards and rational deliberators of behavior. The shift to the description of an active, choosing, and interpreting actor led to the interest in achievement striving. Achievement motivation is the idea that individuals have a need for achievement that is learned and shaped in childhood by associations between achievement and positive emotional states (Atkinson, 1964). The tendency of a person to approach or avoid an activity is calculated in terms of motive for success, probability of success, and the incentive value of success (pride associated with engagement and achievement). The common theme among the different theories that were proposed during this time was that motivation was centered on the mathematical relationship among motives, probability of success, incentives, and values.

CONTEMPORARY COGNITIVE THEORIZING

Graham and Weiner (1996) have characterized the post-1970 phase of motivation research as extending earlier theorists' interest in cognitive influences, including causal ascriptions, anxiety, and perceptions of control, to explore individual differences in motivation. Research interest continued to focus on understanding individuals' perceptions and how they interacted with and were shaped by learning environments to influence motivation. The continuing trend, the authors observed, was to apply a variety of constructs to make sense of students' motivation. These principles are discussed below. But first, consider a view of motivation that is of growing interest.

A SOCIOCULTURAL VIEW OF MOTIVATION

A seemingly alternative view of motivation in contemporary theorizing falls under the banner of socioculturalism. Educational psychologists who promote a sociocultural perspective on motivation have expressed concern that researchers have focused too narrowly on individual processes, states, and conditions without adequately accounting for the relations between students and their environments (Hickey & Zuiker, 2005; Rueda & Moll, 2012). Rueda and Moll (2012) have stated, "Sociocultural theory argues for a reconceptualization of cognitive activity (and by extension, motivation) as a within-child, context-independent phenomenon towards a perspective that highlights the *interdependence* of cognitive and sociocultural activities. Accordingly, from this view, motivation is not located solely within the individual without reference to the social and cultural contexts within which individual actions take place" (p. 120; emphasis in original). From a sociocultural perspective, motivation researchers have focused on the qualities of activities, students' cultural backgrounds, school culture, classroom structure, and relationships. Sociocultural researchers do not ignore or discount students' aspirations, perceptions, beliefs, and values but, rather, argue that these individual qualities are contextually bound. Hickey and Zuiker (2005) explained this view as follows: "A sociocultural perspective leads to a specific way of reconciling assumptions about the activity of individuals and assumptions about the functioning of broader social systems. Rather than using aggregated assumptions about the behavior or cognition of individuals to understand social systems, a sociocultural approach treats assumptions about individual behavior or cognition as 'special cases' of sociocultural functioning" (p. 291). The conceptual and pedagogical shift in this view is movement away from treating motivation as resulting from individual cognitive conditions to motivation as a manifestation of sociocultural worlds. Researchers have taken this starting point and theorized the relationship between the individual and social world in a variety of ways. One merit of this view is that it invites a shift in focus away from motivation as a purely psychological and physiological phenomenon. Thus, addressing so-called motivation problems can move away from the conditioning of behaviors and perceptions.

Approaches to Motivating Students

The different perspectives inform different approaches to motivating students. Although theorists have departed from the endorsement of a purely mechanistic approach, the idea of motivating students by conditioning their behaviors via reinforcements is still prevalent. Another prevalent approach is to condition students' perceptions. While these approaches vary significantly, they both involve targeting students directly. Another approach to addressing issues with students' motivation is to change something in their environment, since environments can thwart students' natural capability to organize behavior to achieve a goal. This approach is characterized by a commitment to structure environments in order to tap into and harness students' drive to pursue mastery. The foundational assumption of this approach is that problems with students' motivation result from environments not allowing for the expression of their nature. The goal is not to motivate students by consequences, but rather by means of acknowledging, validating, and expressing emotions, needs, desires, and dispositions. The logic here is that if their

needs are met and proclivities expressed, students will not need to be co-
erced, bribed, threatened, or prodded to engage.

CONDITIONING BEHAVIORS

Knowing how to condition behaviors using reinforcements and punishments can be a powerful and efficient way to motivate students. To motivate this way, teachers must be equipped with principles of behaviorism
(see chapter on classroom management). Although potentially effective for
motivating students, this approach is concerning because it can invite an instrumental approach to learning. Thoughts and behaviors are performed as
an instrument to attainment of something else and not an end in itself. Being
motivated by consequences can undermine intrinsic value for a task. Students
may learn to engage only when there is a desired reward or the potential to
avoid a punishment. If motivated by consequences, students may only do
what is necessary to receive a reward or avoid punishment. Motivation via
consequences invites a performance orientation.

Another issue with motivating using consequences is that extrinsic motivation is more difficult to sustain than its intrinsic counterpart (Deci &
Ryan, 2008). Consequences can be effective for energizing and directing
thinking and behavior as long as there is an association to those consequences. Once the reward is no longer offered or if the reward loses value,
the assumption is that students are not likely be motivated to engage with
the targeted task. However, if there is value for the task in itself, the assumption is that students will enact behaviors and thoughts to engage with
tasks independent of a consequence. If there is little value, students may
strategically maneuver to do the minimum required in order to elicit a desired consequence.

Aside from the potential to undermine intrinsic value and sustain commitment to goal pursuit, Kohn (1999) argued that motivating by consequences could invite self-interest. Kohn reasoned that frequent attention to
consequences encourages students to remain concerned about and motivated
by ways they can maximize their rewards and avoid punishment. Extrinsic
motivation encourages students to perform if it satisfies the pursuit of some
type of gain. This concern should be taken seriously during a time when personhood is increasingly self-interested and less concerned about the social
good (Twenge, 2014). It is important to note, however, that a commitment
to intrinsic motivation may not address this concern. Intrinsic motivation is
about personal meaning, satisfying needs, validating emotions, pursuing interest, and individual expression. Although opposing a commitment to foster intrinsic motivation might seem counterintuitive, such a focus, as with

efforts at extrinsic motivation, can communicate the problematic message that the self is of heightened importance, distinct, unique, the pedagogical center, and entitled.

CONDITIONING PERCEPTIONS

Rather than behaviors, targeting perceptions is a way to motivate students. If students perceive themselves and the learning task in particular ways, they are more likely to value tasks for their own sake, which is associated with persistence and challenging goal-setting—markers of the motivated student. In contemporary theorizing, being motivated to learn is largely a result of students' perceptions, which include self-efficacy, attributions, self-determination, expectancy, and value. Students should (1) attribute success and failure to things that are internal, unstable, and controllable, such as the amount of effort exerted (locus of control); (2) perceive themselves as capable to master challenges (self-efficacy and expectancy); (3) perceive themselves as connected to students and teachers (belonging); (4) perceive environments as safe and trustworthy; (5) have a sense of autonomy and personal control (self-determination); and (6) value tasks.

Self-efficacy

Self-efficacy is the belief in one's capability to achieve a designated level of performance for a specific task. Evaluations of these beliefs are task-specific and are not universal evaluations of capabilities. Self-efficacy is described in terms of high and low. Students with low self-efficacy may doubt that they can perform well on, for example, a spelling test. Low self-efficacy is associated with disengagement and task-avoidance. Whereas, the higher the self-efficacy, the more challenging goals individuals set for themselves and the stronger the volition to achieve those goals (Bandura, 1989). The thinking is that if students believe that they can be successful with tasks through their own efforts, they are likely to enact behaviors to succeed with those tasks and seek challenges. If students believe they cannot be successful with specific tasks, then they are less likely to engage with those tasks and persist in the face of challenge.

Although high self-efficacy is important, the goal is not necessarily to foster inflated efficacy (Zimmerman, Bonner, & Kovach, 1996; Bandura, 2001; Linnenbrink and Pintrich, 2002). The accuracy of these personal evaluations is critical. If students over- or underestimate what they can do, the result can be lack of preparation or task avoidance, respectively. Zimmerman, Bonner, and Kovach (1996) stated, "Pessimism can lead to poor motivation, and over-optimism can lead to insufficient preparation" (p. 30).

According to these authors, inaccurate self-efficacy, whether too high or low, can create the mismanagement of learning and contribute to motivation problems. As complicated as this idea of accurate self-assessments might be, the goal of targeting self-efficacy is to ensure that it is high and reflective of what students actually can do.

Expectancy and Value Theory

According to Wigfield and Eccles (2000), achievement behaviors are determined by two factors: expectancies for success and subjective task values. Expectancy and value interact to predict engagement, interest, and academic achievement. Expectancy refers to the confidence individuals have in their ability to succeed. This assessment is not unlike self-efficacy. This theory contributes to the understanding of motivation by bringing value into the equation. Task values refer to how important, useful, or enjoyable individuals perceive a task to be. Theorists have contended that if either expectancy or value were zero, students would not be motivated. For example, if students fully expect to be successful with a task, yet assign no value to it, they will not engage with the task. Conversely, if students assign high value to a task and have no expectancy for success, they will not engage with the task. According to this theory, there must be at least a little of each in order for students to be motivated to engage. The challenge is to figure out which quantities facilitate the motivation to learn.

Learned Helplessness

The absence of expectancy for success and having a low self-efficacy can result from learned helplessness, which is the perception that one has no control to influence outcomes. This notion is associated with the research of Seligman, Maier, and Geer (1968), who strapped dogs to a harness so they could not escape the administration of electrical shocks. Seligman, Maier, and Geer found that after repeated failed attempts to escape the shocks, dogs remained in place when shocks were administered without the harness restricting their movement. Generalized to students, the idea is that from experience, individuals may learn that they can and cannot affect their outcomes through their own efforts. The latter is the phenomenon known as learned helplessness. Students may perceive themselves and environments in ways that bring them to conclude that no self-generated action can shape outcomes. Therefore, they are less likely to be motivated to engage in tasks to pursue those outcomes. Learned helplessness is considered a faulty perception because the assumption is that students have agency in situations even though they may not perceive it.

Self-determination Theory

According to Deci and Ryan (2008), individuals have an innate desire to grow and gain fulfillment. Human nature, they have argued, shows persistent positive features, such as effort, agency, and tendencies for growth. This nature surrounds three innate psychological needs that are the basis for motivation: competence, relatedness, and autonomy. Individuals need to feel masterful, related to others, and agentic. That is, in contexts where students perceive themselves as belonging, they need to have opportunities to master tasks and increase skill while believing that they are in control of that learning. Deci and Ryan suggested that meeting these conditions fosters self-determination and intrinsic motivation. This idea is referred to as self-determination theory, which is geared toward facilitating what Deci and Ryan have referred to as "autonomous motivation" (14).

The big idea here is that individuals will be highly motivated to learn and pursue achievement for its own sake (i.e., be intrinsically motivated) if the three aforementioned innate psychological needs are met. This theory is perceptual because of the interpretations of one's sense of competence, relatedness, and control. To foster autonomous motivation, teachers must convince students that they are competent or can develop competence. Although not unlike self-efficacy and expectancy theory, self-determination theory adds the importance of perceiving oneself as belonging and having control.

Locus of Control

What is responsible for individual success and failure? This question is the foundation of attribution theory. According to Weiner (1986), people try to understand the causes of their outcomes by considering personal and environmental forces. Weiner specified three dimensions of causality: locus (internal/external), stability (stable/unstable), and controllability (controllable/uncontrollable). Locus is about the source of control or influence, which is categorized as internal or external. Internal are those sources that are featured within individuals, such as ability, effort, talent, and intelligence. External sources include teachers, subject matter, luck, peers, curricula, and institutional structures. Stability relates to perceptions of change over time and how likely the sources of control are likely to change. Talent and intelligence may be perceived as stable sources, whereas effort and ability are unstable. The third dimension relates to perceptions regarding one's ability to control the source of influence. For example, some students might perceive intelligence, talent, institutional structures, and curricula as sources that they cannot control. Given that these are perceptual variables, individuals will determine the stability and controllability of sources differently. For example, some students may perceive intelligence as incremental (changing over time), whereas others will view it as an entity (a stable feature of persons). The notion of growth mindset, which is argued to be associated with academic achievement, is based on this idea that ability, talent, and intelligence can be developed through effort (Dweck, 2006).

For attribution theory, the perceived source of success and failure and the perception of those source's stability and controllability affect motivation. Some attributions can demotivate while others can motivate. The optimal attribution is internal, unstable, and uncontrollable. The idea is that individuals must believe that the source of their success and failure is something internal that can be changed and controlled through their own efforts. For example, if a student attributes a successful experience to effort, which is generally understood as unstable (amount of effort varies) and controllable (one can choose their level of effort), that student is likely to develop pride in the accomplishment and exert effort on future tasks. Attributing failure to a different internal source such as ability, which might be perceived as stable and uncontrollable, could lead to a lack of trying, as students may believe that there is little they can do to affect outcomes. Attributions to external sources, especially ones perceived as stable and uncontrollable, could foster a lack of trying and disengagement, as students may believe outcomes are independent of what they think and do. Like self-determination theorists, attribution theorists contended that students are likely to choose valued academic behaviors, persist with tasks, and exert effort if they perceive themselves as having control (Weiner, 1986; Alderman, 2013). Thus, the pedagogical goal is to foster the perception of personal causation and controllability for academic outcomes.

TARGETING PEDAGOGICAL ENVIRONMENTS

As a second approach to directly targeting students' perceptions or behaviors, teachers can work on motivating students by structuring environments, which can range from classrooms to school-wide organizations. The idea is that environments must be organized around a commitment to meet students' developmental, emotional, social, or cognitive needs, which will be referred to as motivational material (MM). The guiding commitment is not to change students directly but rather to change the structure and practice of the classroom or school. The assumption is that carefully constructed learning environments can help to avoid or curtail issues with students' motivation by allowing needs to be met and proclivities expressed. The idea is that environments can curtail or suppress students' natural drive and impulse to learn and pursue mastery.

This assumption is the foundation of major educational theorists (Dewey, 1910/1997; Montessori, 1948; Piaget & Inhelder, 1969). For example, one of the foundations of Maria Montessori's educational philosophy is that students will spontaneously self-discipline and be attentive and hardworking if contexts are structured in ways that allow their natural tendencies to be expressed. According to her philosophy, motivational strategies are about shaping contexts, not necessarily students' perceptions, although that very well may be the target or the consequence of her pedagogical environment. Rather, her philosophy is underpinned by the idea that children have natural motivational structures that will surface in the right environment.

The focus on MM for motivation is regarded as a humanistic approach. The goal is to render pedagogical environments compatible with MM. Researchers such as Kohn (1999) are optimistic that if students' MM is taken into account in the construction and evolution of learning environments, students are likely to be motivated without coercion, bribery, prompting, or teacher surveillance. On the other hand, failing to satisfy needs, allowing for tendencies to be expressed, and quelling proclivities can lead to behaviors, emotions, and thoughts that can thwart students' motivation to learn. From this approach, the emotional, physical, and psychological needs and states of students must be met in order to optimize motivation and support students' well-being.

What is students' MM? Many educational theorists have had something to say about this question (Dewey, 1916/2004; Montessori, 1964/2014; Maslow, 1968; Piaget & Inhelder, 1969; Perry, 2002; Deci & Ryan, 2008). For example, Maslow (1968) emphasized the importance of self-actualization and other human needs, including physiological and emotional. He contended that individuals have a positive human nature that needs to be expressed and fulfilled. The task, he argued, is to discover that nature, which shares some universal commonalities across students (see Maslow's pyramid scheme) but is also unique to individuals. Maslow argued that suppressing what he termed the "essential core of a person" could lead to negative behaviors, emotional turmoil, and undesirable personality traits. Human nature, he reasoned, is not overpowering and is easily invalidated, suppressed, and thwarted. Although this nature is weak and easily suppressed, Maslow contended that it does not go away but rather continues to press for actualization. Therefore, when environments do not validate, affirm, support, and allow the expression of human nature, internal and external conflicts abound. Therefore, the goal of teachers is to discover that natural essential core of students' beings and construct environments that allow for the actualization of that nature.

MM can also be understood in terms of developmental needs, innate human dispositions (e.g., curiosity, creativity, and experimentation), or the needs associated with self-determination theory, which are to feel competent, interested, connected, and autonomous. Developmentally appropriate practice can guide this orientation to motivation. This discourse is often based on universal depictions of human nature. If there were essential qualities to students, one must consider if the importance of needs, dispositions, and proclivities were also universal. For some students, certain needs and proclivities may be more important than others. Given the potential for variability, the requirement is that teachers observe and evaluate their students to figure out their needs and proclivities.

Whereas targeting perceptions or behaviors assumes a deficiency in students, MM centers attention on problems in the environment that are precluding the realization of students' spontaneous goal-directed behavior. As noted, this approach may involve the reconditioning of perceptions, but that is not achieved through individualistic interventions but rather through environmental restructuring. From this approach, perceptions are important, but they are a consequence of environments and, therefore, changed in relation to environments. Problems with motivation occur when environments are incompatible with psychological and physiological characteristics of students. This misalignment can affect perceptions. However, from this approach the pedagogical goal is to change those perceptions by changing the environment to create an alignment.

Although the ingredients are known, the formula for producing the motivation to learn is not algorithmic. Contemporary researchers are concerned with understanding which structures of classroom environments can be most effective for validating and changing, if necessary, perceptual conditions for optimal motivation. The result of this research does not always yield universal practices that can impact students in the same way. A great deal of attention has been focused on individual differences in perception as well as the generalized interactions between students and pedagogical environments. The thinking is that not all students will perceive themselves and their pedagogical environments in the same way. Teachers are therefore encouraged to use motivational principles and constructs when deliberating over pedagogical decision-making and student engagement.

Critical Analysis

The very notion of criticizing motivation discourse may seem counterintuitive, especially since "tapping into" students' stores of energy in order to shape their perceptions is tied to the realization of their potential. Furthermore, motivating students, whether to perform or learn, could support the achievement of schooling goals. Can't effectively motivating students by any means be rationalized as supporting their own good? A critique of motivation discourse does not necessarily mean that teachers need not concern themselves at all with motivation or that a pedagogical commitment should be made to limit students' potential. Rather this critique is about examining the values and norms that underpin accepted principles and practices. The following analysis considers (1) the limitations of the metaphors of motivation; (2) the context in which students are to be motivated; (3) the dangers with attributing motivation to perceptual variables; and (4) and the ethical function of motivation research. Although some motivational strategies may seem more humanistic than others, all strategies are dangerous.

METAPHORS OF MOTIVATION

Different theories and principles rely on different assumptions about the mechanisms responsible for motivation and the factors that affect it. In contemporary discourse, these assumptions are revealed by the prevailing metaphors, which are that motivation is a code to be unlocked, a resource to tap into, or an energy source to be harnessed. These metaphors are examples of what Lakoff and Johnson (1999) referred to as ontological metaphors that project substance onto something that does not inherently have a substance but is substantiated via the association to a concrete experience. In the instance of motivation, an inherently intangible force is conceptualized as inside a person, ready and waiting to be expressed. This metaphor is aligned with another prominent one, which is the extrinsic (originating and operating from "outside") and intrinsic (originating and operating from the "inside") binary. These metaphors are underpinned by the assumption that motivation to learn is within individuals and requires some intervention or pedagogical structure in order to ensure its proper outlet.

But there are dangers with the inner/outer metaphor. First, this metaphor is underpinned by a conception that students have psychological lives that are distinct and separable from a physical world, including their bodies, brains, and context. In other words, quite explicitly, the conception is that there is an outside and inside world and that motivation originates and results from either of these physical locations. This affirms the dualism of inner and outer, which has been the subject of much philosophical critique (e.g., see Sugarman & Martin, 2010). New and emerging theories of persons and learning challenge this binary; for example, embodied cognition, a theory that unites bodies, minds, and the physical world as inseparable. As key contributors to the development of this notion, Lakoff and Johnson (1999) reasoned that conceptual systems take form in relation to spatial experiences. In this regard, that which is understood as internal is grounded in the body's relationship and experience in the world. The notion of embodied cognition is about the rejection of a neat separation between an internal and external world.

As we have seen, sociocultural theory can also be used to challenge the inner/outer metaphor. Sociocultural theorists explain motivation in terms of activities, relationships, and tools. As noted, according to Hickey and Zuiker (2005), a sociocultural view of motivation does not rest on the qualities of the individual for understanding and explaining motivation, but rather the context. From this view, student motivation occurs in situations, with others, and for particular purposes. Rueda and Dembo (1995) described this view as conceptualizing motivation as "an individual-in-action in specific contexts" (257). Hickey and Zuiker's corresponding suggestion that motivational issues must be understood in terms of context, which includes purpose, authenticity of task, other participants, identity, and meaning, thus implies that motivation is not understood as resulting from students' perceptions but from shared value in the pursuit of knowledge for a particular purpose.

Despite these emerging theories, contemporary theorizing is still fixed firmly on the individual, even if context is now considered more influential than it was in the past. Part of the problem is that traditional psychological research has defined motivation as an inner property of the individual. Although emphasizing activity and purpose, sociocultural theorists tend to preserve individuals as the source of motivation and context as influential. As Sugarman and Martin (2010) have argued, context is not merely influential but constitutive. They meant that students are not inherently fragmented via internal and external worlds, but that individuals take shape through these types of metaphors, statements, and ways of reasoning. Contemporary theorizing points to the limitations of these conceptual limitations to adequately capture the complexity of human subjectivity.

Another issue with motivation metaphors relates to the ontological certainty for the contents of persons. In this context, ontological certainty means asserting unequivocally, ahistorically, and objectively the contents of students' motivational capacities and qualities. If one assumes motivation originates from within or without, then the empirical and intellectual task is to "uncover" the qualities and features of both. This commitment can be dangerous as these qualities of persons and their surroundings may be normalized. For example, one might claim that students are naturally and inherently competitive, despite the fact that competitive environments are not always motivating. However, in assuming the ontological certainty of the internal, human nature to be competitive, researchers and teachers may strive to understand the conditions that best support this natural proclivity. They may ask questions such as (1) what kinds of competitive structures are most motivating for students; and (2) what perceptions must students have to be motivated in competitive environments? Given the assumed ontological certainty of human competitiveness, interventions to harness this capacity can normalize competition and strive to change students in ways to get them to value and thrive in competitive environments. Such pedagogical practices may be rationalized as intellectual innovation by tapping into students' internal, natural motivational sources.

Alternatively, critical educational psychologists tend to eschew claims of ontological certainty, especially those that normalize and validate neoliberal ideology. One might espouse the belief that human nature is competitive in order to justify capitalism and modern neoliberal educational reforms. Any claim of ontological certainty is situated within a particular cultural, historical, political, and ideological context. Even those claims that are less controversial are contextually bound. When researchers and teachers make claims about what is natural and internal to students, they are relying on a conceptual system, types of evidence, and styles of reasoning that are historical, cultural, philosophical, and ideological. The understanding of innate, internal, and natural drives is shaped by conceptions of persons, historical narratives, philosophical commitments, and values for certain types of evidence. Thus the idea that students have inside and outside worlds should not be taken for granted as locating sources and mechanisms of motivation.

MOTIVATING STUDENTS IN SPECIFIC CONTEXTS

Another critical concern with the motivation discourse relates to the contexts in which students are to be motivated. Educational theorists and researchers have contended that students have a natural desire to learn and take satisfaction in that learning. But if one agrees that learning is a natural and satisfying drive, then why is it necessary to understand and apply principles of motivation to support students' success and satisfaction in schools, which is where learning is supposed to take place?

Brophy (1983) provides insight into this question when he described schooling in the following way: "The vast majority of classrooms . . . are work settings in which students must cope with activities that are compulsory and subject to evaluation, rather than play settings offering free choice according to personal preferences. . . . During academic activities, students . . . are responding to intellectual challenges in a public setting, under conditions in which their performance will lead not only to subjective judgments of success or failure but to external evaluation and subsequent reward and punishment" (202). This characterization seems appropriate for many classrooms. Students have to engage with tasks that they might not otherwise choose to engage with were those tasks not compulsory and consequential. Many students are likely to experience schools as forced, judgmental, and constraining, which Brophy argued is counter to play, wherein persons pursue their interest, exercise choice, and manage their own time. Brophy's characterization of schooling can immediately signal problems for students' motivation to learn, especially if one takes the ontological certain position that students are optimally motivated when given choice, opportunities for autonomy, and experiencing manageable levels of anxiety. Assuming this MM, modern educational environments can thwart students' capabilities and proclivities.

The narrative that humanist psychologists tell about students' motivation is incompatible with current curricula structures and reforms. Students have to learn specific content in a particular way at a universalized pace—all for the purpose of an economic goal. Much of what drives educational reform and policy today is rationalized in terms of improving students' outcomes across global assessments, producing "good" workers for the economy, and advancing science and technology for economic and environmental purposes. The result is the contemporary focus on science, technology, and math (STEM), twenty-first-century competencies, and so-called "higher" standards. Students are socialized as early as prekindergarten to start along the path for college and careers with a tightened focus on developing specific skills and content knowledge expertise. Within this environment, the curriculum narrows, teachers' autonomy steadily declines, and student outcomes are predetermined and specifically tied to the economy. Specific ideas about what students need to know and be able to do fall along a well-defined learning trajectory. Hyper-evaluative classrooms and high-stakes testing are mechanisms to encourage movement along this trajectory. The pressure on teachers and parents to motivate students within these contexts is high.

Modern schooling seems to conflict with humanist assumptions about motivation, which is that students are likely to be motivated to learn when given choice, control, and opportunities to pursue interest and achieve mastery. However, initiatives to homogenize and script teaching can make it difficult to center students' motivational material. Researchers and teachers are unlikely to argue that students are motivated to learn in standardized, prescriptive, homogeneous learning environments. For that reason, knowledge of motivation is necessary because teachers have to figure out how to motivate students despite an ostensible incompatibility with individuals' needs, drives, and dispositions. Hence, there is pressure to differentiate instruction and personalize learning, all while achieving curricular mandates. Although teachers operate in contexts that are increasingly scripted and based on universals, they are expected to figure out how to make pedagogical adjustments that are within the boundaries of the school structure but which affect students differently. Therefore, teachers are expected to figure out ways to work within and mediate curricular structures so that the schooling environments align with students' MM.

TARGETING STUDENTS' PERCEPTIONS

Motivating students by targeting their perceptions is problematic for a couple of reasons. As argued above, classrooms are becoming more and more regulated and homogenous, potentially making it difficult for students to experience autonomy, control, and choice. If necessary for motivating students to learn, the pedagogical task then is to convince students that they do in fact have autonomy, control, and choice. Perhaps, the masterful teacher is one who convinces students that they are autonomous choosers who pursue their own academic interest, despite the regulatory mechanisms in place. Herein lies a point of concern. As Carver and Scheier (2000) argued, those who are interested in autonomy, choice, and self-determination have focused mainly on individuals' need to "perceive" themselves as in control as opposed to "actually" being in control. In other words, it matters little if students are "actually" exercising control and choice. The belief and perception that they are is key for motivation. Although the distinction between "actual" control and the perception of control is challenging to discern, deliberations about this complexity are not typically a concern for educational psychologists who study motivation.

The perception that one has choice and control increases motivation, as well as is linked to resilience and mastery (Zimmerman, 2000; Bandura, 2001). Perceiving oneself as in control and making choices is likely to reduce rebelliousness and resistance to the source that is identified as quelling these natural proclivities. Students may be unmotivated in schools because they perceive themselves as not having control, autonomy, choice, and opportunity to explore interest. Therefore, the pedagogical task is to ensure that students perceive themselves as in control, making choices, and pursuing interest. This task can be carried out in a number of ways. For example, teachers can elicit students' contributions for setting classroom rules and consequences, determining assessments for learning, and choosing tasks in which to engage. Teachers can give students choices for which books to read to fulfill a classroom requirement. In regards to these strategies and countless others, there are certainly questions about whether this type of control and choice are "actual" in classrooms that continue to be scripted and driven by predetermined outcomes. The question of actuality is inconsequential when it comes to trying to foster optimal motivation. The point is that students must perceive themselves as having control in order to motivate them.

In addition to perceiving oneself as in control, having choices, and having the opportunity to pursue interest, students must also perceive themselves as responsible for their success and failure. The main premise of attribution theory is that students are likely to be motivated when they attribute the sources of success and failure to internal factors that change and can be controlled. One of these factors is effort. The thinking is that if students believe they were successful on tasks because of effort, which is something they can control and varies in degree, they are more likely to be motivated in situations in which they want to successfully achieve a goal. If students attribute failure to effort, the assumption is that motivation will increase if they want to be successful. If students perceive themselves as having no control over outcomes, they are unlikely to be motivated with those tasks. Although these conclusions make sense, there are a number of dangers with trying to shape students' perceptions to attribute success and failure to internal factors that they can control.

Fostering the perception that success and failure are attributable to internal factors that students can control aligns with meritocratic thinking. Meritocracy is the idea that talent, hard work, and effort determine one's position in life. Regardless of one's starting position, experiences in schools, disparate privileges, or any type of institutional or structural discrimination, students must attribute performance to effort. This attribution aligns well with zero-tolerance policies, a "no excuse" way of thinking, and motivational concepts such as grit. The assumption is that opportunity is wide open and hard work will translate into gaining access to opportunity. This perception is associated with a politically conservative view in which individuals are deemed solely responsible for their place in the world. This assumption underpins attribution theory, which promotes a particular explanation for academic success and failure. Although this explanation has come under heavy attack, the political implication and questions about the reality of the locus of control is of little consequence. The perception matters for motivation. If students perceive schooling as unfair, discriminatory, unchanging, and ultimately responsible for performance, they are unlikely to be motivated.

Several educational theorists have challenged a view of schooling as meritocratic. Students may also have these perceptions, which can be associated with disengagement and resistance to schooling. For these students, a problem with fostering internal, unstable, and controllable attributions invokes the idea that schooling environments are fair, misjudged, and misread by students. If students communicate external and uncontrollable causal explanations for success and failure, teachers must operate with the belief that such perceptions are faulty. Therefore, fostering certain attributions can lead teachers to invalidate students' interpretation of the world. Any perception that students have that might compete with motivation, such as value for tasks, low self-efficacy, and feelings of powerlessness must be viewed as perceptual delusions that must be changed. Viewing perceptions this way puts teachers in a difficult situation. Validating students' perceptions that they lack control can contribute to problems with motivation. On the other hand, invalidating students' perceptions can be demotivating because teachers may communicate a sense of distrust in the students' ability to interpret the world.

As Graham and Weiner (1996) argued, trust is important for motivating students. Graham and Weiner argued that the most pervasive motivational problems are children not wanting to learn, which is connected to their perceptions. Graham and Weiner frame the problem in the following way: "How can we get 'unmotivated' children to accept the basic premise that learning, school, and mastery of the material that adults prescribe are important? That is, how can there be internalization of attitudes that reflect, 'Trust us. We know what is best for you, and if you do it, you will not only like it, but it will help you better yourself in our world?'" (81). The authors seemed to have accepted that schooling is neither inherently satisfying nor perceived as immediately having value. Therefore, motivating students comes down to convincing them that they can trust school personnel to always act in their best interest. The pedagogical task is to shape students; perceptions so they see value and satisfaction in schooling because adults know how to guide them in ways to achieve self-betterment.

Students must trust teachers, the institution of schooling, and the promises of schooling.

The trust Graham and Weiner (1996) pointed to is trust is in teachers, tasks, and the promise of schooling for self-betterment. However, not all students have this trust. Graham and Weiner argued that the lack of trust in teachers and schooling extend beyond the classroom and into American culture. But this distrust is more salient among certain groups than others. In particular, the distrust among African Americans and working-class students is well documented (Auerbach, 2007; Ogbu & Simons, 1998). As Graham and Weiner argued, some students recognize the lack of equality in society as well as within specific institutional structures. As a consequence, some students may perceive meaningful goal attainment as an impossibility. Resistance to engagement and a general lack of motivation may reflect this state of affairs. However, treating perceptions as misreadings that need to be changed invalidates the political implications of decreased motivation. The lack of student motivation can be a political act that can invite reflection on asymmetrical power relationships in classrooms, schools, and the broader society.

Targeting students' perceptions in order to motivate them is about shaping particular perceptions about schools, teachers, tasks, and society. This focus is underpinned by the assumption that schools are stable and fair, and that students' lack of motivation results from faulty perceptions, or that perceptions must change without changes to schooling environments. Therefore, motivating students involves changing something about their way of interpreting the world. As Freire (1968/2000) argued, when a change in students' psychology is targeted in order to support their motivation and engagement while preserving environmental conditions, students are dehumanized. Critical theorists start with the premise that schooling is unequal and inequitable. However, for students, this perception is not conducive to motivation and academic engagement. Yet, rather than change the structures of schooling, the motivation discourse supports an orientation to change students' perceptions. In this case, the teacher is the authority regulating students' reading of the world and the protector of schooling structures.

THE FUNCTION OF MOTIVATION KNOWLEDGE

Targeting students' perceptions in order to motivate them, either through a psychological intervention or some form of environmental change, is about changing psychological states to render students amenable to institutional lessons. Arguably, this amenability and adaptability to schools is a key function of motivation research. Consider that problems with motivation are only in relation to those who do not perform in expected ways. If workers perfectly achieved corporate goals, which are most likely to maximize profit, then knowing how to motivate them is unnecessary. If children did everything their parents wanted them to do, then motivating them would be unnecessary. If students achieved all goals outlined by schools, then figuring out how to motivate them would be unnecessary. Problems with motivation become such when there are challenges with directing persons in particular ways and when their behaviors do not align with the rationality of an institutional goal.

Typically, challenges with students' motivation are in relation to those who are disengaged or those who are motivated to perform rather than to learn. Another motivational problem arises when students pertinaciously engage with a task and pursue a goal. Researchers refer to this type of motivation as grit, which is about perseverance in the face of long-term challenging goals (Duckworth, Peterson, Matthews, & Kelly, 2007). Researchers generally view grit as a positive and highly desirable trait that can contribute to the mitigation of educational inequalities (Tough, 2013). There are several reasons to be skeptical of the grit discourse. One reason is that although researchers call for grit to be taught in schools, this so-called trait may not be conducive to classrooms that require shifting attention to different subjects and the mastery of many tasks, behaviors, and concepts—not just one. To be valuable for schooling, students have to have a broad goal of mastering schooling and see all tasks as part of this goal, or they must shift their goals and scale back intensity so they can adapt to schooling requirements. Being motivated too intensely to achieve a goal can pose challenges for teachers who need students' goals and attention to shift in accordance with structures and pace of schooling.

Student motivation must be intense enough to achieve a particular goal but must be redirectable, malleable, adaptable, and responsive to situational demands. Thought about in this way, the discourse of motivation is not about motivation in the abstract sense. That is, it is not about getting students just to do something. Rather, the motivation literature is about helping teachers elicit certain behaviors and thoughts from their students so they can achieve certain goals in a particular time frame and with a certain level of intensity. Teachers are tasked to adhere to curricula and pedagogical mandates while trying to motivate students to be successful with those tasks. If students are already successful with school tasks, then they might not be seen as having motivation problems. When students' ways of engagement make the achievement of schooling goals difficult, then they might be perceived as having a problem with motivation.

If students are perceived as having motivation problems, then the discourse of needs, aspirations, perceptions, and states can come into play. Motivation problems are generally understood at the level of the individual. What if it were possible to unequivocally know students' proclivities, needs, desires, and states? What if it were possible to use that knowledge to implement pedagogical interventions in order to motivate students to learn? What if it were possible to shape students' perceptions in the ways associated with optimal motivation? Although alignment between schooling goals and student outcomes is created in different ways, the function of motivation research remains the same, namely to ensure that students' energy manifests in ways that align with schooling goals and demands. Even the so-called humanistic approach functions in this way. Ensuring that pedagogical environments meet students' needs could be viewed as a form of seductive compliance. The focus is on meeting students needs so they are more likely to do what they are supposed to do, when they are supposed to do it, and in the way that is required.

Compliance and amenability are not generally recognized as a function of motivation research. Rather, educational psychologists reason that knowing and applying knowledge of students' motivation is about helping them realize their potential. These functions, however, are not opposing; complicity and amenability to schooling lessons can be understood as the means to unlock potential. For that reason, the notion of potential might be invoked to explain the discrepancy between student engagement and the achievement of school goals. One obvious problem is that students' potential will be judged on their perceived adaptability and amenability to schooling contexts. That is, if students are not meeting institutional expectations but are believed to be capable of doing so, then their potential is not realized. Motivation research is driven by the humanist commitment to help students realize their potential.

Although it might seem highly controversial to problematize a commitment to the realization of students' potential, the idea present some concerns. The notion of potential can be situated within neoliberal thinking. The realization of students' potential or progress toward it is often understood in relation to curricula benchmarks and schooling authorities. For this reason, a student's potential, its suppression or realization, is determined by adaptability to schooling environments and judgments about performance. Legitimacy about students' state of potential is granted to others and situated within a particular context. Furthermore, the notion of potential is well suited for a neoliberal ethic of selfhood. The idea of potential evokes the assumption that students are not yet realized; something is lacking and a pedagogical intervention is necessary to move them toward a particular endpoint. The pedagogical imperative to help students realize their potential constructs students as in need of improvement and subject to expertise on how to achieve that improvement. This imperative contributes to students and teachers casting doubt on the present-ness of being and projects one into the future that is guided by human capital accumulation.

The ethical commitment to realize potential, which is associated with humanism and empowerment, makes sense within a neoliberal climate that endorses a view of persons as always in need of improvement and requiring expert guidance on how to manage the pursuit of self-betterment. So the notion of potential is caught in a dangerous ideological context. This danger is not addressed by centering students' "internal" goals, as if they have goals that are independent of social, political, cultural, and ideological contexts. The problem is not about whether potential is defined by others or by oneself. Rather, the problem is about the ways this notion can be used to engender complicity to schooling demands, shape subjectivity, and endorse a particular ideology.

Within motivation discourse, it is not enough to energize students to achieve an institutional goal in a particular way and in the expected time frame. Motivating students is not just about behavioral complicity but also about helping students to find personal satisfaction in pursuing and achieving school goals. Motivation research is intended to support the alignment between institutional goals and students' aspirations and goals. Some students may already have achieved this alignment. In those cases, students are not motivational problems, but for those with a misalignment, some type of intervention is required. If applied well, motivation research can ostensibly support academic achievement, while preserving a sense of individual accomplishment and personal satisfaction. That is the goal of motivation research: to use scientific understanding of motivation in order to get people to conform to institutional expectations for behaviors that are deemed necessary to achieve certain outcomes, while at the same time fostering a sense of personal satisfaction.

Given this dual goal, motivation research is caught up in efforts to regulate subjective capacities (Rose, 1999). Cruikshank (1999) argued that "the line between subjection and subjectivity is crossed when I subject my self, when I align my personal goals with those set out by reformers . . . according to some notion of the social good" (p. 25). This effort at alignment is what critical theorists refer to as a struggle for the soul. Critical theorists use the notion of "soul" as an analytical concept to explain the operation of power. For example, Foucault (1977) examined the way discipline shifted from the body (i.e., corporeal punishment) to the soul (i.e., inner beliefs, feelings and sensitivities that generate action). Hacking (1995) wrote, "Philosophers of my stripe speak of the soul not to suggest something eternal, but to invoke character, reflective choice, self-understanding, values that include honesty to others and oneself, and several types of freedom and responsibility" (p. 6). Similarly, Rose (1999) treats the soul as personality, subjectivities and relationships. The soul does not ahistorically signify psychological phenomena such as personality, beliefs, perceptions, and attitudes, but rather the constitution of psychology via the categories and styles of reasoning that are available at the moment.

In contemporary theorizing, psychological constructs are used in the struggle for the soul. Students are constructed as perceiving beings. Perceptions are responsible for a host of beliefs, dispositions, behaviors, attitudes, and sense of purpose that can hinder or decrease optimal motivation in schools. Students' success within these structures is made possible by harnessing or changing perceptions and the corresponding attitudes, dispositions, and desires in order to facilitate optimal performance. These changes must be done in such a way as to communicate a sense of personal control and autonomy. The goal is to invite motivation that is seemingly "intrinsic," "self-generated," and aligned with schooling objectives.

Conclusion

Why is knowledge of students' motivation so important? One response already considered is that it can facilitate engagement and success with school tasks while helping students to realize their potential. The goal of motivation research is to construct a picture of the mechanisms responsible for students' motivation and help teachers reflect on the relationship between those mechanisms and pedagogical environments. The assumption is that this understanding can support students' success by helping teachers unlock students' potential by shaping classroom structures in order to motivate students to learn.

Although couched in positive terms, the discourse of motivation is as we have seen entangled in specific political, ideological, and philosophical contexts. Thus, whatever the dominant discourse, it is important to ask certain questions: (1) what assumptions about people underpin ideas about motivation; (2) in what contexts are students to be motivated; (3) what are the ethical implications of approaches to motivating students; and (4) what function does motivation research serve? Motivation discourse and the role of motivation knowledge in teaching have ethical, philosophical, and ideological underpinnings. Critical scrutiny of the discourse is not about rendering students disengaged, motionless, and directionless but rather about understanding the assumptions on which the practice of motivation rest.

CHAPTER THREE

Higher Order Thinking

I N CONTEMPORARY EDUCATION CONVERSATIONS, policy makers and researchers endorse pedagogical and curricular structures that support the development of problem solving, self-regulation, critical thinking, and creativity, which in educational psychology are categorized as higher order thinking (HOT) skills. Individuals with varying philosophical and ideological commitments rally behind efforts to shape curricula and pedagogy in ways that are centered on teaching these skills. Advocates include those who endorse a purpose of schooling based on civic engagement, humanization, and democratic processes (Dewey, 1916/2004; Shor, 1992; Lipman, 2003), as well as those who endorse a seemingly incompatible purpose of schooling based on benefits to the economy (e.g., Pithers & Soden, 2000; Azzam, 2009; Järvelä, 2011; Robinson, 2011; Marzano & Heflebower, 2012). Although there tends to be agreement about the need for HOT skills, there is not always agreement about what they are, how they develop, or the best way to teach these skills. To resolve debates, researchers generally focus on methodological, pedagogical, and conceptual developments, which are aimed at increasing the understanding of and efficacy for teaching HOT. However, little scholarship has been dedicated to critical analysis of HOT skills.

A critical analysis of HOT is not about advocating for the teaching of lower order thinking. In fact, the terms higher and lower are problematic because they limit the understanding of thinking to a binary system. In this system, thought exists on a hierarchy made concrete by the metaphor of levels. Certain values and norms underpin what is perceived as higher and lower, as well as shape who is perceived as displaying those types of thinking. Aside from propagating norms and marking students thinking qualities, Harré (2002) suggested that this binary exists as part of an effort to create psychological taxonomies, which he argued was necessary to position psychology as scientific. Another impetus for the distinction between higher and lower relates to efforts to separate psychology from biology (Harré, 2002). The purpose was to show that humans neither merely respond to stimuli nor are governed by the limitations of their perceptual system but rather they can reason about, and of course control, their perceptions, feelings, emotions, and thoughts. As Harré pointed out, specific motivations underpinned the formation of the distinction between higher and lower. While identifying thinking as either higher or lower has its utility, this classification is a hierarchy of thinking that is constructed for particular reasons and should not be treated as an objective, universal way of conceptualizing thinking.

Despite the philosophical, historical, and cultural underpinnings of the different levels of thinking, terms such as higher and lower are taken for granted as representing students' thought. A well-known and often used taxonomy of thinking is often associated with Benjamin Bloom. In what is referred to as Bloom's taxonomy, HOT signifies developed and evolved thinking processes. In his framework for thinking, Bloom (1956) did not discount the value of lower order thinking, which he described as involving memorization and recollection of knowledge claims. He argued that this type of thinking is necessary for eventually progressing toward higher forms of thinking, such as problem solving, critical analysis, and creativity. Rote learning, exerting habitual behavior, and following simple procedures stand in contrast to HOT, which typically connotes intentionality, reflection, self-control, awareness, and self-determination.

HOT skills are lauded in contemporary discourse because of the value associated with both civic virtue and the modern labor market. Schools that promote only lower order thinking are considered obsolete for the twenty-first-century political, economic, and democratic environments. Although associated with democratic ideals, the push to institutionalize HOT skills comes from policy makers, researchers, and theorists who tie the purpose of schooling to the modern economy. The twenty-first century is represented as rapidly changing, competitive, unpredictable, riddled with problems, vulnerable to foreseeable problems, and susceptible to problems not yet known. In this representation, the nature of work in the United States is changing. Manufacturing jobs continue to decline and in some cases machines have replaced workers. Workers are no longer required to engage in rote tasks but must have the knowledge, skills, and dispositions to fix machines. Some researchers reasoned that HOT is important to drive innovation, stave off corporate mortality, and maintain America's competitiveness in the global market (Pithers & Soden, 2000; Azzam, 2009; Robinson, 2011; Zhao, 2012). Given this depiction of the modern economy, educational policy makers and business owners have argued that all individuals on any level of the economic rung have to think critically, solve problems, be innovative, and self-manage. In this regard, HOT skills have become a form of human capital that is necessary for people to adapt to, compete in, and contribute to the twenty-first-century economy.

The economic value of HOT as emphasized in contemporary discourse is evidenced by twenty-first-century competency frameworks. Several organizations have produced overlapping frameworks that describe competencies that individuals need in order to navigate and succeed in the twenty-first-century economy. These include the Organisation for Economic Co-operation and Development (OECD); Partnership for 21st-Century Skills; Assessment and Teaching of 21st-Century Skills; and the Council on 21st-Century Learning. A competency is understood as skills, knowledge, attitudes, and abilities that enable individuals to attain designated outcomes for specific tasks (Wolters, 2010). In twenty-first-century competency frameworks, HOT skills feature directly and indirectly. The ideal persons, in these frameworks, are positive, adaptable, risk takers, entrepreneurial, creative, innovative, critical thinkers, self-regulated, and good problem solvers. Given the instrumentalism of schooling for the economy, HOT skills are present in contemporary curricula with the goal of making the teaching of these skills effective.

Explicitly shaping pedagogy and curricula to teach HOT is appealing, especially if the alternative is to encourage rote learning, habitual engagement, stagnation, passive acceptance of knowledge claims, and dependence. However, formally teaching and measuring HOT can render these skills a new type of automation and docility. In modern discourse, the "good thinker" is the correlate of the good worker. The "good thinker" is an instantiation of neoliberal selfhood (Vassallo, 2013b). The neoliberal self is a rational competitor in the marketplace, driven by self-interest and betterment as pursued and rationalized through an economic logic of productivity and efficiency. The neoliberal self strives for autonomy, fulfillment, and meaning by strategically deliberating over choices that can optimize personal value. Life outcomes are treated as a matter of personal responsibility, and one's life is a project that is never complete. The neoliberal self is active, calculating, and continuously striving for betterment. Such a self is projected into the future, and strategic control is exercised to shape the self into whatever it wants to be. This type of self requires HOT. Value is arguably bestowed upon students when they embody HOT skills and deploy those skills quickly, efficiently, and effectively in environments that reward those skills.

The critical concern is that the formal teaching and measuring of HOT reflects a commitment to a different type of automation. Rather than promote rote, simple procedures for productive and efficient work, workers must automate HOT to be productive and efficient. Furthermore, they must develop an organizing principle of self that that aligns with representations of the twenty-first-century and neoliberal purposes of schooling. So-called good thinkers are those who can adapt to modern institutional organizations and structures (Fendler, 2001; Dilts, 2011; Vassallo, 2013b). In this chapter, self-regulation, creativity, critical thinking, and problem-solving are connected to neoliberal representations of twenty-first-century persons who can quickly, efficiently, and for personal betterment use thinking skills to achieve institutionally sanctioned objectives.

The purpose of this critical analysis is not to suggest abandoning the teaching of HOT in favor of the seemingly alternative rote learning, habitual engagement, dependence on others, acceptance of knowledge claims with analysis, destructiveness and stagnation, and indifference to problems or inefficiency at problem solving. Although binary thinking in general is replete with problems, this particular instance is especially troublesome in that HOT is a new form of automation. Committing to teach HOT should not be understood strictly as a departure from automation, habit, and docility, but rather as a way to pursue autonomy and independence as defined in neoliberal terms and rationality. HOT has become hijacked by proponents of neoliberal ideology and it is difficult to commit to teaching these skills without endorsing this ideology.

Of course, proponents of neoliberalism do not have sole jurisdiction over HOT. Those who support a democratic vision of schooling, which arguably stands in contrast to a neoliberal vision, also endorse the teaching of HOT. There are two questions to consider: (1) does institutionalizing HOT realize these two contradictory visions of schooling; and (2) if the visions are irreconcilable, how can teachers, researchers, and policy makers ensure that a focus on HOT is actually used to achieve a goal to resist rather than endorse neoliberalism? To answer these questions, conversations about HOT must move beyond conceptual clarity, pedagogical efficiency, and methodological soundness to considerations of the ways in which ideology shapes the understanding of HOT skills and how they function in policy and practice. Considering alternatives to the current HOT framework is helpful for achieving this goal. In the discussion that follows, critical consciousness is presented as an alternative to critical thinking, and problem-posing pedagogy is presented as an alternative to problem solving. There are no such alternatives presented for creativity and self-regulated learning. Bear in mind, however, that one's critical commitments should not depend on the availability of alternatives. Simply critiquing a thinking skill without trying to replace it with something else is sufficient for critical analysis and necessary for inviting ethical reflections on pedagogy and policy.

Creativity
CONCEPTUALIZATION

Researchers define creativity as something that humans do intentionally to produce an idea, behavior, or product that is novel (or original) and useful (or valuable) (Sawyer et al., 2003; Wegerif, 2010; Robinson, 2011; Zhao, 2012). Interest in creativity in schooling burgeoned in the 1990s and continues to grow in educational discourse (Pope, 2005). In the last decade in particular, creativity has received a great deal of attention (Hennessey & Amabile, 2010). Tanggaard and Glăveanu (2013) explored three reasons for this increase: (1) creativity in the form of art and music, for example, helps to cultivate skills that can be transferred to other subject domains; (2) creativity can support nonconformity in a time that requires people to be innovators and entrepreneurs; and (3) creativity enhances the overall education of children and builds them into well-rounded people. These reasons highlight the treatment of creativity as an instrument to achieve a variety of ends, including institutional, economic, and civic ends. The value for creativity does not serve an end itself.

Although there can be debate about its classification as a skill, creativity is featured as such in twenty-first-century competency frameworks and has recently been grouped as a HOT skill in a widely used educational psychology textbook (compare Ormrod, 2003 to Ormrod, 2011). Education reform conversations are replete with calls to shape curricula and pedagogy to foster creativity, which is a goal associated with progress, virtue, democracy, problem-solving, humanization, and innovation (Pope, 2005; Gaut, 2010; Glăveanu, 2010; Zhao, 2012; Arfken, 2014). Yet critics have raised concern that creativity is not taught in schools but rather systematically educated out of children (e.g., Azzam, 2009; Robinson, 2011; Zhao, 2012; Tanggaard & Glăveanu, 2013). Those who are concerned with global competition, innovation, technological advancement, and corporate sustainability tout the importance of making creativity an explicit, formal pedagogical goal (Rose & Nicholl, 1997; Beghetto, 2010; Robinson, 2011; Zhao, 2012).

The notion of creativity has been around for decades, and cognates have been around for centuries (Pope, 2005). Although widely valued, questions and debates persist about the definition and ontology of, as well as pedagogical possibilities for, creativity. Guiding questions include (1) are children naturally creative or does creativity need to be learned? (2) does creativity need to be disciplined and cultivated? (3) what role does intentionality play in creativity? (4) how much of creativity involves unconscious or spontaneous discoveries? (4) are all children and adults creative? (5) what are the roles of persistence and serendipity? (6) how much time is needed for creativity? (7) what are the roles of divergent and convergent thinking? and (8) what are the roles of freedom and constraint in creative activity? Answers to these questions are rooted in assumptions about the nature of persons and social systems. Any conceptualization of creativity is historically and culturally bound to narratives about what people are, how they form, and their relationship to others.

These narratives are shaped by the predominance of psychological perspectives. For example, before the cognitive revolution of the 1970s, behaviorism was the dominant psychological perspective. According to Arfken (2014), behaviorists believed environmental reinforcements were responsible for anything that was considered creative. Behaviors that led to creative outputs were a direct consequence of punishments and reinforcements. This view of creativity is deterministic, reduced to observable behaviors, product-oriented, and controllable by environmental engineering. Although viewed as a product of individual behavior that can be controlled through the environment, there was little room for the idea of personal and intentional control of creativity. From this perspective, the production of something novel or useful occurs through individuals but is the result of environmental conditions.

In the 1970s, cognitive scientists ushered in a new paradigm about persons, and thus a new paradigm about creativity. A cognitive approach to creativity is characterized by a commitment to transform mental operations into an algorithm for creativity (Arfken, 2014). Like the behaviorist view of psychology, this understanding also located creativity within the individual and endorsed the idea that creative capacities can be measured and cultivated. For this paradigm, however, researchers dissected and compartmentalized cognitive capacities so that pedagogical interventions could be shaped to target the sources of creativity, such as divergent thinking, emotions, individual dispositions, imagination, motivation, and intellectual style (e.g., Sternberg & Lubart, 1991). The guiding assumption was that creativity resulted from various psychological phenomena that worked together to lead to the production of novel and useful products. The thinking was that if the cognitive landscape could be measured and relationships between phenomena mapped, creativity could be fostered, cultivated, and managed.

With the surge of sociocultural theory during the 1980s, researchers challenged the cognitive approach (Csikszentmihalyi, 1999; Moran & John-Steiner, 2003; Glăveanu, 2011; Arfken, 2014). Working from this perspective, Glăveanu (2010, 2011, 2013) has worked to change the conceptualization and language of creativity to reflect the historically, culturally, and socially mediated nature of novelty and usefulness. Recognizing the role of others, dialogue, artifacts, historical circumstances, and politics, Glăveanu's work complicates the measurement and assignment of creativity to individuals and dispels the myth of the creative genius. Glăveanu attempted to rewrite the language of creativity by moving it away from isolated and decontextualized individuals to actors situated in contexts. Glăveanu (2010) explained: "The *new artifact* (material or conceptual) is seen as emerging within the relation between *self* (creator) and *others* (broadly understood as a *community*), all three being immersed into and in dialogue with an existing body of *cultural artifacts, symbols and established norms*. This model is not structural but *dynamic* since it is in the 'tensions' between all four elements that creativity takes shape with the 'new artifact' becoming part of 'existing culture' (for self and/or community) and constantly alimenting the creative cycle" (p. 87; emphases in original). The main premise of this view is that individuals, artifacts, conventions, and others exist in a dependent and dynamic relationship that leads to the emergence of activities and products that counts as novel and useful. Even if an individual action can be identified as producing something novel and useful, what counts as such results from the available tools and contexts in which creativity is practiced and products emerge.

Behaviorist, cognitive, and sociocultural accounts of creativity all tell a different story. In both cognitive and sociocultural approaches, creativity is a universal feature of persons that can be learned and developed, as well as suppressed. This HOT skill is not limited to only a select few. Tanggaard and Glăveanu (2013) characterized this universalism as democratizing creativity because all individuals can be conceptualized as creative or potentially creative. The contribution of a sociocultural view of creativity, however, is that creativity is not strictly attributed to individual qualities and intra-psychological relationships.

Glăveanu's sociocultural theorizing reflects a paradigm shift that can avoid many dangers associated with behaviorist and cognitive conceptualizations. His work can bring the discourse closer to resemble critical educational psychology, a perspective in which radical individualism, claims about intentionality, individual authorship, universalism, and ahistoricism are put under serious scrutiny. To move toward a critical approach, taking up the aim to cultivate creativity in schools should draw heavily on the insights and developments exemplified in Glăveanu's work.

However, even if sociocultural theorizing was the dominant paradigm, there are other concerns. One can exhaustively explore the limitations of and assumptions surrounding ideas about creativity in hopes to teach it better. Perhaps a sociocultural approach can be conducive to this goal in a way that is democratic, communal, and humanistic. However, one danger is that sociocultural theorizing can be used to improve the conceptualization of creativity in ways that support pedagogical applications. As Glăveanu (2010) argued, a sociocultural approach can offer examples of good practice surrounding aims to foster creativity by showing its social origins and its evolution within a social setting. This author hoped that teachers, policy makers, and researchers would understand the situated and distributed nature of creative activity so they might be able to strategically structure environments in ways that most optimally invite and recognize creativity from all participants. However, getting better at conceptualizing and teaching HOT is not necessarily the aim of critical educational psychology. Rather, the aim is to illuminate the ideological and political foundations of the conceptualization of creativity and its elevated importance in modern schooling and twenty-first-century selfhood.

THE IDEOLOGY AND POLITICS OF CREATIVITY

Conceptual, methodological, and pedagogical debates are abundant. The nuances of these debates are not captured here. Suffice it to say that the ideological underpinnings of creativity are seldom part of these conversations, especially in education discourse. Creativity has become a means or instrument for achieving particular ends that are economic and individualized as opposed to democratic and humanizing. Implicit in the instrumentalism of creativity is the tension between an economic (e.g., profitability and global competition) and a social (e.g., humanization, opportunity, equity, and democratic engagement) good. In neoliberal discourse, social, economic, and individual goods are thought about as the same thing. From this perspective, humanization is constructing, celebrating, expressing, and mobilizing oneself in economically useful ways that might be reasoned to support equity and virtue.

Pope (2005) has argued that for years the need for creativity has been tied to economic purposes, in particular those associated with capitalist production. He reasoned that the "dynamic of capitalism requires the perpetual abolition of current market values and their replacement with others as yet unknown" (p. 29). In other words, for consumption to replace existing products, there must be a continued production of commodities. For this reason, Pope (2005) wrote, "Creativity . . . is one of the most prized commodities of capitalism" (p. 29). Novelty and usefulness, which are generally accepted as double criteria for creativity, are about the perpetual creation of commodities and the simultaneous devaluing of extant ones. In addition to the production of commodities, advocates continue to push for institutionalizing creativity because it is believed to drive and lead innovation, which can support job creation, corporate profit, and national prosperity. It is no wonder that researchers housed in departments of business have taken keen interest in creativity (e.g., Amabile & Kramer, 2011; Furnham, Batey, Booth, Patel, & Lozinskaya, 2011; De Stobbeleir, Ashford, & Buyens, 2011).

These types of economic rationalizations underpin many calls for institutionalizing creativity in schools (Rose & Nicholl, 1997; Beghetto, 2010; Zhao, 2012). In an interview with Sir Ken Robinson, who was knighted because of his work on creativity, Azzam (2009) asked Robinson, "Why creativity now?" Robinson responded that the twenty-first century is unpredictable and rife with economic problems related to health care, education, and financial institutions. As suggested, the mantra of the unpredictable, shifting, and problem-prone twenty-first century informs rationalizations for fostering students' creativity (Rose & Nicholl, 1997; Beghetto, 2010; Robinson, 2011; Zhao, 2012). In the interview, Robinson stated, "I work a lot with Fortune 500 companies, and they're always saying, 'We need people who can be innovative, who can think differently.' If you look at the mortality rate among companies, it's massive. America is now facing the biggest challenge it's ever faced—to maintain its position in the world economies. All these things demand high levels of innovation, creativity, and ingenuity. At the moment, instead of promoting creativity, I think we're systematically educating it out of our kids" (p. 23). The neoliberal rationales are clear in this quotation. Creativity is needed for staving off the mortality of companies and supporting global competition.

Creativity has become a key feature of human capital, a thinking skill that is argued to be necessary for individuals to solve twenty-first-century economic problems. The logic is that creative capacities must be harnessed and cultivated so that individuals have the skills and capacities to fix financial, economic, and social problems. Creativity has become an important asset for occupations in the twenty-first century and can enable individuals to compete for those positions. In this regard, institutionalizing creativity can serve as a means to level the playing field. Those who demonstrate creativity have a credential that, if measurable, is marketable for the twenty-first century.

Even if not to stave off corporate mortality, creativity has become important because of changing conditions in workplaces. For example, with the workforce downsizing, burdens are placed on managers and workers to be creative and innovative in ways that enable them to maintain productivity and profit with diminishing resources. Doing more with less requires creatively managing workers and working in creative ways. This requirement speaks to a broad function of creativity. Workers must have the skill and competence to adapt, of course, in efficient and productive ways, to whatever corporate conditions present themselves. Thought about this way, however, creativity is a quality of workers that renders them amenable to adopt, adapt to, and pursue a corporate mentality to survive and remain profitable.

Humanitarianism's Neoliberal Guise

Creativity can serve a neoliberal agenda even when it is not so explicitly organized around corporate survival and profit. Creativity can be masked as humanitarian while justifying and validating neoliberal structures. For example, in Detroit, a restaurant owner started a nonprofit organization called The Empowerment Plan. The owner's goal was to provide basic needs for homeless people in an attempt to break the city's generational cycle of poverty and homelessness. Homeless women were employed in a formerly abandoned warehouse to make coats that could transform into sleeping bags and backpacks. These coats were distributed to homeless people at no cost to the recipients. This organization was featured on a National Public Radio program and discussed as a great example of entrepreneurialism, ingenuity, and innovation that served a humanitarian aim. If creativity can be causally associated with the emergence and operations of this nonprofit organization, then creativity can be reasonably associated with serving a social good and not necessarily one solely driven by profit. In this example, however, the creative enterprise is not disassociated from neoliberalism. Perhaps this organization was necessary because of the bleeding of public funds to social services, the increased demand on private organizations for providing social services, the intense concentration of wealth in the top 5 percent of the population, and the movement of jobs overseas in the pursuit of profit. Thus neoliberalism can help to produce conditions that make creativity necessary. Neoliberal policies require creative people to manage the conditions that these policies help to create.

Another way creativity can be masked as humanitarian relates to identity. A humanitarian perspective is based on the idea that everyday living is creative and that individuals' vocations are to fashion themselves in a variety of ways (Arfken, 2014). In this sense, novelty and usefulness serve a goal of self-determination and expression, not of producing novel and useful commodities. Boden (1996) made this distinction by using the terms H-creativity and P-creativity. The former refers to ideas and products that no other has had before. The latter refers to ideas that are new to a particular individual. H-creativity is associated with cultural and historical transformation, whereas P-creativity is new and transformative for the individual. Similarly, Sawyer et al. (2003) made the distinction between creativity (with a lowercase "c") and Creativity (with an uppercase "C"). The former refers to the everyday activities that bring novelty and joy, usually found to be ubiquitous with children. The latter refers to cultural-transforming products, usually associated with adult activity. These distinctions are about conceptualizing novelty and usefulness as either self-referencing (i.e., novel and useful from a personal standpoint) or determined by their places and contributions to a community, culture, and economy. Although both forms of creativity can be aligned with a humanitarian perspective, both P-creativity and lower case "c" creativity appear to be more strongly aligned with a humanitarian view than their counterparts.

This view, however, does not disentangle creativity from neoliberal reasoning. Identity and selfhood have become economic commodities (Davies & Bansel, 2007; Fitzimmons, 2011), challenging the distinction between humanitarian and economic aims of creativity. From a humanistic perspective, the creative task is to lead an authentic lifestyle of nonconformity and personal empowerment. For humanists and neoliberals, the appearance of a nonconforming, authentic identity is appealing. Tanggaard and Glăveanu (2013) suggested that one reason research is rapidly expanding is because creativity can support nonconformity in a time that requires people to be innovators and entrepreneurs. However, there is a paradox. Novelty and usefulness for self-expression align with the neoliberal push to harness personal resources in order to create an entrepreneurial, innovative, risk-taking person. The paradox is that although persons may take different risks, pursue different changes, and start different businesses, they organize and conform their conception of self around this market logic.

SUMMATIVE REFLECTION

Creativity is gaining a great deal of attention in order to better support its institutionalization. The push for formalizing it in schooling is entangled in economic instrumentalism. The discourse surrounding creativity is concerning because creativity has become a feature of human capital that teachers will be expected to measure and cultivate so that students can be marketable and adaptable in twenty-first-century environments. Creativity is not a product of neoliberalism but is discussed and mobilized in ways that are complementary to neoliberal aims. If educators and policy makers want to resist neoliberalism, there must be conversations about how creativity can be divorced from this ideology. Humanistic conceptions and practices of creativity may foster resistance to neoliberal values but still can be tied to production of entrepreneurs and innovators. Insights from a sociocultural view may enable one to resist the attributions of creativity to isolated individuals and support resistance to creativity as human capital. However, this perspective might be mobilized for pedagogical purposes without critically analyzing the conceptualization, functions, and purposes of creativity in schooling.

Self-Regulated Learning
CONCEPTUALIZATION

Self-regulated learning (SRL), as described in the chapter on knowing students, is a self-steering process in which individuals target their own cognition, feelings, and actions, as well as features of the environment, for the modulation of personal learning goals (Boekaerts & Cascallar, 2006; Hadwin & Oshige, 2011). From its inception in the early 1980s, research on SRL has continued to show steady increases in each subsequent decade (Martin, 2004; Post, Boyer, & Brett, 2006). Educational psychologists almost exclusively consider SRL a valuable and empowering form of engagement that is associated with academic success. This HOT skill is associated with individual control over the conditions that affect academic outcomes. The underlying assumption is that SRL involves self-initiated adaptations to oneself and the environment in ways that enable students to achieve their learning goals.

Although generally valued, researchers reason that SRL is particularly important for modern educational conditions (Zimmerman, 2002; Boekaerts

& Cascallar, 2006). With "high" standards, getting a classroom of students to direct themselves is more efficient than working individually with each student to prompt activity, set goals, plan courses of actions, and make adjustments. Furthermore, As Zimmerman (2002) argued, student diversity makes it difficult for teachers to attend to the learning needs of individuals using generalized teaching strategies. He reasoned that teaching students to monitor, direct, and adapt their own learning is more effective and efficient than adjusting instruction for every student. Even if personalized instructional adaptations were possible, Zimmerman contended that a key purpose of education is undermined, namely to help students develop lifelong learning skills. He reasoned that students must learn to make their own adjustments in order to achieve their learning goals.

The discourse on SRL is not without theoretical debates, and it includes different theories of academic self-regulation (e.g., see Zimmerman & Schunk, 1989, 2001; McCaslin et al., 2006). In contemporary discourse, these theories can be organized by three concepts: self-regulated learning, co-regulated learning, and socially shared regulated learning (Hadwin & Oshige, 2011). This grouping reflects differences in the understanding of persons, the social world, and the mechanisms, sources, and ontology of regulatory activity. A major difference relates to the role of the social world. Those who use the term SRL are likely to believe that students are naturally self-regulating and have a priori cognitive mechanisms that mediate the use of socially learned scripts for learning (e.g., Bandura, 2001). Whereas those who use the terms co-regulated learning and socially shared regulated learning are likely to assume that the foundations of regulatory activity are social in nature and only after internalization of scripts can individuals self-regulate (e.g., Hadwin and Oshige, 2011). Although these and other differences persist, prominent SRL researchers argued that theoretical variations do not lead to a fundamental departure of a core understanding (Zeidner, Boekaerts, & Pintrich, 2000; McCaslin et al., 2006;). At the core is adaptation and self-direction (Schunk & Zimmerman, 1997; Bandura, 2001; Zimmerman, 2002; Chong, 2006; McCaslin et al., 2006; Wolters, 2010; Järvelä, 2011).

An assumption underpinning conceptions of SRL is that strategic activity is initiated and directed independent of an external source. Some researchers use the notion of proactivity to describe self-direction (e.g., Zimmerman, 2000; Cleary & Zimmerman, 2004; McInerney, 2011). Proaction means setting goals, evaluating tasks, and developing plans without being prompted or reacting to an environmental consequence. McInerney (2011) captured this conceptualization when he described SRL in the following way: "Self-regulation views learning as an activity that students do for themselves in a proactive way, rather than as a covert event that happens to them reactively as a result of teaching experiences, self-regulated learners are self-starters" (p. 442). Being proactive is associated with setting and seeking challenging tasks in order to improve skill and performance (Zimmerman, 2000; Bandura, 2001). Reactivity has a role in self-direction as well (Zimmerman, 2000). Reactivity involves reflecting on environmental consequences (e.g., score on an exam) to evaluate goals and strategies. Self-regulated learners treat feedback as valuable pieces of information to prompt reevaluation of thoughts, behaviors, goals, perceptions, as well as the impetus to institute adjustments if necessary.

One must not only self-direct thoughts and activities but must make careful assessments of situational demands and personal resources in order to make strategic adjustments to thoughts, behaviors, emotions, and, when possible, environments in order to achieve learning goals. Researchers have suggested that effective and productive self-regulated learners do not adopt a habit or a routine set of skills or strategies. Rather, they respond to new learning challenges in productive ways by strategically adapting tasks, task perceptions, goals, plans, identities, and strategies. The mark of productive self-regulating learners is adaptation in the face of new learning challenges. To be self-regulated, students must initiate and control these adaptations.

Despite the value, importance, and widespread endorsement of SRL, it gives rise to critical concerns. Critical analysis of SRL is not about endorsing dependence on others for initiating tasks, adapting, setting goals, and evaluating performance. In fact, researchers have argued that SRL is actually entangled in efforts to support dependence (Martin & McLellan, 2008; Vassallo, 2013b). Like creativity, SRL is caught up in neoliberal discourse and is an instantiation of the neoliberal self (Vassallo, 2013b). Given this association, students must depend on authorities to enact institutionally validated regulatory thoughts and behaviors. They must conform to the logic of neoliberal ideology by shaping their understanding of and relationship to their self. Another critical concern is that class norms are embedded in the discourse of SRL. The conception of self that underpins SRL also is embedded in class values. The self of SRL reflects a version of personhood that is endorsed, valued, rewarded, and normalized in middle-class culture.

SRL AND SOCIAL CLASS VALUES

The notion of the self is a foundational component of SRL, even in the conceptions of co-regulation and socially shared regulation. Although inseparable, the complexity surrounding the self in SRL remains under-acknowledged. An examination of SRL literature reveals the persistence of a particular assumption about the self. The starting point of critical education psychology is that the self is a cultural artifact, not to be understood as a universal, ahistorical, and pre-ontological phenomenon (Mead, 1934; Martin, 2007; Sugarman, 2009). "Self" designates a particular way of constituting a biophysical being. As such, the self can take different forms. Key to that form are social, cultural, historical, and political contexts.

The underlying, and often implicit, conception of self of SRL is aligned with neoliberal and middle-class norms (Vassallo, 2013b). As sociological researchers have argued, class shapes different values for and endorsements of selfhood (Eckert, 1989; Kusserow, 2004; Schutz, 2008; Weininger & Lareau, 2009). Middle-class selfhood is constituted in ways that reflect expressive and scientific selves, which are the selves of SRL. Martin (2007) described the former as an organizing principle of self that is based on understanding and expressing. People are taught that they have unique characteristics, strengths, weaknesses, preferences, and desires that must be explored and expressed. The scientific self is an understanding of selfhood based on the idea that one must carefully monitor and observe behaviors, thoughts, and emotions in order to direct improvements. This self is about knowing, controlling, and improving.

The expressive and scientific selves align with the brand of self that is associated with middle-class culture. Kusserow (2004) described middle-class parents as encouraging self-expression, pursuing self-interest, constructing uniqueness, and conceptualizing psychological states as causally related to actions. Schutz (2008) contended that middle-class families celebrate children's "unique" characteristics and capabilities. He also argued that middle-class children learn at an early age to monitor themselves and use techniques of surveillance to achieve personal learning goals. Weininger and Lareau (2009) argued that middle-class guardians work closely with children to develop their dispositions and skills for self-management.

Schutz (2008) argued that parents from working-class backgrounds treat the self of middle-class culture as "wasteful indulgence" (p. 411). Working-class children are not oriented toward identifying and expressing their unique characteristics. These children tend not to rely on psychological language and psychology causation to describe actions. Kusserow (2004) argued that individuals from working-class backgrounds are committed to a self that is oriented to protection, toughness, and action. Note the component of expression in her depiction of working-class selfhood. However, Kusserow argued that such expression is not organized around psychological descriptions, evaluations, and measurements. Rather, expression is through the recollection of narratives that reflect class-based struggles. Echoing this assertion, Schutz (2008) argued that working-class children's dramatic storytelling reflects narratives about struggle and long-term relational ties and not about their so-called unique and distinct psychological qualities. A cursory consideration of class-based values for selfhood points to a clear alignment between the self of SRL and the self of middle-class culture.

Connecting SRL to middle-class selfhood with its values for expression and scientific management is not to suggest that people from working-class backgrounds are not self-regulated. It is dangerous to apply deficit-based thinking (middle-class kids are self-regulated and working-class kids are not) to individuals who are not middle-class. However, it is also dangerous to conclude that all students are self-regulated because it normalizes a particular brand of selfhood. Such a conclusion might lead researchers and teachers to consider how working-class students uniquely self-regulate, or they might evaluate these students' activity in relation to dominant ideas about what SRL looks like. The point is not to encourage deficit-based evaluations or to normalize SRL as a necessary feature of persons but to show that dominant ideas about SRL are underpinned by a particular understanding of selfhood that aligns with middle-class values.

SRL AND NEOLIBERAL VALUES

Another concern surrounding SRL relates to the neoliberal self. SRL involves a commitment to make strategic choices in order to efficiently and productively pursue academic enhancement and increase personal value (Zimmerman, 2002; Boekaerts & Cascallar, 2006; McCaslin et al., 2006; Järvelä, 2011). The emphases on choices, efficiency, and personal value are foundational to neoliberal selfhood. The values and purposes of SRL are steeped in the language of efficiency, productivity, and self development—all features of the discourse of neoliberalism. Furthermore, the scientific and expressive selves are key requirements for the neoliberal selfhood. Although seemingly neutral, the notion of SRL is intertwined in neoliberal discourse.

The Emergence of SRL

One way to understand the relationship between SRL and neoliberalism relates to the time of their emergence. The notion of SRL entered in scholarly discourse at the same time that neoliberal policies were being pushed in education. Research on SRL began to be published in the early 1980s. Although cognates, such as self-control and self-management, have been around for decades, something different happened with the emergence of SRL. That is, SRL became a trope to describe, make sense of, and measure students. Based on conceptualizations and measurements, it became possible to describe students as self-regulated or not self-regulated, or as having high or low quality self-regulatory ability (Zimmerman, 2002; Hadwin, 2012). The popularity of SRL has grown significantly from its inceptions, with research increasing substantially in subsequent decades.

Alongside that growth is the continued influence of neoliberalism for shaping pedagogy and policy. At the time when SRL was formally studied, neoliberal educational policy was being pushed by the Reagan administration. The parallel emergence may be a coincidence. However, one could argue that SRL was researched and applied to schooling because it reflected an aesthetic for a particular brand of selfhood. One might even question whether or not the discourse of SRL would have experienced the growth it did if not for a neoliberal backdrop. Whether causal, coincidental, or otherwise, there is a historical relationship between the emergence of SRL and the push for neoliberal educational policy. This relationship continues in contemporary discourse; the popularity of SRL grows in conjunction with the continued spread of neoliberal ideology.

SRL supports a specific narrative about the makeup of persons, the sources of academic success, and the operation of schooling that aligns with neoliberal thinking. This narrative is underpinned by a belief neoliberal idea of meritocracy, which is an ideology that ability, hard work, and talent determine students' outcomes. The idea is that social systems require people with certain talents, skills, and ability to fill various functions within a political and economic system (Hurn, 1993). Some functions are more valued and compensated than others. For meritocratic thinking, sociocultural factors, such as wealth, class privilege, race, and sex, do not influence individuals' achievement, nor do they limit opportunity to compete for and fill any position in a system. Outcomes are a result of what students earn via their effort and ability. Given the assumption that these efforts and abilities are controllable, the corollary assumption is that inequality results from sources of personal control. From a meritocratic perspective, addressing inequality means working on students so they can improve their abilities and increase their effort to succeed in schools. Herein lies one appeal of SRL. Explanations of academic achievement in which individuals can overcome limitations by relying on personal sources for their academic outcomes are dynamic and controllable. For a narrative of meritocracy, supporting students' success means helping them regulate their learning. Part of this effort involves shaping students' perceptions that they are intentional actors who are in control of and responsible for their learning outcomes.

Even without a causal link between the emergence of SRL and neoliberalism, it is difficult to deny that the self of SRL aligns with neoliberal selfhood. Davies and Bansel (2007) argued that the model neoliberal self is responsible for outcomes by virtue of choices. Those who are successful make appropriate choices for which goals to pursue, plans for actions, strategies to use, personal adjustments, and how much to persist. The neoliberal self uses all resources and information to (1) set goals; (2) operate with as little oversight as possible; (3) respond to environmental changes; (4) commit actions to a purpose; and (5) strive for improvement. This model neoliberal self is strikingly similar to the self-regulating learner. Like the self-regulated learner, the neoliberal self is personally accountable and "responsibilized" (Clarke, 2005; Davies & Bansel, 2007). This type of self benefits a neoliberal agenda by emphasizing individual accountability, which also preserves a sense of society as a meritocracy.

Adaptability

Aside from the broad alignment between SRL and neoliberal selfhood, both specifically emphasize the importance of adaptability (Wolters, 2010; Vassallo, 2013b). In an OECD (1989) report, which is a representation of neoliberal values, the ideal self is described as one who "has a positive, flexible, and adaptable disposition toward change, seeing it as normal rather than a problem. To see change in this way an enterprising individual has a security borne of self-confidence, and is at ease when dealing with insecurity, risk, difficulty, and the unknown" (p. 36). Although arguably a natural human process, adaptability has become a marker of selfhood that must be measured, evaluated, and, if necessary, developed. Those who are adaptable can be useful for neoliberal twenty-first-century environments. This adaptation requires intense attunement to environmental configurations. One must recognize changes in the context and respond accordingly. For this reason, adaptation is also a way to efficiently govern individuals from afar (Fendler, 2001; Dilts, 2011; Martin & McLellan, 2013).

If all individuals effectively adapt themselves to changes that are introduced into the environment, then authorities no longer have to govern individuals directly. Rather, authorities can shift and structure environments to govern from a distance, allowing for the perceived self-determination of actions, thoughts, and changes. Individuals must be attuned to situational demands and adjust themselves accordingly. This response is important for managing workers, who ideally adjust themselves to align with institutional aims and mandates. In neoliberal contexts, individuals must be attuned to situational demands and figure out how to strategically change themselves in order to be marketable and useful for handling those demands. The adaptable person is focused on self-transformation for the purpose of an institutional, political, and economic aim. Although not determined by environmental cues and configurations, adapting requires dependence on them for prompting responses and evaluating the effectiveness of those responses. If adaptations were not made in relation to cues and configurations, then responses might seem maladaptive, incoherent, inefficient, and willy-nilly. Although individuals may seem to implement personal changes independently, to count as adaptable they must be prompted by the environment to act.

It is not enough to have the disposition to be adaptable. One must make the right kinds of adaptations. SRL researchers distinguish between maladaptive and adaptive self-regulation, with each having specific requirements. Adaptation involves certain attitudes, goals, dispositions, and processes. As Walkerdine (2003) argued, the adaptable person is "propped up and supported by a whole array of psychological support, most particularly forms of counseling and therapy" (p. 241). The point is that with guidance from others, individuals must learn to adapt in ways that support the efficient and productive pursuit of a goal. Shifting environments to invite particular responses works only if individuals are attuned to those environments, and if they have the knowledge, skills, and dispositions to institute appropriate responses, evaluate the consequences of responses, and adjust personal variables if necessary. Thus to adapt in acceptable ways persons must be guided and conditioned by others.

Purposes of SRL

The underlying conceptions of proaction, self-direction, and adaptation in SRL are featured in neoliberal conceptions of self. Although already show to be well aligned, by considering the purposes of SRL, the relationship between neoliberalism and SRL is deepened. McCaslin et al. (2006) distinguished between three not necessarily mutually exclusive purposes: efficient production, pursuit of self, and social participation. The first is most clearly aligned with neoliberalism. Efficient production involves optimal self-control and refers to setting and prioritizing goals, staying focused on a task, ignoring competing demands, and enacting strategic behaviors—all in service of adapting to situational demands with as little misdirection, meandering, and waste as possible.

Pursuit of self involves the construction of identity, which is made possible through the development of self-knowledge via the choices people make. The idea of taking up oneself as a project through the formation of a unique identity is a feature of neoliberalism. Bansel (2007) writes that "opportunities for self- and professional development, become means for securing identity and investing in oneself and one's future" (p. 289). Researchers suggest several ways to pursue the development of self. McCaslin et al. (2006) reasoned that choice enables learners to reflect on interest and self-knowledge, as well as deliberate over possible selves. That is, self is made possible by giving students choices, helping them construe their choices as indications of self, using that knowledge to perform strategic actions, and recognizing that they have personal responsibility for their outcomes.

Social participation, informed by sociocultural perspectives of SRL, involves contributing to a community and pursuing a shared goal. Arguably this last purpose does not align neatly with neoliberalism. However, McCaslin et al. (2006) steeped their discussion of social participation in individualism and optimization. They maintain that the individual is a distinct actor who contributes to a shared goal, and who must strategically work to shape their environment to efficiently and effectively contribute to that goal. Arguably, this last purpose does not align as neatly with neoliberalism as the previous two. It is not surprising that this last purpose receives the least amount of attention in SRL literature. The misalignment between this purpose and neoliberalism stems from the emphasis on a shared communal goal, as opposed to an individualistic one. Despite the seeming departure from neoliberal discourse, McCaslin et al. (2006) used the language individualism, optimization, productivity, and efficiency. For example, these writers pushed for researchers and educators to consider how social contexts can be optimized to support the efficient production of a shared goal. Neoliberalism might shape what counts as an acceptable goal, but this ideology can also be connected to the language of efficiency and productivity.

In sum, shaping curricula and pedagogy to foster SRL is appealing, especially if considered in opposition to dependency and apathy. A number of positive educational practices and outcomes are associated with SRL, such as empowerment, adaptability, control, and achievement. However, the binary between SRL and dependency is false. The norms and values that inform the conceptualization and purposes of SRL align with middle-class culture and neoliberal ideology. Fostering SRL requires practices of legislation in which students must understand themselves in particular ways. In this regard, SRL requires dependency on others and situational demands for self-management. As environments continue to be shaped by neoliberalism, adaptation may involve developing the knowledge, skills, and dispositions to navigate and function within so-called free-market conditions. Proponents of neoliberalism value accountability, radical individualism, efficiency, productivity, and adaptability. SRL can be empowering in that it is a form of neoliberal subjectivity that enables individuals to navigate and be successful within neoliberal contexts.

Critical Thinking

Critical thinking (CT) is another HOT skill that is frequently mentioned in educational policy, curricula, and pedagogy. This skill is featured in Common Core and is prominent in twenty-first-century competency frameworks. It is widely agreed that students need to think critically. However, the conceptualization of CT and what counts as CT is a source of debate. Commonly, CT is conceptualized as the evaluation of epistemic validity of knowledge claims by considering issues, ideas, artifacts, and events before accepting or formulating an opinion or conclusion (Lipman, 2003). This conceptualization relies heavily on the tools and methodology used by analytic philosophers, including conceptual and argument analyses, recognizing false inferences and logical fallacies, and distinguishing between fact, opinion, and evidence (Brookfield, 2007). Although this type of reasoning is valuable, Brookfield (2007) argued that this view of CT tends to be focused on cognitive processes that require a facility with language and logic, while neglecting social and political critique. Herein lies a key point of critical reflection.

Brookfield (2007) argued that CT has been interpreted to reflect self-interested analysis of knowledge claims that are used for predetermined tasks that are deemed valid by others. He and other critical theorists have argued that the current discourse has moved away from the original intention of CT, which is social, political, and cultural critique related to issues of power and oppression (Burbules & Berk, 1999; Kincheloe, 2000; McLaren, 2007). Neoliberal ideology can be implicated in supporting the current understanding. More so than the other HOT skills, CT is at the center of debates between those who endorse democratic and neoliberal visions of schooling. Proponents of CT view this skill as promoting autonomous thinking and reasoned judgment, which can be associated with a citizenry that can contribute to democracy and the economy. However, if teachers and policy makers want to support a democratic vision of schooling, they must consider how CT is aligned with and mobilized to serve neoliberal interests, and they must be willing to adopt what Brookfield (2007) argued was the original conception and purpose of CT, which is social and political critique.

A NEOLIBERAL VISION OF CRITICAL THINKING

The call for CT is loud in neoliberal discourse; it is present in all frameworks for twenty-first-century competencies (Vassallo, 2013b). Business leaders lament the lack of critical thinking from their employees (Pithers & Soden, 2000). Pithers and Soden (2000) contended that employers demand that "education, no matter in what discipline or at which level, ought to enable graduates to 'think smarter'" (237). The authors associated thinking smarter with thinking critically. CT ostensibly enables individuals to interpret the bombardment of information and make reasoned decisions in a sea of technological advancement and shifting economic conditions. To use Burbules and Berk's (1999) phrase, the student is to be a "critical consumer of information" (48). Within modern corporate structures, researchers suggested that CT is important because it supports adaptability, problem solving, and fast learning—which are said to add value to organizations (Pithers & Soden, 2000).

Given the economic value, it is not surprising that CT is prominently featured in Common Core. The prominence of this thinking skill may seem to bring some favor to an otherwise unfavorable set of benchmarks. CT is identified as an essential skill for school success and college-readiness. The assumption is that honing CT skills will develop competence in thinking about history, math, science, and literature. Although there is debate about whether CT is an abstract thought process that can be applied across domains or if it is a subject-specific thought process, there tends to be acceptance that fostering CT is valuable.

One problem with CT, however, is that this skill is tied to the radically individualized self (Burbules & Berk, 1999; Brookfield, 2007; Vassallo, 2014). CT is understood in individualistic terms and mobilized to serve personal interests. For example, Paul and Elder (2005) described CT as self-directed, self-disciplined, self-monitored, and self-corrected. Not only described as an individual process, CT is understood to serve personal gain, such as grades, favor from teachers, and the advancement of views. Prescripted curricula are provided for which students are rewarded for reasoning in ways that are recognizable as critical. CT requires a particular style of reasoning, facility with language in relation to predetermined tasks. One must use CT when asked or expected to do so in schools. If students do not display CT in recognizable ways, then the teacher must work on shaping students' thinking. CT is a skill that requires a disposition to enact a thinking script for analyzing and drawing conclusions in relation to predetermined tasks that are evaluated by a source of authority.

When understood in this way, CT aligns with and is a component of neoliberal subjectivity. CT involves the consumption of material and immaterial products for personal goal attainment. This skill encourages reflection, analysis, and evaluation of information and processes not as a means of advancing justice, but of understanding how one can maximize personal benefit by becoming savvy with language and logic. This HOT skill focuses on the self and self-expression in a clear and rational manner; the emphasis is on evaluations and assessments that serve personal interest, rather than on a dynamic thinking process that contextualizes information and thought processes within existing power structures. CT encourages flexibility, adaptability, and self-reliance within well-scripted contexts (Burbules & Berk, 1999). These three characteristics are essential for neoliberal subjectivity. CT is supposed to free persons from the limitations of knowledge claims by using reasoned judgment to determine truth and accuracy of information. By engaging with the validity of knowledge claims, individuals can adapt their assumptions, propositions, and presuppositions. The major concern is that such adaptations must be institutionally validated.

A DEMOCRATIC VISION OF CRITICAL THINKING

Those who endorse a democratic vision of schooling also tout CT as an important thinking skill. The assumption is that reasoned deliberation is essential to democracy and an egalitarian life (Brookfield, 2007). CT seems to be a much more natural fit for a democratic vision than a neoliberal one. However, it is important for a democratic vision that the conceptualization of, justification for, and the purpose of CT are distinguished from neoliberal discourse. Kincheloe (2000), who is known for working with both teachers and students on shaping schooling to support democracy and justice, conceptualized CT as "the ability of individuals to disengage themselves from the tacit assumptions of discursive practices and power relations in order to exert more conscious control over their everyday lives" (p. 24). He promoted resisting dominant perspectives (i.e., elitism, patriarchy, imperialism) in order to create authentic, practical (learning) opportunities for students to build relationships with communities in order to foster social change. In order to resist dominant perspectives and implement change, Kincheloe argued that individuals must have consciousness about how power operates.

Brookfield (2007) asserted that a democratic treatment of CT is not the same as being logical or making decisions to solve problems, although these aspects are sometimes present and essential. Theorists acknowledged that there are some common features of CT in neoliberal and democratic visions of schooling (Berbules & Berk, 1999; Kincheloe, 2000; Brookfield, 2007). However, these theorists also depart from the neoliberal view by suggesting that CT is much more than just logical thought, higher order rationality, and an examination of evidence for the purposes of making a reasoned argument. In fact, Brookfield argued that enacting this type of CT is psychological and ideological dogma. He explained that CT tends to function as a skill to achieve good scores on standardized tests and serves as a mechanism to garner complicity to particular institutional, economic, and political structures. Rather than conceptualizing CT as making clear, well-reasoned assumptions, judgments, and arguments that support personal and economic goals, a democratic vision is about interrogating dominant ideologies and making ethical choices about ideals, intents, and purposes that serve a social good.

For critical theorists, CT is about understanding, challenging, and changing the world (Burbules & Berk, 1999; Brookfield, 2007; McLaren, 2007). Brookfield (2007) explained that "Critical thought is not the blind dismissal of the school status quo with no consideration as to what might replace it. It is thinking manifest in active claims by students of the right to be involved in shaping the classroom practices to which they are subject. On a broader level it is thinking through how schools might become sites that challenge dominant ideology and exclusionary practices. And on a macro-societal level it is thinking used to abolish the exchange economy of capitalism that commodifies human relations" (p. 323). From a democratic perspective, CT is about ideological critique for the purposes of shaping contexts in ways that support justice and equity. This type of thinking is not about being better at reading texts to look for meaning and logic that is not seemingly obvious. Brookfield stated, "Critical thinking . . . helps us understand how we learn political ideals, morality, and social philosophy within the institutions of civil society such as schools, associations, clubs, families, and friendship networks. It shows us that the constructs and categories we use instinctively to understand our daily experiences are ideologically framed" (Brookfield, 2007, p. 324). Like other critical theorists, this author contended that the ideas, skills, and ways of reasoning learned in school are political, cultural, and ideological. Particular student practices and outcomes serve a particular set of interests. CT is generally not directed at the examination of these interests, and that neutralizes this skill from oppressive cultural, political and economic structures (Burbules & Berk, 1999; McLaren, 2007).

If CT is merely a thinking skill, McLaren (2007) argued that the notion "critical" is neutralized in ways that serve dominant power structures and contributes to students' subordination to those structures. He stated that "neoconservatives and liberals have neutralized the term *critical* by repeated and imprecise usage, removing its political and cultural dimensions and laundering its analytic potency to mean 'thinking skills.' In their terms, teaching is reduced to helping students acquire higher levels of cognitive skills. Little attention is paid to the purpose to which these skills are to be put. The moral vision that grounds such a view encourages students to succeed in the tough competitive world of existing social relations" (p. 188). McLaren does not discount the potential usefulness of thinking skills. However, the crux of his criticism is in regards to the ends toward which these skills are directed and toward the lack of understanding of the context in which the skills are shaped and employed. McLaren argued that isolating thinking skills from the contentious debates and contexts runs counter to the original aims of CT. This concern captures the broad goal of this chapter, which is not to say HOT should not be a pedagogical goal, but that there are ideological, political, and economic reasons for teaching these skills and that modern context is implicated in shaping the understanding and teaching of them.

Given concerns with the neoliberal interpretation of CT, Burbules and Berk (1999) distinguished between CT (as a thinking skill) and critical consciousness. The latter is associated with the work of Paulo Freire. Freire (1968/2000) conceptualized critical consciousness as the awareness and resistance to oppressive social arrangements in order to avoid (re)inscribing, validating and (re)producing asymmetrical power relationships. Action and reflection, which Freire referred to as praxis, are key features of critical consciousness. Critical consciousness is an orientation to participate in the (re)formation of social configurations that affirm humanity of others. This consciousness involves "learning to perceive social, political and economic contradictions, and to take action against the oppressive elements of reality" (Freire, 1968/2000, p. 35). In Freire's philosophy, critical consciousness is communal. Individuals are critically conscious to the degree in which they construct their reality in solidarity with others to produce better democratic processes that mitigate injustice. Rather than invalidating claims about their truthfulness, critical consciousness is about situating truth claims in a system of power and understanding the political, cultural, and institutional purpose of those claims. These insights are starting points for working with others to transform inequitable and undemocratic relationships.

Unlike SRL and creativity, CT offers an alternative concept that can serve as a compass for resisting the neoliberal influence on HOT. Shifting the language from critical thinking to critical consciousness can orient HOT toward democratic ideals. This shift can encourage the understanding of CT that aligns with democratic processes, rather than the dehumanized completion of intellectual tasks for pursuit of self-benefit. To realize a democratic ideal, students can use thinking skills to apply knowledge in a way that contributes to a social good. If students are to be encouraged to think critically, let this skill be directed at dominant structures that weaken our hope for sustainable and effective democracy.

Problem Solving

Problem solving (PS) is another HOT skill that is assigned increasing importance (Kwan 2009). Simply stated, this skill involves finding solutions to problems. The critical complexity is not so much in defining this skill, but rather in the consideration of the types of problems that are to be solved, what counts as a valid solution, the processes involved, the role of the teacher, and the purposes of developing PS skills. As with the other HOT skills, researchers are focused on understanding the psychological, social, and cultural mechanisms that contribute to "effective" and valued PS (e.g., Azer, 2001; Goodnough & Nolan, 2008). This knowledge is intended to improve the teaching and learning of this skill. Against this trend, a comparison between problem-based learning (PBL) and problem-posing pedagogy (PPP) is offered to highlight some of critical concerns with the discourse of PS. PBL is a widely used model for PS and is increasingly researched and applied to learning situations. Like CT, PS in a PBL model can be associated with a neoliberal agenda for producing good workers who can function well within a twenty-first-century economic setting. In comparison, PPP, which is associated with the work of Paulo Freire, is not as widely applied as PBL but can be considered an orientation to PS that can serve a democratic vision of schooling.

PROBLEM-BASED LEARNING

PBL is inquiry driven learning (Kwan, 2009; Etherington, 2011). The idea is that students learn new content knowledge by exploring "real-world" problems (Kwan, 2009, p. 91). Kilroy (2004) contended that PBL derives from a theory that, for effective acquisition of knowledge, learners need to be stimulated to restructure information they already know within a realistic context, to gain new knowledge, and to then elaborate on the new information in the context of solving a problem. Kwan (2009) argued that as a formal pedagogical model, PBL originated in 1965 with the work of Howard Barrows, who was a medical educator. Barrows (1980) was interested in improving medical students' clinical reasoning by giving them clinical experience in the learning process. The goal was to support learning through guided practice and reflection on that practice. The adoption of PBL outside of the medical field gradually occurred in other professional schools such as engineering, higher education, and K–12 school settings (Kwan, 2009; Hodges, 2010; Etherington, 2011).

Kwan (2009) described PBL as more than just an instructional method that can be integrated into any pedagogical situation. Rather, she contended that PBL is about structuring environments organized around an entire commitment to nurture students by providing opportunities for PS to guide the achievement of particular learning outcomes. PBL can be considered an example of student-centered learning. Kwan listed the following characteristics of PBL: (1) learners explore real-world problems as the starting point for learning; (2) learners engage in self-direction by evaluating their own learning process; (3) learners work collaboratively in small groups; (4) teachers assume the role of facilitator; and (5) learning outcomes emphasize content knowledge acquisition, as well as skills and attitudes.

For some models of PBL, there are steps to solving problems (Wood, 2003; Kwan, 2009). According to Kwan (2009), PBL begins with a teacher presenting an ill-defined problem to students. Next, students work in teams to evaluate and analyze the problem. Kwan argued that in this stage of the process, students' reasoning and knowledge should be evaluated, challenged, and developed. Then students identify areas of need, which is supposed to lead to individualized study. The skills and knowledge learned are shared among team members and then applied back to the problem. This part of the process provides a context to evaluate the quality of the learning. This process can be iterative, some steps can be repeated, and goals can be adapted. Although this process seems well scripted, Kwan argues that adopting a commitment to PBL is complex and challenging, with many factors contributing to this challenge.

Educational psychologists are generally interested in students' PS without necessarily endorsing any particular pedagogical format. Their interest is studying processes and states that impact PS. For example, PS involves using working memory capacity, which for information-processing theorists is the mechanism that is responsible for processing, storing, and retrieving information. As this capacity is limited, a good problem solver reduces the cognitive load by offloading information, organizing, strategically asking for assistance, and delegating responsibilities. By reducing the cognitive burden, students can then use working memory to retrieve relevant information for solving the problem. Students must retrieve what they know, whether it is declarative, procedural, or conditional knowledge, and know how to use that knowledge for PS. In so doing, students are supposed to build on, revise, and acquire new knowledge. This expectation can invite frustration because students may believe that they do not have the requisite knowledge, skills, and schema to solve problems (Kwan, 2009). For that reason, this author argued that PBL can take time to implement and should involve explicit instruction.

PROBLEM-POSING PEDAGOGY

PPP is a pedagogical philosophy that, like PBL, is not reducible to an instructional method. PPP involves a particular understanding of what it means to teach, the relationship between teachers and students, purpose of schooling, and what counts as knowledge. Solving problems within PBL environments is vastly different than solving problems in environments that are aligned with PPP. However, there are points of overlap between PBL and PPP. One overlapping feature is that problems are not contrived, abstract, or hypothetical. Rather problems are situated within the communities, classrooms, and world. By focusing on these types of problems, the hope is that students get a sense that they can (trans)form their worlds. Another similarity is that both PBL and PPP are not a method of instruction but an entire commitment to schooling. That is, solving a problem is not ancillary to lecture or modeling but is itself the means of constructing knowledge. Another similarity is the emphasis on collaboration. Students work with teachers and their peers to solve problems. Despite these similarities, there are also significant differences that illuminate critical concerns with PBL. These differences relate to the role of teachers, the origination of problems, pedagogical processes, and the purposes of solving problems.

The Role of the Student-Teacher

A key characteristic of PPP is authentic dialogue and action. For such dialogue, both teachers and students must be recognized as possessing valuable experiences and knowledge that when shared stand as representations of the world. In this regard, PPP undermines conventional roles of students and teachers. In a conventional role, the teacher is an authority whose job is to regulate the way students perceive and construct the world. Teachers deposit information, an approach Freire (1968/2000) called banking, and evaluate students' understanding of that information as measured by some assessment. In this pedagogical relationship, knowledge is treated as static, pre-determined, and possessed by an authority (i.e., teacher) who is responsible for bestowing such knowledge upon others (i.e., students), and students are treated as passive recipients of that knowledge. For PPP, the teacher and student roles are fluid; the students teach the teacher, as the teacher teaches the students; both gain experience and knowledge in constructing new ideas. From this construction of the teacher and student relationship, acts of knowing can be grounded in individual experience and circumstance. New knowledge is neither predetermined nor prescriptive but emerges through dialogue and action.

The Origin of Problems

Like PBL, PPP is centered on problems. However, for PPP a teacher does not present an ill-defined problem to be solved by students for which they apply a well-defined process. As might be argued by critical pedagogical theorists, the construction and presentation of a problem from a teacher privileges a particular perspective about what problems are deemed worthy of engagement. Furthermore, although there might be mutual interest in a problem that is presented by the teacher, the danger is that students will not exercise their critical capacities to reflect on how the problem relates to injustices surrounding their communities. Another danger to teachers presenting problems is that they may already have ideas about the solution to the problem. Freire (1968/2000) is opposed to teachers presenting students with problems, especially those for which answers are already known. For PPP, the problem must emerge in dialogue between students and teachers.

The Purpose of Problems

The purpose of solving problems also distinguishes PBL from PPP. For the latter, the problem must be directed at ending the cycle of oppression via the pursuit of social change and the advancement of democracy. Problems must be tied to a social justice purpose as participants advance their literacy and knowledge (Leonard & McLaren, 2002). McLaren (2007) argued that PPP is not actually a pedagogical model but a commitment to social justice, which means affirming humanity through dialogue with the distinct purpose of mitigating unjust social hierarchies (Freire, 1968/2000; Apple, 2002; Greene, 1988; McLaren, 2007; Giroux, 2009). The purpose of PS in PPP is to understand and change conditions of oppression beginning and grounded in local communities.

In order to achieve this goal, teachers/students and students/teachers must perceive structures of oppression and believe that, through dialogue and action, such a reality is transformable. Freire (1968/2000) stated, "In problem-posing education, people develop their power to perceive critically the way they exist in the world with which and in which they find themselves; they come to see the world not as a static reality, but as a reality in process, in transformation" (p. 252). The continuous production of a new and just reality is collective and in solidarity with others, not for personal gain, material consumption, and individual betterment. From a Freirian perspective, it is essential that pedagogy be committed to dialogue and love, while avoiding commitments to transmit a static form of knowledge and encourage adaptation to existing norms and structures. Such an education dehumanizes students by invalidating their knowledge and experiences, silencing their voices and decision-making capacities, affirming an oppressive social order, and rendering individuals in the world, not part of its production. Critical pedagogy is committed to affirming humanity of all individuals. This effort is characterized by the logic of integration, which means that through dialogue and solidarity, individuals participate in the transformation of their worlds in ways that mitigate oppression and discrimination.

Neoliberalism and the Purposes of Solving Problems

Though PBL can be tied to the purpose of mitigating injustice, the purposes of problems in PBL environments are more likely to be rooted in neoliberal objectives. Those who support PBL emphasize the importance of local, community-based problems. However, the problems of local communities can be perceived differently. If teachers pose or discount emerging problems, the problem itself and the purpose of solving it may be based on a narrow perception of the states, needs, and values of a particular community. More important to consider are the purposes of engaging with local problems. For Smith and Sobel (2010), grounding problems in local community environments helps to (1) sustain student engagement; (2) build social capital; (3) connect students to natural world; and (4) build leaders. The authors treat these purposes as aligned with a democratic vision of schooling, but they can be interpreted as aligned with neoliberalism. For example, sustained engagement may be about (1) improved performance on state-mandated tracks and assessments; (2) rendering students amenable to curricular mandates; or (3) efficiently moving students through a curriculum superhighway. Building social capital may be about students having the networks to advance their own individual, economic interests. Building leaders can be about socialization and sorting based on normative criteria about qualities of a leader.

In recent years ExxonMobil put out a series of ads that tout the importance of students' developing PS skills and teachers getting better at supporting its development. The ads justified the importance of PS in economic and imperialist terms. The ExxonMobil website included the statement that "if the next generation of U.S. workers lacks the skills to solve the problems of the future, it's not just U.S. leadership in energy that's at risk—it's also our leadership in medicine, research, technology, and other pillars of the American economy" (Cohen, 2012, paragraph 5). For this corporate campaign, ExxonMobil supports initiatives to improve students' performance in science and math, and to improve teachers' ability to teach these subjects. This message is not unlike those in relation to other HOT skills. If students do not learn to think, none of the problems in the United States can be solved and the nation's future for global, domestic, and local leadership is threatened.

SUMMATIVE REFLECTION
An appeal of PBL is that schooling reflects a commitment to solving problems that are relevant to students' lives and to their communities. However, like criticism of CT, PS in PBL environments is connected to individual human capital development for the purposes of adapting to institutional mandates. PPP, on the other hand, can be a compass for committing to PS in ways that align with a democratic purpose. The purpose of PPP is not to script environments so that students can develop and mobilize PS skills when they are given a problem. Rather, the purpose is to mitigate injustice and create and practice democratic processes. Like other HOT skills, PS is subject to neoliberal highjacking and can be connected to a narrow curricula focus, human capital development, self-interest, and corporate interest. Adopting PPP can support movement away from a neoliberal version of PS.

Critically Engaging with Higher Order Thinking

Calls to foster HOT come from business leaders, teachers, critical theorists, and educational policymakers across political and ideological spectra. Critical engagement with HOT is not intended to invite schooling that focuses on so-called lower order thinking, which is one end of a problematic binary. Rather, the goal is to recognize that the HOT skills featured in educational psychology need to be critically engaged. Although specific conceptual, philosophical, and cultural concerns relate to each skill, a neoliberal current runs throughout HOT. Institutionalizing HOT in an effort to prepare students to compete and navigate the twenty-first-century economy is a clear endorsement of a neoliberal agenda. Thinking skills have become a feature of neoliberal selfhood and are implicated in rendering individuals "ready-made" for a twenty-first-century market. Thus HOT is not neutral and value-free but is intertwined in dangerous assumptions about persons and the purposes of schooling, as well as underpinned by specific political, philosophical, and cultural positions.

When curricula and pedagogy are focused on cultivating these skills, one must be aware of the ideological context that is endorsed and validated. To resist neoliberalism does not necessarily require one to reject HOT. In order to untangle the discourse on HOT skills from the project of neoliberalism, a straightforward effort to divorce these skills from economic instrumentalism, individualism, efficiency, consumption, and self-betterment may be considered sufficient. However, severing an explicit connection to the economy does not adequately resist neoliberalism. Rhetorically divorcing thinking skills from neoliberal values does not mean that such skills will not serve a neoliberal function. This point is important because although individuals may not rationalize thinking and learning skills in neoliberal terms, teaching these skills may ultimately support this agenda and validate neoliberal structural arrangements. An important pedagogical commitment is to continuously reflect on how HOT can be validated in schools without serving a neoliberal aim.

CHAPTER FOUR

Theories of Development

D EVELOPMENTAL PSYCHOLOGY is the study of progressive changes in physical states, identity, behaviors, emotions, and reasoning that occur across the lifespan (Bornstein & Lamb, 2011). The core tenets of this branch of psychology are applied within the domain of schooling in an attempt to understand the needs and states of students at any given time within their presumed developmental trajectory. Understanding developmental characteristics ostensibly supports teachers' efforts to produce congruence between schooling environments and their students, known as developmentally appropriate practice (DAP). For some, DAP is the gold standard of teaching. To achieve DAP, teachers must (1) construct developmental profiles of students by assessing cognitive, emotional, and psychological needs, states, and capabilities; (2) judge which tasks are congruent with those profiles; and (3) have an understanding of developmental trajectories so that new and challenging tasks can guide or avoid hindering change.

DAP is positively associated with student engagement, motivation, and academic outcomes. However, developmental theories and the broad idea of thinking developmentally about students pose concerns. The idea of development itself, the categories used to delineate it, and the dominance of certain theories are rooted in political, historical, ideological, and cultural contexts. Developmental ideas are used to propagate normative values, justify student deficiencies, reproduce social hierarchies, and endorse the neoliberal emphasis on competition (Walkerdine, 2003; Lesko, 2001; Packer & Tappan, 2001; Burman, 2008 Kaščák & Pupala, 2013). Thinking critically about development means recognizing these possibilities and integrating them into reflections about the value and consequences of using developmental theory in teaching.

Background

Developmental psychology is the study of growth and change across the lifespan. However, educational psychologists tend to focus on development during school-age years. Regardless of focus, the foundational feature of any conceptualization of development is change, which is not a synonym of development (Packer & Tappan, 2001; Bornstein & Lamb, 2011). To count as development, Bornstein and Lamb (2011) argued that change must (1) be influenced by earlier changes; (2) be enduring and signify improvements in functioning and harmony between oneself and the external world; and (3) demonstrate progress toward a particular endpoint along a trajectory. Given such conditions, the authors have reasoned that development is change that is organized, continuous, progressive, adaptive, enduring, and successive.

Development is a concern for educational psychologists because children spend a good portion of their lives in schools, which are places that can support, quell, steer, or limit changes for students. In an effort to support certain developmental achievements, educational psychologists attempt to describe and explain students' needs, states, and trajectories in relation to a number of areas, including intelligence, reasoning, language acquisition, self, attention, perspective-taking, attachment, morality, and personality (Baltes, Reese, & Lipsitt, 1980). These areas of development tend to be treated as separate domains; educational psychologists might argue that teachers need to account for all of them in order to teach the "whole child." Achieving DAP thus requires knowledge of these domains, the mechanisms responsible for change, and what change should look like.

THE VALUE OF DEVELOPMENTAL KNOWLEDGE

There are a number of reasons to strive for DAP. In general, DAP is associated with humanistic pedagogy, student success, and well-being (Covin, 1974; Elkind, 2007 Powell & Kalina, 2009). Pedagogical environments that do not reflect DAP are associated with student misbehavior, academic failure, teacher frustration, and student disengagement (Eccles et al., 1993). By knowing needs, states, and trajectories, teachers can shape environments to ensure student success while also pushing them to complete more complex thinking and behaving than what they can already do. In other words, teachers can consider what students are "ready" to learn and tailor the pace and approach for that learning. Requiring students to think, feel, and communicate in ways outside their developmental potential can cause them to feel either incompetent or unchallenged, both of which conditions can decrease motivation. Developmentally inappropriate practice can create and exacerbate academic problems.

Developmental knowledge can also be a tool for leveling the academic playing field. Students who do not meet developmental expectations or are not adequately progressing on a trajectory may be considered "behind" and at a disadvantage. Developmental knowledge arguably supports the identification of those students who need an intervention in order to "catch up" to reflect normalized expectations. Teachers can use developmental knowledge to construct an appropriate intervention as well as monitor, chart, and evaluate students' progress toward developmental goals. Developmental knowledge can serve as a compass to shape interventions and ensure that students are adequately moving along the targeted trajectory so they can develop the same cognitive resources as their peers.

THE STATUS OF DEVELOPMENT IN EDUCATIONAL DISCOURSE

Developmental psychology is prominently featured in education discourse. Development is a defining feature of the field of educational psychology and is integrated into all areas of scholarship extending beyond the conventional domains to include higher ordering thinking (e.g., self-regulated learning, metacognition, and critical thinking), competencies, intelligences, and attention. For teaching, the value of development is evidenced by the contents of professional standards (e.g., NAEYC, 2009a; NBPTS, 2012; CCSSO, 2013). The standards for teachers' national certification are structured in terms of developmental ranges. Teachers can be certified for specific age ranges: early childhood (ages three to eight), middle childhood (ages seven to twelve), early and middle childhood (ages three to twelve), early childhood through young adulthood (ages three to eighteen plus), early adolescence (ages eleven to fifteen), adolescence and young adulthood (ages fourteen to eighteen plus), and early adolescence through young adulthood (ages eleven to eighteen plus). The assumption underlying the need for certification in a specific age range is that teachers must demonstrate mastery of the specialized knowledge relating to a particular age group. Implementing DAP is an essential requirement for national certification.

The Interstate Teacher Assessment and Support Consortium (InTASC) is a group of state and national education agencies and organizations that is dedicated to reforming the preparation, licensing, and ongoing professional development of teachers. InTASC has proposed ten standards for quality teaching, the first of which pertains to the ways learners grow and develop (CCSSO, 2010). For this standard, teachers must recognize that patterns of learning and development vary individually within and across the cognitive, linguistic, social, emotional, and physical areas. Teachers must also be able to design and implement developmentally appropriate and challenging learning experiences (CCSSO, 2011). The original 1992 InTASC standards, from which the current standards have been revised, did not employ the term "developmentally appropriate," nor was there a standard that explicitly focuses on learner development (Henson, 2009). The latest version's prominent inclusion of a standard for learner growth and development illustrates the growing prominence of developmental knowledge for teacher quality and professionalization.

Dominant Theories

Although few disagree about the importance of DAP, conceptual and philosophical debates have given rise to the following questions: (1) do all individuals develop the same way (universalism) or is everybody different (individualism); (2) does development occur as a result of biological forces or culture; (3) is development linear and predictable or messy and unpredictable; (4) how much of development is controllable and what are the sources of control (e.g., personal, biological, parental, and environmental); (5) does development occur in discrete stages and at corresponding ages; and (6) are there different domains of development, and if so, how do they interact? Responses to these questions will be shaped by epistemological commitments, whether one adheres to constructivism (associated with Jean Piaget) or socioculturalism (associated with Lev Vygotsky). These authors are foundational figures in developmental debates and are typically treated as having opposing views.

CONSTRUCTIVISM

Constructivism describes a theory of knowledge underpinned by the idea that development manifests from personal processes. This particular education philosophy is student-centered and assumes that students have knowledge, attitudes, states, schema, interests, and experiences that they bring to learning situations. Such qualities shape meaning, engagement, performance, and understanding. The key tenet is that knowledge is built upon personal experiences, and learning occurs when students are interacting with subjects (as opposed to passively absorbing information from a teacher). According to Jean Piaget, the construction of knowledge results from developmentally determined schema, which are mental structures that people use to engage with and make sense of experiences. Schema change over time and shape possibilities for the kinds of reasoning and knowledge students develop.

Before researching children, Piaget was a biologist by trade. He was interested in the biological basis for the emergence and changes in children's logico-mathematical reasoning. Piaget and Inhelder (1969) conceptualized children as incomplete beings who learned to reason in qualitatively different ways by progressing through stages. These changes occurred in stages and had corresponding ages: sensorimotor (ages zero to two), preoperational (ages two to five), concrete operational (ages five to eleven), and formal operational (ages eleven to fourteen). Each stage is associated with specific qualities of reasoning that provide the underlying mental structure for making sense of experiences and building concepts. According to Piaget (1952), the movement through stages unfolded and resulted from changes in biology. Piaget contended that each stage laid the foundation for the next one. In this regard, Piaget proposed a theory of development that is linear and progressive. His theory is universal in that he posited that each person, regardless of time and place, progresses sequentially and linearly through these four stages.

Several other constructivist theories have related to other domains of development (see, e.g., Selman's stages of perspective taking, Kohlberg's stages of moral reasoning, and Erikson's stages of personality development). Typically, stage theories are associated with specific age ranges. These theories inform a portion of developmental thinking in educational psychology and rest on the assumption that development follows a linear, predictable, sequential, and universal path. In other words, regardless of time, place, cultural variation, and individual differences, there is a predictable sequence and pattern of development. A foundational assumption across all these developmental domain theories is that natural processes are responsible for developmental changes.

From a constructivist approach, DAP is achieved when teachers purposefully and intentionally align their classroom environment and pedagogy with stages and ages. For stage theories, the structure of the pedagogical environment is important for ensuring the proper unfolding of development by avoiding the suppression and thwarting of naturally occurring changes. Implementing DAP from a constructivist view requires one to operate with universalist and predetermined assumptions about what children are and what they need. For example, Piaget and Inhelder (1969) believed that throughout the first stage (sensorimotor), infants and toddlers develop comprehension through sensory experiences. Therefore, in early childhood education, DAP incorporates sensory practices and manipulatives. In another example, in the formal operational stage, Piaget and Inhelder proposed that students could reason deductively, as well as comprehend abstract ideas, such as moral consequences of actions and events. DAP is giving students multiple opportunities to explain and explore suppositional situations. If one were teaching about the US Civil War, DAP could involve a discussion on the ethical issues that divided the country. Broadly, to implement DAP from a constructivist perspective, a teacher must know the qualities, needs, and states that are specifically related to children at certain ages and shape teaching accordingly.

SOCIOCULTURALISM

The major tenets of constructivism are often presented in contrast to those of socioculturalism, which are a group of perspectives that are unified by the idea that development results from interactions between individuals, other people, tools, and activities. Although sociocultural theory is specifically associated with Lev Vygotsky, the work of several theorists falls under this category (e.g., Lave & Wenger, 1991; Cole, 1998; Rogoff, 2003; Bronfenbrenner, 2009). Some of these theories emphasize different social functions and processes. However, a uniting assumption among the theories is that psychological materials emerge, rather than unfold, and change as a consequence of social interactions that take place during a particular moment in time. From this group of perspectives, developmental phenomena are not solely attributed to persons, but rather a result of disciplinary knowledge, assessments, actors, ideology, politics, historical moment, and individuals. Psychological material is not a priori or a given, nor is sequentially evolved or predetermined. Rather, psychological material is cultural and historical. Ways that people remember, the qualities of reasoning, the formation of the self, and the contents of that self are artifacts.

Unlike Piaget, who contended that developmental stages shape possibilities for knowledge construction, sociocultural theory's foundational figure Lev Vygotsky believed that experiences and the accumulation of knowledge drove development. Thus, the accumulation of knowledge and experiences precedes qualitative changes in reasoning. Terms to explain this view of development include internalization and zone of proximal development (ZPD), or the range of tasks that children can complete with support. ZPD is the distance between person's actual development as determined by independent engagement and their potential development as determined by engagement with guidance or collaboration with more capable others (Vygotsky, 1978). Internalization is the movement of interactions from a social plane to a cognitive one. Internalization occurs as support is gradually removed to give individuals opportunities to autonomously perform the targeted thought process or behavior. As support is removed, other support is given to continue the development of even more complex thought processes and behaviors. Pedagogical terms that are associated with Vygotsky are scaffolding and guided participation, both of which emphasize structural supports for developmental achievements.

An example of Vygotsky's ideas can be gleaned from the Woods and Middleton Pyramid Puzzle Experiment conducted in 1975, in which researchers provided three- and four-year-olds with a puzzle that was beyond their own comprehension and ability. In this experiment, mothers provided different levels of assistance. The children were then assessed on whether they could construct the pyramid on their own. Results showed that when children were given varied support from mothers (low levels of support when the child was doing well, and high levels when the child struggled) they were able to construct the pyramid. However, when the mothers consistently provided the same support, this seemed to make the children conclude the activity was beyond their comprehension, and they soon lost interest in constructing the pyramid. The idea is that varied levels of scaffolding are needed in order to support students' completion of tasks within their ZPD.

In contrast to stage theories, DAP through a sociocultural lens must incorporate lessons and activities that merge what children can do independently with what they can do with support. Given that experiences drive development, the teacher must provide lessons and activities that are just beyond students' capabilities. DAP, therefore, requires knowing students' capabilities and the right amount of assistance to complete a task. DAP also involves knowing when to remove support. Ensuring that learning experiences are meaningful, relevant, and respectful to children and their families, teachers must have some knowledge of the social and cultural contexts in which children live (Bredekamp, 1987). Such knowledge helps teachers build on students' prior experiences and learning so they can help them progress to more complex thoughts and behaviors than their existing levels. It is important to note that not every pedagogical support is universally applicable to students. A Vygotskian view of development complements contemporary requirements for differentiating instruction.

Contemporary Theory

Packer and Tappan (2001) have argued that up until the late twentieth century constructivism dominated development discourse in the United

States. The grip loosened as sociocultural theory began to be integrated into educational conversations during the 1980s. Since that time, a number of sociocultural views have emerged. Despite this shift, constructivist views still have a firm place in policies, practices, and representations in educational psychology. However, Elkind (2007) doubted the actuality of constructivist influence and contended that educational policies and practices are actually concerned with "hurrying" development. This charge makes sense in the context of Common Core, which provides a set of well-defined, predetermined benchmarks. Although Biggam and Hyson (2014) made the argument that DAP is possible with Common Core, this set of benchmarks can invite teachers to ignore student "readiness," an idea of which Piaget and Inhelder (1969) were strong advocates. According to them, attempting to teach children concepts before they have arrived at them is harmful to students and frustrating for teachers. However, the well-defined structure of Common Core can pressure educators to focus more on adhering to a learning structure than to giving students opportunities to "arrive" at concepts.

Controversies persist about how to understand students' developmental states and what kinds of experiences they need to support their progression. Notwithstanding, it cannot be ignored that sociocultural theory has been growing in acceptance in policy and in the rationalization of teaching. One reason for its prominence, Kaščák and Pupala (2013) contended, results from the interpretation of Vygotsky's theory to fit a neoliberal emphasis on individualism and competition. The acceptance of socioculturalism, however, has not led to the rejection of constructivism but to the reconciliation between these views. Few researchers operate strictly on either side of the constructivist and sociocultural binary (Kindermann & Skinner, 1992; Martin & Sugarman, 1999; Rogoff, 2003). Kindermann and Skinner (1992) stated, "It is almost impossible to find a developmental psychologist today who would argue against a contextualized understanding of individual development. Development is widely viewed as a joint function of organismic and environmental forces and as processing within a frame of organizing contexts" (p. 155). Rogoff (2003) captures this view by stating, "It is clear that there is not just one way for children to develop. At the same time, there are regularities. The variations that become apparent with a cultural lens are not infinite and random" (p. 5). The integration of constructivist and sociocultural theory is captured in a variety of developmental models, albeit with significant variation.

Integrating these perspectives can produce a broad view of development that can open up possibilities for interpreting students and implementing

DAP. Notwithstanding, integration does not answer all developmental questions, such as (1) are some developmental phenomena affected differently by biology or culture; (2) are some phenomena only biological and some only cultural; (3) does biology and culture work in concert to affect the same phenomena; (4) what specifically does biology and culture affect; (5) can biology and environment be controlled; and (6) can personal characteristics override environmental factors? Answering these questions is important for advancing developmental psychology and ensuring educators have the nuance to apply developmental knowledge in their classrooms. As important as these questions are, their answers do little to illuminate the political, ideological, and cultural underpinnings of developmental theory.

Critical Analysis

The use of developmental theory in teaching is, on the one hand, intended to be democratic, humanistic, and empowering. Environmental congruence is supposed to reflect a humanistic commitment to students' success by focusing on their needs and potential. Some researchers have suggested that a focus on development in teaching can support efforts to mitigate economic poverty (Doyle, Harmon, Heckman, & Tremblay, 2009). Integrating development in teaching can also be used to resist neoliberal educational reforms, which overly formalizes school by endeavoring to move students efficiently and effectively through a curriculum. Rather than conforming children to the needs of policy makers and politicians, as well as the purported needs of an economic order, a developmental perspective can lead to the centering of students' needs and invite the pathologization of schooling environments for what might considered developmental aberrations.

On the other hand, developmental thinking is implicated in a number of problematic educational commitments, philosophies, and practices. The notion of development invites philosophically and culturally narrow ideas about change and growth—whether conceptualized as universal stages or culturally determined trajectories. Also, the contents of developmental trajectories are steeped in culture, history, governance, and ideology. In particular, the discourse of development is linked to cultural reproduction, utilized to achieve economic and political aims, and entangled in the scientific management of people, surveillance, and control (Lesko, 2001; Packer & Tappan, 2001; Burman, 2008; Vagle, 2012; Reich & Albarran, 2014). In addition, although developmental discourse can be mobilized to resist neoliberal reforms, developmentalism can also endorse such ideology, which is not typically associated with humanism, emancipation, freedom, and democracy.

Normative Cultural Underpinnings

Development is a story about how people change that is underpinned by assumptions about progress. If developing correctly, students change toward or achieve particular endpoints. The previous state, which signifies incompleteness, may be viewed as inadequate or inferior to the emerging or developing state. Development does not typically signify movement toward a worse state, but something more valued, favorable, and complete. In this regard, development connotes goodness and progress. There is a great deal of uncertainty, however, surrounding the evaluation of states, changes, and endpoints. What one might call development, another might call devolution. There is also concern for the idea that something more needs to happen for one to embody valued states and become a finished being. This way of thinking about persons invites a perception of lacking and an orientation to self that is centered on needing improvement.

The narratives of progress and incompleteness are cultural and historical. Developmental stories are told differently across time and place, creating cultural rifts and ideological battles. Not everybody views children developmentally or agrees with dominant narratives about development. Packer and Tappan (2001) explained: "Clearly the trajectory of change that we call 'development' is not natural and pregiven, nor uncontested and agreed-upon by all. Communities in which a single pathway to adulthood is accepted unquestionably are found rarely, if at all. In postindustrial societies any apparent consensus over the value of ubiquitous movement towards ends such as 'freedom' and 'autonomy' disguises 'profound rifts' and disparate appeals to moral ends thin enough to permit multiple interpretations and implementations" (p. 29). The authors pointed to the existence of multiple and contested trajectories and endpoints, which are underpinned by diverse narratives of growth, change, and endpoints. Narratives shape what is viewed as developing, how life is fragmented, what is believed to be possible at certain ages, and the categories of life stages, such as child, toddler, adolescent, and so on (Rogoff, 2003). Different narratives contribute to entirely different trajectories, categories, and developmental achievements (e.g., see Menon & Shweder, 2001; Rogoff, 2003).

Despite this diverse landscape, developmental norms, values, standards, and trajectories are underpinned by a narrow and specific set of cultural values (Carta, 1995; Hsue & Aldridge, 1995; Lesko, 2001; Packer & Tappan, 2001; Burman, 2008; Vagle, 2012; Reich & Albarran, 2014). In particular, critics associate developmental norms with a white male Western middle-class population. Historically, using this population to construct norms resulted from explicit efforts to shape people in accordance with a particular vision for society (Lesko, 2001; Burman, 2008; Reich & Albarran, 2014). That is, researchers studied dominant populations and developed norms, which were applied to the measurement and evaluation of subordinate groups. The purpose was to identify developmental shortcomings of certain groups in order to reform them to align with a particular vision for a social order. This agenda was the driving force behind the study of adolescence in the 1800s (Lesko, 2001). White Western middle-class individuals informed standards and norms for evaluating and reforming all individuals in ways to solve specific economic, social, and cultural problems.

Contemporary developmental norms continue to be underpinned by particular populations. For example, researchers charged that the NAEYC guidelines for DAP reflect white Western culture (Carta, 1995; Hsue & Aldridge, 1995). Hsue and Aldridge (1995) pointed to conflicts with traditional Taiwanese culture and early childhood education practices. They contended that the NAEYC guidelines for DAP encourage the development of autonomy in young children, promote the American interpretations of equity and justice, and focus on success. However, Taiwanese culture and early education practices are centered on the development of respect for elders, promote the values of tolerance, benevolence, and consideration of others, as well as encourage a balance between success and failure. Williams (1994) also raised concern about the NAEYC by suggesting a conflict with Native American communities. Whereas the guidelines emphasize individual development, learner autonomy, and creating opportunities for children to speak, Native American communities emphasize the growth of an individual as it relates to the group, learning from a mentor or model, and creating opportunities for children to listen. Although the comparisons discussed above are oversimplifications of variation and homogeneity, the cultural underpinnings of developmental norms and guidelines cannot be ignored.

Consider research on self-regulated learning (SRL) as another example of the ways developmental norms continue to be underpinned by particular groups and values. Although treated as a universal human capacity, certain conditions are associated with the development of students' effective and adaptive forms of SRL. For example, certain practices and structures in the home are implicated in SRL development (see, Vassallo, 2013b). These include parent-child interactions, extracurricular activities, structure of leisure time, childrearing logic, fluidity between home and school, and parents' behavior. As Vassallo (2013b) pointed out, the specific qualities of these structures and practices map onto middle-class cultural norms, values, and material realities. Therefore, Vassallo reasoned that taking up the aim to explicitly facilitate SRL development in the home means embodying and propagating middle-class practices and ideals. Although arguably an unintended consequence, it is difficult to avoid propagating cultural norms when, as Pino-Pasternak and Whitebread (2010) charged, researchers who study parent involvement and SRL tend do so with well-schooled middle-class white families.

There are several ways in which development reflects norms and standards of particular populations. These narrow underpinnings result in part from the populations who are studied and represented in research (Reich & Albarran, 2014). Like other developmental theorists, Piaget is accused of conducting research with a racially and socioeconomically homogenous population, leading him to normalize the values and thought processes of that population (Goodman, 2008). Lesko (2001) and Burman (2008) argued that researchers choose particular populations with the intent to propagate certain values and norms. At times, however, researchers study populations that are accessible. As Reich and Albarran (2014) argued, middle-class individuals are more likely to participate in research studies on development than working-class or economically disadvantaged individuals. However, studies involving the latter groups are not likely intended to inform dominant representations of normal development. Rather, they are likely informed by a commitment to understand groups for the purpose of reforming them in ways to reflect dominant developmental norms and standards.

In conjunction with population selectivity, as Packer and Tappan (2001) argued, the production, interpretation, and application of development theory reflects the values of policy makers, researchers, parents, and educators. These individuals operate with cultural frames of reference that seep into and inform standards, narratives, trajectories, evaluations, and interventions. Developmental norms, along with their associated DAP, are subject to the biases of their creators, despite efforts to generate abstract, unbiased, universal theories of development. A consequence is that developmental norms fail to capture a range of diversity. Given culturally normative underpinnings, teachers must consider who produced the theory and what vision of persons informs the theory.

The normative underpinnings of developmental theory may not pose the greatest challenge to teaching because there is no such thing as a neutral and value-free theory. Values, norms, and frames of reference shape the content of theories, which includes assumptions about states, needs, trajectories, rates of change, and endpoints. The trouble is the failure to recognize such underpinnings. If invisible, developmental theory can present significant problems for students. If students are not part of the group represented in developmental standards and assumptions, they can be marginalized, silenced, and pathologized. If one is operating with a developmental narrative that is taken for granted as neutral, value-free, and natural, then students who do not fit into, conform to, or exceed developmental expectations may be viewed as deficient and abnormal. Espousing and applying developmental standards without recognizing its cultural foundation can endorse cultural hegemony and cultural deprivation theory.

Cultural Hegemony

Cultural hegemony describes the operation of power by dominant groups to normalize and naturalize their beliefs, perceptions, experiences, logic, behaviors, and, in this case, developmental patterns. Hegemony involves accepting and propagating the cultural patterns associated with dominant groups. It also involves an effort to shape individuals in accordance with these norms or to use norms to justify social, political, and economic hierarchies. The normalization of development can create perceptions of deficiencies and pathologies for those who do not conform, justifying their disenfranchisement, marginalization, and position in hierarchies. Explanations for developmental deviations can be attributed to individuals and their environments. This attribution deflects attention away from issues with developmental thinking, as well as contents of developmental theories that made it possible to brand one developmentally behind or ahead.

Theorists explain student deviations from developmental norms in a number of ways. These include natural variations in persons, culture differences, impoverished home environments, parent deficiencies, poor teaching, lack of access to quality early childhood education, or curricula inadequacies. In much of the contemporary political discourse, deviations are typically attributed to access to early childhood education, especially for individuals from economically disadvantaged backgrounds. In a schooling context, this attribution makes sense. Believing that all children can develop "normally" given the right kinds environments could avoid blaming students, as well as ascribe power for pedagogy to shape development. The push for early childhood education is driven by the goal to expose children to environments that facilitate the development of the academic and social skills that are required for K–12 classrooms. Although there is a positive side to this effort, it assumes that children from these backgrounds have inadequate environments and parents who cannot and do not support the right kinds of development.

Regardless of the source for deficiencies, which are debated and contested, there is often a source left unacknowledged: the developmental theory. Seldom is developmentalism to blame or the contents of those theories, as they are often taken for granted as representations of growth and change. Fendler (1999) argued this point:

> Educational discourse generally takes it for granted that children's growth can be understood as conforming (or not conforming) to a pattern. Moreover, if a child's growth does not conform to a given pattern of development, then the child is judged to be "abnormal." This sort of judgment is significant because in an analytical organizing schema, the theory of developmentalism is held to be "true" and the child is held to be "deviant." The principle is believed to reflect the norm, and the lives of individual children are evaluated with reference to that norm. The analytical generalization takes precedence over the broad range of variations by calling some children "normal" and some children "abnormal." . . . In another schema, the theory of developmentalism might be judged faulty because it cannot account for the range of empirical data—namely the wide variations in the ways children grow. (pp. 170–171)

Fendler does not advocate an individualistic approach to development, but instead points out that both the principle of developmentalism and the contents of developmental theories invite deficit-based thinking for those individuals who do not conform to norms and standards. Developmentalism and theories of development are not pathologized, but rather students, parents, and cultures—explanations connected to cultural deprivation doctrine (CDD).

Cultural Deprivation

Coined in the 1960s, CDD is the idea that low student achievement from traditionally underrepresented groups results from inadequate child-rearing, unstimulating home environments, and cultural practices. This doctrine focuses on what is lacking in home structures, interactions, routines, and experiences, as measured against and validated through particular norms. Lubeck (1994) argued that the DAP in the NAEYC guidelines are both a subtle and explicit form of CDD. Whereas CDD is explicitly centered on what is lacking, the DAP guidelines focus on what should be present by describing "best practices" for early childhood education programs. However, this difference appears to be rhetorical; assumptions in the guidelines suggest deficit-based explanations for developmental variations.

In the 2009 version of the NAEYC guidelines, closing the learning gap is named as one of the current educational challenges that can be addressed with DAP. In these guidelines, the gap, which refers to differences in academic performance between African-American and Hispanic students as compared to their white counterparts, exists because of disparities in children's early experiences and access to good programs and schools, a mismatch between the school culture and the students' backgrounds, and "dramatically less rich experiences" with language in their homes (NAEYC, 2009c, p. 3). These reasons for the achievement gap suggest that parents cannot provide the "proper" experiences for "healthy" development. The second explanation is less of an endorsement of cultural deprivation than the first and third ones, unless one argues that parents need to change the home to match those at school. It is often the case, however, that parents must change home structures to match school, not the other way around. Offering these explanations is underpinned by the assumption that development theories are valid, giving credibility to cultural deprivation for those developmental aberrations.

Universal Child to Superchild: Neoliberal Expectations

The narrow selectivity of populations, as well as the backgrounds of researchers and policy makers, contributes to the production, interpretation, and propagation of a normative set of developmental norms and standards. In addition to this cultural normativity, ideology operates in and through developmental theory. In contemporary discourse, neoliberalism is implicated in the commitment to developmentalism, as well as shifting values and expectations for developmental norms (Kaščák & Pupala, 2013). These authors made this argument by analyzing contemporary discourse on early childhood education in Europe. Although the focus of this study was situated overseas, the authors' argument is applicable to the United States. Kaščák and Pupala (2013) argued that over the last several decades, developmental discourse was geared toward ensuring that every child reflected what they termed the "universal child." The idea is that each child has the potential to develop in the same ways. The authors described the universal child as locked within programs that measured what was lacking in order to intervene and reform. Those who fell behind, as measured and validated by a particular framework, were exposed to an intervention with the goal of helping them "catch up." In this regard, the study of development, although still problematically underpinned by cultural norms, was thought to be applied to promote and achieve universal and democratic ideals.

Kaščák and Pupala (2013) contended that there has been a paradigmatic shift in developmental discourse. They argued that no longer are children expected to embody universal norms, but expected to exceed them. Rather than a commitment to the universal child, development has become about the cultivation of the "superchild." Stated the authors, "In contrast to the preschool child of the past, imprisoned in a network of developmental programmes, tables and lists of lacking competences, the superchild is a child who is full of potential, prepared for the new challenges that lie ahead, both in terms of education and career. The superchild is a competitive, individualised, risk-embracing being, capable of exceeding itself. The superchild is . . . a promise of knowledge economy workers to come" (p. 320). This notion is an instantiation of the good neoliberal subject, guided by an ethic to exceed capabilities for the purposes of outcompeting others and being economically useful. In addition, the superchild is highly individualized and is documented, measured, and calculated for the purposes of evaluating developmental status. The notion of the superchild is tied to the neoliberal values of economic instrumentalism, constant need for excelling, and intense individualism. Universal developmental norms, ideals, and values still underpin the evaluations of the superchild. However, these norms serve as reference points for determining level and pace of acceleration. As Kaščák and Pupala stated, "In this [neoliberal] context pedagogical intervention no longer monitors whether universal norms are being achieved, but whether individual performance is being heightened" (p. 323). In other words, universal developmental norms no longer serve to determine which students need interventions to catch up to their peers; rather they serve as points that must be exceeded.

Kaščák and Pupala (2013) further contended that the shift from universal to superchild is powered by the neoliberal imperative to produce persons that are good for the twenty-first century economy. This commitment is evidenced by the emphasis on early childhood education for the development of competencies. The authors argued that calls for early childhood education are guided by a commitment to cultivate competencies for the twenty-first-century economy, which is a representation of a neoliberal vision of schooling. Some of the well-known competencies include self-regulation, creativity, critical thinking, problem solving, and information literacy. In educational psychology, these are typically referred to as higher order thinking skills. In the United States, a great deal of research is focused on the development of these competencies, especially on self-regulation and creativity.

To foster the cultivation of competencies, researchers have to standardize them, study their development, and provide pedagogical suggestions for facilitating them. This information is necessary to structure environments for optimal competency development. Although these competencies may seem relatively innocuous and humanistic, Kaščák and Pupala reasoned that a focus on standardizing and developing competencies derives from visions for producing a particular type of worker. They stated, "The competences model, in the form of standardised educational goals, is derived from the model of the 'knowledge worker'; someone who is autonomous, intellectually agile, creative and flexible, socially competent in interpersonal relations, self-motivating and capable of self-realisation in the tireless effort of exceeding the normative skills required in his/her job" (p. 330). The authors suggested that individuals are expected to excel at the development of certain competencies in order to exceed work requirements. A major concern with this focus is the pressure on children to resemble premature adults, ones whose developmental trajectories are instrumentally tied to the economy. Students as early as kindergarten are pressured to meet state-mandated learning goals, which are rationalized in terms of college and career-readiness. Kaščák and Pupala argued that schooling is preoccupied with producing certain types of children who resemble the kinds of adults who can function well within a neoliberal world order. It is no wonder that business owners rally behind a curricula focus on competency development (Ananiadou & Claro, 2009; Trilling & Fadel, 2009).

Aside from problems with economic instrumentalism, Kaščák and Pupala (2013) are concerned that a commitment to cultivating superchildren by efficiently and effectively developing competencies is a form of "hurrying" childhood. In a hypercompetitive environment, developmental knowledge serves this function. There is a predetermined curricular road map that functions as a pipeline to move students into and render them useful for a twenty-first-century economy. Success is determined by how quickly and efficiently children can move through this pipeline. In this context, one can evoke a Piagetian view of development to highlight the educational and psychological dangers of this commitment.

Elkind (2007), who is a neo-Piagetian, is well-known for his criticisms of hurrying childhood. He warns of educational commitments that are intended to create the most productive adults for the economy while ignoring natural developmental trajectories. Elkind argued that schools need to approach curriculum in a way that is sensitive to the ecologies of different developmental stages of life, not developing a predetermined pipeline for children to move through as efficiently and effectively as possible. This means shifting a focus away from testing and benchmarks, which leave few opportunities for students to engage in developed and developing capacities, to providing students with hands-on, experiential learning opportunities that take place in the context of their developmental needs. This approach requires a negotiation of curricula and pedagogical mandates, not strict adherence to them or a commitment to exceed them. It also requires the centering of students' developmental needs.

Proponents of neoliberalism want to accelerate development especially in the area of competencies. There are developmental theorists who argue that efforts to accelerate development conflict with natural developmental trajectories and are a form of hurrying childhood. Although each position requires a great deal of unpacking and critical reflection, there is a broad concern about this debate. Theorists on both sides are interested in competency development. Like proponents of neoliberalism, Elkind is interested in the most effective ways to foster children's creativity. For him, that includes play, optimizing autonomy, remaining patient, being less rigid, and providing student-centered environments. The danger is that if empirical evidence is convincing enough to show that competencies develop from these pedagogical commitments, then schools may adopt this approach but for the same purpose, which is to efficiently and effectively cultivate competencies for the twenty-first-century worker. Perhaps, a curricular pipeline, standardization of competencies, hurrying children will be viewed as inefficient. The broad concern is that knowledge of competency development equips teachers, parents, and school personnel with the knowledge to achieve a neoliberal objective to cultivate superchildren—just in a different way.

EXPERTISE: TEACHERS AS DEVELOPMENTAL DIAGNOSTICIANS

Whether one is propagating norms that are underpinned and produced by narrow populations or endorsing developmental norms shaped by neoliberalism, thinking developmentally about students makes it necessary to establish developmental diagnosticians—professionals who measure, diagnose, and reform students (Lesko, 2001; Burman, 2008). Those who are, or are perceived as, well versed in developmental knowledge apply their expertise to the evaluation of children and parents. Expertise is traditionally granted to developmental psychologists and early childhood educators. However, today all K–12 teachers are expected to take on the role of developmental experts. Specifically the NAEYC (2009b) guidelines include a call for early childhood educators to be knowledgeable of human development, with such calls especially strident amid the standards and accountability movement. As experts, teachers must assess, measure, monitor, and chart students' development to ensure pedagogy is shaped to address shortcomings or advance toward a trajectory. In order to achieve this goal, teachers must construct developmental profiles of their students, as well as figure out how schooling environments align with, complement, harness, and are congruent with norms and trajectories. Teachers must make judgments about students' capabilities and potential as it pertains to the readiness for curriculum and pedagogy. An assumption is that the more that is known about students, the better learning environments can be tailored to meet their needs.

In addition to applying expertise in their classrooms, teachers are expected to communicate their developmental knowledge to parents and guardians (NAEYC, 2009b). The NAEYC guidelines suggest a "professional-client" relationship by encouraging teachers to advise families on what is developmentally appropriate for their children. The NAEYC assumes that their developmental ideas are universal and objective and that being educated about these ideas renders teachers more knowledgeable than parents and other community members. One danger as suggested in Lubeck's (1994) analysis of the NAEYC guidelines, parents who have different ideas about children's development or those who may not be interested in viewing children through a developmental lens may be positioned as uninformed. Assuming developmental expertise opens up the possibility of invalidating diverse perspectives and can contribute to marginalizing and silencing students and parents.

The function of developmental experts also contributes to governance and surveillance. Historically and today, development is underpinned by ideological, economic, social, and political aims (Burman, 2008; Lesko, 2001). Burman (2008) argued this point: "Developmental psychology participated in social movements explicitly concerned with comparison, regulation and control of groups and societies, and is closely identified with the development of tools of mental measurement, classification of abilities and the establishment of norms. It is associated with the rise of capitalism and science, subscribing to a specific gendered, alienated and commodified model of scientific practice" (pp. 13–14). The author pointed to the role of regulation and governance in developmental psychology. As an example, Burman discussed the legislation of mothering. Research and popular media messages are replete with claims that mothers are a primary and major influence on children's development. Therefore, children's failure to meet developmental norms provides grounds to pathologize mothers. If there are specific developmental achievements that children must reach, then mothers must be coached and trained in ways that enable them to achieve that goal. In particular, mothers have to be "nurturing" and "bonding" and adopt a commitment to concerted cultivation, which means strategically engaging with various community members to ensure that children develop the cognitive and social skills to be successful in schools. The assumption about the importance of mothering and the qualities of "good mothering" reflect middle-class values. The application of expertise to conform individuals to developmental norms is not about recognizing variation in growth, but more about realizing a narrow vision for persons and society.

HISTORICISM: INSTRUMENTS, TOOLS, AND DESCRIPTIONS

An analysis of the normative underpinnings of development is important and necessary. However, there is a danger of reifying the objectivity of development. As part of the critical project, developmentalism itself must be questioned as well as the concepts that give it form. As Walkerdine (2003) stated, "In the world of developmental psychology, it has seemed since its inception that there was no problem with the real. That children were children and develop has appeared so common-sense a notion that the arguments that have raged have been about models of development not about the existence of those objects called 'the child' and 'development' " (p. 451). Walkerdine is speaking about conventional debates in which one might defend, for example, constructivism over sociocultural theory. Within each perspective, certain models might be defended as more valid and scientific than others. Other debates circulate around questions pertaining to the role of the social world, individual variation, and biology. Walkderine's point was that amid debates and controversies, the objectivity of categories or a commitment to developmentalism have remained unquestioned.

One example can be gleaned from debates on the development of creativity. One position is that creativity develops in structured environments wherein students acquire a certain level of knowledge and discipline to produce something novel. A different position is that creativity develops with minimal adult interference and naturally manifests in students' efforts to construct their worlds. Debates such as these reify positions that students must be developed, development happens systematically, and that development is happening. The debate on the development of creativity ignores why there is concern about it now and what values underpin the developmental narrative. Although there is benefit to inquiries about mechanisms and processes of development, conversations must include examinations of the historical conditions that contribute to the production of developmental concepts and their corresponding narratives. As Walkerdine (1993) argued, developmental concepts and developmentalism should not be taken as given, unchangeable, and independent of historical and political contexts.

Political, methodological, ideological, and historical contexts give shape to the possibilities for thinking about development and its categories, such as child, adolescence, progress, and adult.

From this perspective, developmental phenomena are not characteristic of and featured within people. Rather, the individual as the site of developmental achievements is replaced by an understanding that is bound to interactions between historical context, language, actors, instruments, tools, culture, and ideology. Looking historically at development is not about engaging in conventional debates about valid and objective models and categories, nor is it about defending the real and scientific. It is not about uncovering a "true" developmental narrative that has been distorted by certain developmental ways of seeing. Walkerdine captured this treatment by stating:

> Developmental psychology claims to be . . . a grand, totalizing story, the
> story of children's development, a scientific story testable, within limits,
> in relation to the methodological guarantees given about the treatment of
> scientific data, science's claim to truth. But this [referring to her argument] is
> no mere debate about true scientific stories versus false pseudo-scientific or
> ideological ones. Rather it is about the place of developmental psychological
> stories not in telling a biased or distorted story, and so obscuring a true and
> proper story about children, but in actually producing, fashioning "the
> child" and "development." The claim is that these objects are not simply
> well or badly represented but actually produced within signifying relations
> themselves. (p. 452)

Thinking historically about development means bracketing debates about whether or not developmental narratives are scientifically valid or distorting, but examining the terms and conditions that produce people as developed and developing beings.

Instrumentation: Constituting Phenomena

Walkerdine (1993) pointed to the idea that constructing students' developmentally is a specific way of constructing them. This construction is made possible by available tools, concepts, theories, ideals, and ways of reasoning about persons. In this regard, development is more in the eyes of the evaluator than the one who is purportedly developing. Students may not experience development in the way it is described, classified, and categorized. That gives a great deal of power to evaluations and frameworks than to experiences of being. Experiments, developmental frameworks, and available categories give credibility to the existence of developmental phenomena. Burman (2008) made this argument in a critique of Piaget's theory.

Piaget constructed a picture of development that resulted from presenting well-defined tasks to children that required specific kinds of reasoning. Based on interviews and observations over several trials, Piaget posited a universal theory of children's reasoning capabilities across ages. As Burman (2008) argued, however, engagement with and performance related to these tasks may not necessarily reflect reasoning capabilities as inherent features of persons. She defended this argument by noting that slight modifications in tasks produced significantly different results related to children's thinking than what Piaget postulated. Her point was that assessments, tools, and instruments contribute to the production of students' developmental representations. Improved and "scientifically valid" assessments cannot provide an actual and neutral representation of development. As Burman argued, tools and instruments contribute to the production of developmental phenomena.

The tools and categories that are used to make sense of people help to construct them as developmental beings. Students do not experience themselves as developmental beings outside of assessments, frameworks, theories, and benchmarks that brand them as such. Burman (2008) depicted Vygotsky as recognizing this historical nuance. She stated, "Vygotsky depicted developmental research as indistinguishable from teaching and instruction contexts . . . the context for discovering what children know is inseparable from teaching them. . . . This model of the research process is a far cry from mainstream British and US developmental work in which the variables under investigation are located firmly within the child (rather than constructed in relation to the child) and the context of investigation is seen as neutral or invisible" (Burman, p. 247). Burman spoke to an idea that is well accepted in critical educational psychology discourse, namely that the act of and context around studying and naming something changes that which is studied and named. Rather than naming what exists, what psychologists tend to assume they are doing, tools, instruments, ways of reasoning, descriptions, and categories shape how life is described, experienced, understood, and acted. Tools for measuring and naming do not determine what people are; rather they shape possibilities for meaning making. Developmental ideas and categories are used to assess and name experience, which changes that experience.

Naming and classifying is an iterative and pedagogical process. For this reason, developmental metaphors, such as behind and ahead, are especially dangerous. In a context based on competition, hierarchy, and sorting, being ahead and behind are useful and necessary metaphors. Developmental assessments locate students somewhere on a continuum. The point is that the notions of behind and ahead makes sense in a particular ideological and economic context. These evaluations are made possible because of the production of developmental benchmarks. One might be branded "behind" only because this categorization aligns with the type of thinking that is validated within a particular context and buttressed by normative evaluations of what children should be thinking and doing. The evaluation also makes sense within a context of developmentalism broadly.

Categories and Descriptions

Walkerdine (1993) was also concerned with how developmental terms emerge and come to produce persons as developmental beings. A historical analysis involves recognizing the conditions that make categories and descriptions possible, as well as the conditions for the evolution of those categories. For example, Lesko (2001) explored the historical emergence of the notion of adolescence, which is often taken for granted as a natural stage of an individual's life that is characterized by mood swings, puberty, imaginary audience, insecurity, identity development, and need for a peer group. Many of the contemporary assumptions about this stage are attributed to G. Stanley Hall (Lesko, 2001). Although the idea of adolescence existed prior to Hall, during the nineteenth century this notion took a different form. Lesko explained. "The line between youth and adult became sharper, more intently watched, and democratically applied to all youth. Hall emphasized adolescence as a new birth, a new opportunity to move upward and downward on the Great Chain of Being. He and his colleagues also issued 'pedagogical imperatives,' that is, disciplinary and instructional techniques that were essential for each stage of boyhood and adolescence. Thus laissez-faire approaches to youth were deemed likely to lead to moral anarchy, and the administrative gaze of teachers, parents, psychologists, play reformers, scouting leaders, and juvenile justice workers was everywhere cultivated" (p. 88). According to Lesko, social upheaval, national uncertainty, and nervous masculinity drove this change. Adolescence was treated as the period that was essential for steering development in ways to realize a particular social order. The adolescent was looked upon as an object that could be discussed, diagnosed, differentiated, quantified, and familiarized in terms of unsettled race relations, economic prospects, emerging manliness, purity, and future preparedness. This stage was used to govern the youth in order to cultivate a particular type of citizen. More important, this category became something different and meant certain things. It was a discrete stage that could be calibrated and controlled for particular purposes.

Burman (2008) made a similar argument in relation to the notion of the child, contending that at different historical moments the beginning and ending of childhood was different, along with assumption about children's capacities and parents' roles in child development. Walkerdine (1993) cited historians who argued that the notion of the child and childhood, as a separate life period from adulthood, emerged with compulsory schooling. Before this time, Walkerdine argued, childhood did not exist in any systematic sense. That is, it was not a distinct category that could be studied, measured, calibrated, and steered. In the 1800s, criminality and pauperism were threats that motivated the study of childhood development. Walkerdine argued that knowledge of children was necessary to develop pedagogy to facilitate children's usefulness and industriousness. Lesko (2001), Burman (2008), and Walkerdine (1993) are all speaking to a similar practice, the production of developmental phenomena to solve social, economic, and political problems. They have not contended that these phenomena do not exist. They exist in relation to a network of statements, practices, instruments, tools, and norms. They exist in relation to particular purposes.

Theoretical Prominence and Selective Uptake

Another way to historicize development involves recognizing the conditions that shape the acceptance and interpretation of theories and ideas. As Burman (2008) argued, the acceptance of one theory over another does not reflect inherent value, nor does it reflect movement toward scientific progress. Shifts are less about science correcting itself, and more about political, cultural, ideological, technological, and economic changes. For example, since the 1980s, Vygotsky's theory of development has gained traction in education. Although some developmental theorists might see this change as progress, Kaščák and Pupala (2013) have offered another explanation, suggesting that the acceptance of Vygotsky's ideas is tied to neoliberalism and the commitment to cultivate the superchild. The authors contended that Vygotsky's theory lends itself well to the emphasis on radical individualism and the ethic of excelling. That is, it can provide a framework to construct all students as unique and having their own developmental paths. This theory includes a sense of control. Students can act on themselves and their environments, and teachers can act on students and their environments. In this theory, actions can be taken to support the accumulation of experiences that lead to changes in thinking and behaving. If DAP is implemented correctly, students should continuously experience improvements in their thinking and behavior. Vygotsky's theory of development provides the necessary framework for continuously conceptualizing ways that students can exceed their existing abilities. It is for this reason that Kaščák and Pupala argued that Vygotsky's work is well suited for the production of superchildren.

Context influences not only the acceptability of theories but also their interpretation. Burman (2008) raised concern that Piaget's theory was interpreted to fit within Western culture. She contended that the popularity of Piaget's theory is attributed in part to values for logic-mathematical reasoning that prevailed in the early to mid-twentieth century. Burman argued that Piaget's theory was accepted in the United States because it satisfied a need for understanding scientific thinking, as well as aligned with individualism and male chauvinism. She reasoned that Piaget's theory emerged during the time when there was value for objectivity, reason, truth, and science—all values which at that time were associated with males. Kaščák and Pupala (2013) raised a similar point in relation to the growing acceptance of Vygotsky's ideas. They argued that in the West, theorists tend to interpret Vygotsky's work in individualistic terms whereas, Eastern-based theorists viewed his work in collective ways. Kaščák and Pupala argued that Vygotsky's theory is now more broadly accepted than three decades ago because his ideas were easily adaptable to align with a US value for individualism and the neoliberal emphasis on excelling standards.

A New Starting Point

As we have seen, in both educational policy and educational psychology, the understanding and application of developmental psychology is viewed as serving students' interests, and thus teachers are expected to master and apply developmental knowledge. But underpinning development theory and developmentalism are specific normative values that can be administered to populations to achieve ideological, political, and social aims. This point was illustrated in the preceding exploration of the (1) normative values underpinning developmental frameworks; (2) role of ideology in shaping the developmental trends; (3) influences on the uptake of developmental theories; and (4) the ways development discourse is used for governance and surveillance. As I have suggested, states and trajectories of development are not natural or neutral features of persons that can be objectively measured and universally enacted but are instead situated in complex and dynamic relationships among persons, history, ideology, culture, and tools.

From this analysis, I trust it is clear that I do not endorse (1) an individualistic approach to development; (2) a sense of optimism that knowing all possibile narratives will solve problems with development; and (3) the idea that there is a real development not yet known because objective tools have not been adequately developed. The main objective of this chapter is to show that development is inseparable from culture, ideology, power, politics, and history. There is no such thing as a neutral and value-free developmental idea, but rather, viewing students developmentally is a political, cultural, ideological, and historical act. The starting point for thinking developmentally about children should not be centered on finding a theory that helps make sense of children and what they need. The starting point instead should be centered on understanding the ways that development informs teaching and curriculum, the values that underpin developmental ideas, the purposes for applying developmental ideas, and the effects that applying those ideas have on students.

CHAPTER FIVE

Teaching as Management

ANAGEMENT IS THE INTENTIONAL ORGANIZATION of environmental conditions intended to shape the actions of individuals in order to achieve a particular purpose. A common assumption in education discourse is that quality teaching and learning are not possible without effective classroom management (CM) (Kumashiro, 2009). In schools, management can manifest in teachers arranging the physical environment, establishing rules and procedures, administering reinforcements and punishments, and maintaining students' interest in lessons. The aim of managing classrooms is to support both academic and social-emotional learning (Brophy, 2006). CM requires teachers to design effective instruction, deal with students as groups, respond to individual needs, and administer discipline (Emmer & Stough, 2001). For this reason, teachers and researchers contend that CM is an essential component of a teacher's knowledge base (Evertson & Weinstein, 2006). However, teachers often feel unprepared to manage their classrooms (Brophy, 2006; Evertson & Weinstein, 2006).

Evertson and Weinstein (2006) argued that teacher preparation programs generally fail to provide preservice teachers with a "*comprehensive*, coherent study of the basic principles and skills of classroom management" (p. 4; emphasis added). The authors suggested that teachers are unprepared to manage their classrooms due to a lack of exposure to CM principles and models. The logic is that comprehensive instruction can support teachers' efforts to identify models, strategies, and principles that are congruent with their teaching philosophy and commitments to practice. As Brophy (2006) argued, teachers must be equipped with knowledge to implement management techniques that work best given instructional goals, teachers' personality, and classroom dynamics. This begs the question, given certain classroom dynamics, what structures, practices, and interventions are required to get a group of students to learn academic content in an expected timeframe, while supporting their social and emotional development?

There are several models that purport to best achieve these goals. The discourse of CM comprises several models, strategies, and principles—all with different approaches to teaching and assumptions about students. Some CM approaches emphasize the facilitation of students' self-regulation of their own conduct, while others focus on teachers' administration of reinforcement and punishment (e.g., see the range of management approaches in *Handbook of Classroom Management* [Evertson & Weinstein, 2006] and in *Models of Classroom Management: Principles, Practices and Critical Considerations* [Martin, Sugarman, & McNamara, 2000]). However, arguably no single strategy or approach can be applied in all situations. What works in one setting may not work in others. That said, Evertson and Weinstein (2006) are optimistic that comprehensive instruction can help educators figure out which strategies work best in any given situation. The logic is that with a tool kit of strategies, principles, and models, teachers may be equipped to continuously monitor, evaluate, and, if necessary, adapt their CM to support teaching goals.

The notion of CM seems relatively innocuous and is often conceptualized as serving students' safety and academic needs, as well as teachers' instructional goals. Contemporary CM discourse often centers on a commitment to allow for the expression and development of students' characteristics, states, and dispositions within a group setting. So CM today is not just a set of behavioral interventions, but also pedagogical structuring and psychological conditioning for the purposes of shaping morality, character, and citizenship (Brophy, 2006; Evertson & Weinstein, 2006).

The modern discourse of CM appears to be organized around positive goals. However, the preoccupation with exposing teachers to a vast array of CM models masks a number of concerns that tend to be absent from educational psychology, despite their presence in other academic camps (e.g., Tavares, 1996; Kumashiro, 2009; Casey, Lozenski, & McManimon, 2013). One possible explanation for this absence is that the relevance and efficacy of educational psychology for teaching depends on the promise that models, strategies, and principles of CM can be applied to produce desired outcomes. If teachers have comprehensive knowledge, then they can reliably and predictably produce targeted behaviors and achieve instructional objectives. Rather than challenging this logic, its ethical implications, or critically examining targeted outcomes, the discourse is directed at filling a "void" in teachers' knowledge base. Efforts to address this ostensible void are underpinned by the assumptions that management problems are more or less related to deficiencies with teachers' knowledge or application skills, their preparation programs, and perhaps professional development seminars.

The focus on inadequate preparation masks certain tensions and complexities. One relates to the modern understanding of teaching as management. Although things were different in the first half of the twentieth century, teaching today has become synonymous with management (Tavares, 1996; Casey et al., 2013). This shift is underpinned by the assumption that students need to be managed in order for them to learn (Kumashiro, 2009). However, Casey et al. (2013) challenged this assumption and asked a question that is seldom considered: from where does the need to manage students arise? The authors argued that management is rooted in ideological, cultural, political, and economic rationalities. Critical theorists suggest that teaching as management has roots in industrial efforts to maximize profit by exploiting their labor force. I will extend this argument to the classroom to show that CM plays a role in the governance of students for the purpose of achieving an institutional objective.

Critically engaging with CM requires an examination and exploration of the industrial roots. Furthermore, critical analysis involves illuminating the assumptions of students that are implicit in management techniques, the purposes of schooling implicit in management discourse, and the potential consequences of management strategies. A critical approach raises questions about the outcomes of CM, as well as the ethical implications of construing teaching as management. Discerning models and principles that work best to achieve instructional goals is not the purpose of a critical interrogation. The goal of this chapter is not necessarily to support the administration of effective CM, but to raise questions about the politics, ethics, and philosophical commitments related to this discourse. Educational psychologists and teachers must forefront these concerns and ensure they are included in discussions of CM.

Two Orientations to Management

Countless books and articles on CM have been published. Given the vastness of this literature, a comprehensive review is not possible. Rather, the brief review here is focused on two CM orientations, under which many models, principles, and strategies fall. One orientation centers on behavioral conditioning via the administration of reinforcements and punishments. This orientation captures CM that relies heavily on reinforcement and punishment to condition behaviors. The underlying assumption is that students must be shaped to function within schooling environments using rewards and punishments. It follows that behavioral problems are the result of undisciplined children who have not been conditioned effectively. The other orientation involves the management of students by meeting their needs via environmental engineering. This one requires designing and implementing pedagogy that is sensitive to students' needs, proclivities, dispositions, and cultural backgrounds. From this view, behavioral problems are a consequence of poorly managed environments, not poorly managed students. The idea is that good pedagogy is the best management strategy.

The critical conversation begins with highlighting the limitations of and assumptions implicit in the two orientations, which are underpinned by different ideas about students, the role of teaching, and the purpose of schooling. Furthermore, each orientation is associated with vastly different consequences for students. Although this examination is part of the critical analysis, the discussion is elaborated by considering the political, ideological, and ethical concerns with these management orientations. In addition, critique of the metaphor of teaching as management is offered, as well as the ideological contexts of schools wherein students must be managed. Finally, there is critical discussion regarding the logic that students can be reliably governed through the intentional organization of environments.

DIRECT BEHAVIORAL INTERVENTIONS
Theory of Operant Conditioning

The orientation to condition behaviors via rewards and punishments is rooted in behaviorist theory and called operant conditioning, which is the shaping of behaviors through consequences (i.e. punishments and reinforcements). Behaviorists proposed that the consequences that followed a behavior shaped the likelihood of those behaviors reoccurring. If a behavior was followed by reinforcement (positive or negative), then that behavior is likely to be increased; if a behavior was followed by a punishment, then that behavior is likely to be decreased. Thorndike (1898) called the association between behaviors and consequences (or stimuli) the "Law of Effect." Like other behaviorists, Thorndike came to this conclusion while conducting experiments on animal behaviors in carefully controlled laboratory environments. Although originally applied to animals in laboratories, behaviorists believed that their methods, laws, and theories could be used to study and ultimately shape human behavior. Recall John Watson's statement, quoted in chapter 1 of this book, "Give me a dozen healthy infants, well-formed, and my own specified world to bring them up in and I'll guarantee to take any one at random and train him to become any type of specialist I might select—doctor, lawyer, artist, merchant-chief and, yes, even beggar-man and thief, regardless of his talents, penchants, tendencies, abilities, vocations, and race of his ancestors" (p. 82). As reflected in this statement, behaviorists believed that in a carefully controlled environment consequences could be used to engineer any set of behaviors. The key to achieving this goal was to apply scientific methods to the study of behavior.

In the first half of the twentieth century, behaviorism was the dominant paradigm of learning. This theory was used to explain complex cognitive processes, including higher order thinking and language acquisition. However, given modern ideas about human agency, the separation between behavior and cognition, differences between animals and humans, and the importance of psychological states for actions, behaviorism is seldom used as a theory of cognitive learning. Notwithstanding, operant theory remains influential for CM. This theory continues to pervade CM discourse, both in the production and application of principles, models, and strategies (Kohn, 1996; Brophy, 2006; Casey et al., 2013). Those who endorse an operant approach believe, in accordance with the foundational ideas of behaviorism, in the efficacy and ethics of administering reinforcements and punishments to shape those behaviors that are arguably needed for school learning. This approach rests on the belief that fear of punishments and desire for rewards are powerful motivational forces (Freiberg & Lamb, 2009).

The Behavioral Engineer

The behaviorist orientation of CM requires that teachers assume the role of a behavioral engineer. Teachers must believe that one of their primary responsibilities is to condition students' behavior. Conditioning begins with observing behaviors to determine which actions are out of alignment with classroom expectations. To achieve this goal, a teacher must be equipped with the knowledge of behaviors that are considered normal, good, and desirable for learning. Although ostensibly straightforward, this knowledge is not always clear. Standing up and pacing in the back of a classroom may facilitate learning for some students but certainly falls outside conventional behavioral norms (e.g., staying in one's seat). Once it is determined that behavioral change is needed, teachers must continue to study students in order to discern what is reinforcing and punishing. Therefore, teachers must discern students' desires and what consequences they want to avoid. Although consequences can be generalized across students and appear intuitive, there are challenges. For example, reprimanding a student may be perceived as punishment for one, but reinforcing for another who finds the attention desirable.

There are several types of reinforcements and punishments. Some of them include vicarious reinforcement (being reinforced for a behavior by watching others being reinforced for it), tangible reinforcement (e.g., stickers, grades, and money), intangible reinforcement (e.g., praise, affection, and social acceptance), presentation punishment (adding something unpleasant to decrease behavior), and removal punishment (removing something to decrease behavior). A teacher must decide which types of reinforcement and punishment are most effective. A contemporary trend in behaviorist models is to favor positive reinforcement over punishment. The idea is that positive reinforcement helps to shape positive environments. Punishment can be viewed as negative, whereby teachers are positioned as authoritarian and punitive.

More important than identifying proper consequences, teachers must control access to reinforcements and punishments, as well as effectively administer them. If children are motivated by stickers, the engineer must have stickers and decide who gets them and when. Of course, as objects of desire change, teachers must continuously monitor individuals to learn what consequences will have the greatest strength for conditioning. This knowledge must be accompanied by an understanding of when to administer consequences. Teachers must consider the schedules of reinforcement and punishment. For example, a reward can follow every observation of a particular behavior (continuous reinforcement) or after a fixed number of observations of that behavior (fixed ratio schedule). Or a student could be presented with positive reinforcement after displaying a behavior one time, then not be rewarded again until displayed three times, and then not again until two times (variable ratio schedule). Variable scheduling is typically viewed as most effective for conditioning behaviors (Skinner, 1938).

Although there are general principles that underpin effective administration of operation conditioning, knowledge of students is a key requirement for this approach. Teachers must be equipped with what students find desirable, the intensity of that desire, what they want to avoid, the intensity of the desire to avoid certain consequences, and what scheduling works best.

Contemporary Applications

The pervasiveness of operant theory in CM discourse stems from a preoccupation with seeing behaviors as problems, as well as the familiarity with and efficacy of punishing and rewarding. While administering consequences can provide immediate short-term results for behavioral change (Pink,

2011), many contemporary educational psychologists do not endorse a strict adherence to this behaviorist orientation (Evertson & Weinstein, 2006). However, behaviorist thinking for CM is featured in educational psychology textbooks and informs many models and strategies. This orientation is ultimately about identifying problematic behaviors and conditioning new ones. However, contemporary applications of operant theory are less focused on punishing and reinforcing individuals, and more focused on "preventive" and "proactive" measures.

CM can refer to both school-wide and classroom structures, as some might reason that both are needed for maintaining order in the classroom. In terms of school-wide behavioral management, school personnel can require the repetitive instillation of behavioral codes through student chants and reciting posted rules. Another application of management can involve an institutional enema. Worried about propagating undesirable behaviors from staff and students, school administrators can hire new staff who have a similar mindset, as well as limit interactions between incoming students and existing ones. The purpose is to eliminate remnants of the previous culture in order to shape a new culture, one of discipline and obedience. This practice is not unfamiliar to some charter schools. If students can be indoctrinated into a disciplinary system as part of "establishing" school culture, the source of disciplinary power shifts from a teacher to an abstract source, namely the institution, classroom, or culture. Teachers may not be viewed as behavioral engineers, but enforcers of institutionally sanctioned behavioral norms.

Another notable trend in operant-behaviorist CM is the practice of soliciting input from students for the formation of classroom rules and consequences for noncompliance. In doing so, this strategy creates the illusion that CM is inherently a democratic process. By extension, reinforcements and punishments are rationalized as logical or natural (Martin et al. 2000). Natural consequences are based on the natural flow of events. Just as a child who runs too fast, falls, and scrapes a knee, Martin et al. (2000) suggested that, in the classroom, children who are not listening during a reading lesson might give up their turn for oral reading. In other words, children who commit behavioral infractions are conditioned to believe punishments are a logical, if not inevitable, response to misbehavior. These consequences are viewed as independent of adult interference or at least experienced by students as logical in nature. However, the idea of natural consequences is problematic because the flow of events is structured, produced, and enforced by teachers and administrators. Curricula and pedagogical materials are manufactured by adults and implemented in schools by teachers. The resulting response to student behavior might not explicitly necessitate adult intervention, but is the product of an environment crafted to suit adult interests just the same. However, the thinking is that conditioning might be most effective if consequences appear as not arbitrarily decided by adults.

The Trouble with Operant Conditioning

A common concern with operant conditioning is that it invites a purpose of schooling that misaligns with democratic and critical pedagogical perspectives (Render, Padilla, & Krank, 1989; Kohn, 1996; Lotan, 2006). The latter author reasoned that the purpose of classroom rules and routines is to control students during instruction in an attempt to ensure the timely completion of students' work so as to adhere to extraneous curricular expectations. This approach protects teacher authority, strict adherence to rules, and punishments for infractions (Woolfolk-Hoy & Weinstein, 2006). Fenwick (1998) argued that this approach fosters teacher domination that is designed to improve testing and motivate students to engage in busy-work. This commitment reflects a conception of classroom relations as unidirectional interactions between teachers and students, even if students' voices are solicited in forming classroom rules and consequences (Lotan, 2006). Critics are generally concerned that operant theory invites teachers to focus on needs for instruction and adaptability to a particular pedagogical order.

Another problem with an orientation to an operant theory of CM is that behavioral targets are normalized, prescriptive, and teacher-determined (Freiberg & Lamb, 2009), and the enactment of behaviors get confused with learning (Render et al., 1989). From operant theory, students' "misbehaviors" are targets for change instead of other targets, such as problems with disengaging curriculum, poor teaching, and oppressive schooling conditions. Students are viewed as the problem and solution when it may be the failings of educational structures or broad cultural, political, and economic systems.

Another concern with operant conditioning is that it undermines intrinsic motivation (Kohn, 1996; Emmer & Stough, 2001; Pink, 2011). It is commonly assumed that associating a behavior with a consequence will invite behaviors only when a desired consequence is sought. If students are offered rewards to read, they may only read when they desire the reward. The motivation for behavior is the pursuit of the consequence, not the intrinsic worth of the activity. As a consequence of operant conditioning, engagement with academic tasks as measured by a behavior serves as a means to an end. If students meet the external expectations, they are rewarded; if they do not, they can be punished. Students can be punished with labels such as incompetent, failure, unintelligent, and unmotivated, or can be lauded with labels such as competent, successful, intelligent, and motivated. Motivation to engage academically amounts to avoiding the punishment or gaining the reward.

Incentivized tasks are loaded with extrinsically motivating contingencies with the express purpose of increasing the desirability of engagement. The tasks, however, become a mere means to the incentive. Punishment, in this regard, may not be understood as "that which decreases behavior" and reinforcement may not be understood as "that which increases a behavior." The targeted behavior is secondary to the anticipated reinforcement or punishment. In other words, it is possible for students to receive rewards without performing the behavior—by cheating for example—because it is the reward that is motivating, not the engagement with the task.

Yet another concern with operant conditioning is that targeted behaviors decrease or cease when there is no chance of a reward or if the reward is no longer desired. There is no intrinsic worth for enacting the behavior. Even if intrinsic value was once present, the administration of reinforcements and punishments undermines and quells that intrinsic value. On the other hand, some reason that intrinsic worth can develop following a behavioral intervention, and that some individuals actually need the extrinsic motivation in order develop intrinsic value for academic tasks (Isen & Reeve, 2005). That is, over time individuals who were originally motivated by a reward or punishment may learn to value the activity for its own sake or at least develop "good" behavioral habits, even if not underpinned by intrinsic value (Snowman & McCown, 2015). This idea, however, continues to be challenged (Kohn, 1996; Pink, 2011). There is no guarantee that the value for tasks will change, and the dangers of operant conditioning may not outweigh the slight possibility for a motivation shift.

In addition to undermining intrinsic interest, the application of operant theory can negatively impact moral development. Critics raised concern that rewards and punishments invite self-interest (Kohn, 1996; Emmer & Stough, 2001). Administering reinforcements and punishments invite children to continuously focus on maximizing positive gain, either from a tangible, social, or emotional consequence, and avoiding behaviors and stimuli that are unpleasant. In other words, it invites children to think about how to maximize feeling good and avoid feeling bad. Furthermore, operant conditioning only teaches students that they will suffer unpleasant consequences when they are caught misbehaving and receive reinforcements when responding in accordance with rules and norms (Kohn, 1996). Thus, operant conditioning is accused of impeding the development of long-lasting social and moral values (Kohn, 1996).

MANAGING THE ENVIRONMENT

The second orientation to CM involves shaping behaviors by structuring pedagogical environments in ways that are congruent and aligned with students' emotional, physiological, and psychological states and needs. The primary commitment underpinning this orientation is that behavioral problems are a consequence of poorly managed environments, not poorly managed children. Therefore, rather than administering consequences, CM is about creating curricula, implementing pedagogical strategies, and forming relationships that are sensitive and responsive to students. That means taking into account their developmental characteristics, natural proclivities, needs, and cultural backgrounds. Instead of posturing as a behavioral engineer by directly shaping students' behavior in accordance with school norms, teachers study students in order to structure environments that are likely to shape behavior indirectly.

As with an operant approach, this orientation requires teachers to have knowledge of students. However, rather than focusing on environmental consequences, teachers discern the effects of classroom structures on students' emotional, cultural, and psychological lives. In addition to constructing profiles, teachers must understand how pedagogical structures quell or validate the various dimensions of students' beings, as well as know how to create an alignment between schooling and students. If pedagogical environments can be structured in ways that validate, are sensitive to, and align with various aspects of students, the expectation is that they will be motivated, engaged, and less resistant to instructional goals. Achieving this alignment means that reinforcement and punishment will not be necessary. Reminiscent of educational philosophers such as Rousseau (1762/1913) and Montessori (1948), this idea orientation is aligned with the idea that social environments corrupt positive human attributes, desires, and behaviors.

Developmental Needs and Appropriate Practice

Whether one subscribes to a Piagetian view of universal stage theory or a Vygotskian socially based developmentism, many researchers, theorists, and teachers view students through a developmental framework. That is, they see children as learning and progressing in a particular trajectory. Developmental narratives depict changes and possible futures for children's thinking, emotions, and behaviors. Students can be described as exhibiting behavioral and cognitive characteristics that are specific to an age or period in life.

That is, students have developmental characteristics, which require teachers to implement of developmentally appropriate practice (DAP). Wolfgang (2000) used the term "developmentalist teachers" to describe those who explicitly take students' development into account when constructing pedagogical environments (p. 196).

One concern is that there are several developmental theories, some of which compete and are contradictory. How does one know that the developmental construction of students is correct? Without that certainty, it is challenging to create DAP. Assuming psychologists and teachers can know students' developmental characteristics, then it becomes possible implement pedagogy that is developmentally appropriate. From this orientation, failure to account for developmental states and needs results in behavior problems, such as verbal aggression, physical aggression, or passivity (Wolfgang, 2000). Wolfgang (2000) argued that most behaviors that are deemed problematic can be addressed through DAP. Rather than administer reinforcement and punishment, Wolfgang stated that a developmentalist teacher thinks about several questions: "How does that child separate and bond? Can he cuddle with supportive adults, such as the teacher? How does he eat and handle himself at snack or at rest time? Can he handle demanding activities such as finger painting, water play, or painting? Can he do socio-dramatic play? How do social skills relate to typical developmental stages? Can he express his needs with words while under pressure in a social situation?" (p. 196). These questions may be different with older children. The point is that teachers must be aware of and observe not just academic performance, but patterns of social interactions, interpersonal relationships, communication, and dispositions. Developmentalist teachers use these questions to construct knowledge of their students. The developmentalist teacher will rely on these theories to understand the source of behavior problems and attempt to achieve congruence between states and the instructional environment. Creating this congruence is the CM strategy.

Natural Proclivities and Needs

Students may have needs, states, and dispositions outside of those defined within a developmental framework. For example, as noted in the chapter on motivation, Maslow (1943) proposed that individuals have a hierarchy of needs that must be met in order to support a need for self-actualization. He proposed a hierarchy of needs and motives that range from basic physiological needs to a need for self-actualization. According to Maslow, failure to meet any of these needs resulted in maladaptive personality traits and "misbehavior." Other theorists emphasized need for competence, autonomy, self-efficacy, and control (Deci & Ryan, 2000). Montessori (2014) provided a detailed account of how she created a successful learning environment for poor children who were deemed "unruly." Montessori proposed that young children in her care rejected systems of rewards and punishments and were capable of spontaneous self-discipline in learning environments that respected and valued freedom of choice and self-discovery. Montessori believed that students have natural proclivities, and if you just set up environments in the right way, then children will spontaneously self-discipline. Management is about awareness of and pedagogical congruence with proclivities and dispositions.

Culturally Responsive Classrooms

There is an assumption that students have needs and states that are specific to their cultural background. This assumption underlies the notion of culturally responsive pedagogy (CRP), which is a term associated with Ladson-Billings (1995a). The idea is that school structures should account for and validate culturally specific states and needs. The problem, however, is that schooling structures and practices tends to reward, acknowledge, and validate the cognitive, emotional, and behavioral needs of students from the dominant group (Weinstein, Tomlinson-Clarke, & Curran, 2003). In particular, critical theorists often point to the protection and validation of white, middle-class ways of speaking, knowing, engaging, and thinking. The cultural mismatch for students who have not mastered the dominant discourse is implicated in resistance and disengagement to teachers, curricula, and schooling in general (Giroux & McLaren, 1986; Giroux, 2009). CRP is designed to address this mismatch by valuing and validating different cultures in the everyday operations of the classroom. CRP is a commitment to produce schooling practices that are congruent with all students' cultural backgrounds.

One way to frame problems with CM pertains to the teachers' cultural competence and their action to create an alignment between schooling and students. Problems with CM can be reduced to cultural competence. From this line of thinking, acquiring such competence and using it to inform classroom structures, curricula materials, and interactions can be an effective management approach. This pedagogical commitment is supposed to eliminate mismatch in order to encourage student buy-in and limit resistance. To draw particular attention to the importance of cultural competence and

CM, researchers have developed a model titled culturally responsive classroom management (CRCM) (Weinstein, Tomlinson-Clarke & Curran, 2004). This approach emphasizes teachers' awareness of their own cultural lenses, their knowledge of students' cultural backgrounds, and an understanding of the broad political and cultural contexts of curricula, pedagogy, and policy. This knowledge is supposed to contribute to the production and maintenance of classrooms that value, validate, and reward diverse cultural knowledge. Achieving these goals is possible by connecting with students and their guardians, providing a continuum of support, avoiding deficit-based thinking, and creating relationships based on trust.

The Trouble with Needs, States, and Culture

Managing environments using a CM orientation is more palatable to a progressive, humanistic, liberal, and democratic view of education than the one based on operant conditioning. Contemporary theorists tend to argue that management must go beyond a focus on conditioning behaviors (e.g., Kohn, 2014). Evertson and Weinstein (2006) argued that teachers must develop supportive relationships with students, promote the development of social skills and self-regulation, use group management methods, and optimize instruction. This second orientation reflects these values, as well as general trends in the educational psychology literature (Klem & Connell, 2004; Santrock, 2008). The latter argued that educational psychologists tend to endorse student-centered management (i.e., managing environment based on students' needs) approaches over teacher-controlled (i.e., conditioning behaviors based on institutional norms) ones.

Although centering students seems appealing, there are broad and specific concerns to this approach. Teaching is still framed as management and knowing students is for management purposes. As Casey et al. (2013) argued, although trends in CM have shifted, the control of student behavior is still paramount. They stated, "While the definition of classroom management . . . has shifted to include issues of classroom environment, communication, and planning, discipline and order—in other words, controlling or modifying student behavior—are still key" (p. 41). Accounting for students' cultural and developmental needs can be mobilized to serve the same purpose as operant conditioning, namely to render students amenable and adaptable to schooling structures by shaping behaviors deemed appropriate. Knowledge of students becomes an institutional instrument, one that is cloaked in humanism, individualism, and cultural responsiveness. Managing the environment may just function as a palatable way of garnering behavioral compliance to a particular pedagogical environment.

Ethical Management: A Paradox?
MANAGEMENT AS METAPHOR

The formal practice and study of management has a controversial history. Some historians trace modern systems of management to the development of the railroad system in the mid-1800s (Casey et al., 2013). However, these authors reasoned that systems emerged earlier, considering that during the nineteenth century some 38,000 people were managing an estimated 4 million slaves. Management was centered on a few white people in positions of authority directing the actions of many. Slaveholders had to develop a body of literature and practices specific to the role of the manager so that they could optimize the productivity of slaves. In this context, management required the study and use of knowledge about those who were to be managed. Casey et al. (2013) argued that "if managers did not have racial knowledge that described how Africans best produced and developed, they would have experienced more difficulty managing bodies for production" (p. 37). The purpose of management knowledge was to ensure slaves' absolute obedience for the purposes of profit and material wealth. In addition to the economic benefit, management was justified as supporting the good of Africans, who were conceived of as not having the cognitive wherewithal to manage freedom (Baynton, 2001).

The logic for managing slaves served as a model for factory workers (Casey et al., 2013). Factory managers, like slave managers, were responsible for directing the actions of many, requiring their obedience to authority, an institutional order, and capitalist logic. The goals of labor management were to increase production at lower costs while increasing order, efficiency, standardization, and social control. Frederick Taylor (1914) is recognized as an influential figure in industrial management. In his book *Principles of Scientific Management*, he laid out guidelines for managing tasks and workers. Although he focused on factory labor, he argued that his principles were applicable to the management of people in a variety of contexts. Taylor set out to detail motivational structures, structures of work, and types of interactions between workers and managers that would enable factory managers to optimize worker productivity and efficiency.

For Taylor (1914), management needed to be guided by four principles: (1) replace rule-of-thumb work methods with scientific-based ones; (2) scientifically select, train, and develop each employee rather than passively leave them to train themselves; (3) provide detailed instruction and supervision of each worker in the performance of that worker's discrete task; and (4) divide work so that managers apply scientific management principles to planning the work that workers perform. In sum, Taylor broke down tasks so they could be performed by rote activity, gave explicit instructions for task completion, trained workers to efficiently perform tasks, implemented techniques of surveillance, and relied on the science of human motivation in order to ensure worker productivity and compliance. This kind of management was about using the science of human behavior to control, discipline, and order people for the purpose of efficient production of materials.

Casey et al. (2013) argued that the management of labor as detailed by Taylor (1914) provided a model for schools. Compulsory schooling in the United States began in the era of industrialization. Schools were set up like factories, including bells to signal class changes, students divided into manageable groups, and subjects divided into manageable tasks. Furthermore, the physical layout of school buildings modeled factories (Kliebard, 2004). Educational reformers imported both industry techniques and language to schools (e.g., calling a school a plant, using factory metaphors for curriculum, and applying task analysis to develop curriculum) (Kliebard, 2004). This importation was viewed as necessary because industry needed new kinds of laborers (a specialized worker) in a new kind of workplace (a large factory or corporation). Schools needed to develop management strategies to produce these workers. The management of students was about achieving preparation for factory work by instilling a specific set of knowledge, skills, and dispositions. The aim of schooling was to eliminate waste by properly preparing students for their place in the labor market (Casey et al., 2013). This purpose of schooling is called social efficiency.

Preparation for the labor market resulted not only from the structure of the school day, school building, and curricula, but also from relationships between teachers and students. It was during the time of industrialization that the conceptualization of teachers started to transform into that of managers and teaching as management (Tavares, 1996). With the shifting metaphor, teaching as management resembled the types of socialization that can prepare students to adapt to a modern hierarchy by following the orders of a central authority. Rather than direct monetary profit, however, successful management in the classroom was based on the production of human capital, which is the knowledge, skills, and dispositions that have value for the economy. Management was about socializing students to adapt to a schooling context that was designed to prepare them for the workforce by teaching them skills needed for their respective jobs.

The notion of management involves a source of authority directing the activities of others in order to achieve an institutional goal. Managing students is no different. CM is about achieving instructional goals, regardless if one applies operant conditioning or centers students' needs. One angle for critical inquiry is to consider the contents of those goals, not just the ethical concerns with efforts to elicit compliance to them. In modern schooling, the relationship between instructional goals and the economy is pervasive (Arum, Ford, & Beattie, 2014). Policy, curricula, and pedagogy are often rendered valid insofar as they support the goal of preparing students for the twenty-first-century economy. This purpose of schooling is a product of the growing influence of neoliberalism.

Neoliberal educational policy and objectives function on the same principles as do corporations: to maximize profit, increase productivity, improve efficiency, monitor performance, and stay competitive. These principles shape the understanding of students and purposes of schooling, as well as the curricula and pedagogical goals. In a neoliberal model, students are human capital (future workers) who must develop the requisite skills and dispositions to compete efficiently and effectively in the market place. To achieve this goal, students must be observed, measured, evaluated, and judged to ascribe value to them for filling roles in the social economic hierarchy. Students are commodified and assigned a use-value or practical worth (Casey et al., 2013). Their inability to meet the demands of school threatens their value and contributes to their marginalization and disenfranchisement. This use-value is determined by students' ability to meet neoliberal academic demands and goals of schooling. Their ability to meet these demands is a CM problem. A prevailing motive of CM is to socialize students into the logic of schooling so they can compete with others to meet those demands (Fabricant & Fine, 2012).

Critical analysis must consider the goals of schooling. Being good at CM might mean being good at achieving neoliberal schooling goals, which are arguably incompatible with democratic ones. If the contexts and outcomes of management are changed, then some of the critical concerns with management can ostensibly be assuaged. As Taylor (1914) points out, the scientific management of people is designed to produce competent people for whatever purpose, be it industrial efficiency, reduction of waste, or democratic participation. He argues that management is not about locating unusual people but shaping people in ways that enable them to perform a targeted function. So perhaps CM can be focused for the production of democratic citizens who are committed to social justice and equity. However, even if the goals of CM are directed at more ethical ends than economic productivity, there are still critical concerns with the metaphor that teaching is management.

The notion of management is itself ideological (Tavares, 1996; Casey et al., 2013). Management is tied to efforts to govern populations. Although management serves as a means to achieve instructional goals, CM models, structures, and strategies are pedagogical; they are lessons in themselves about human relationships, positionality, selfhood, value, and role of schooling. Some of these lessons may seem more innocuous than others—for example, the production of good citizens. However, the scientific management of students is still a particular form of governance, especially for those individuals and groups who do not display the behaviors, aspirations, and thought processes that are aligned with institutional goals. Historically, certain groups have been more likely to have been construed as posing management problems and needing management: students from economically disadvantaged backgrounds, immigrants, African Americans, students with special learning needs, working-class students, and any other students deemed at risk.

Although management is important for all teachers, a great deal of discourse on managing students has focused on any combination of the following identity categories: economically poor, working-class, African American, and Latino. More specific, these populations are considered to pose management problems when concentrated in urban schools. In these contexts, Yisrael (2012) argued that problems with CM intensify because these schools are in low socioeconomic areas that are replete with problems related to gang activity, drugs, crime, unemployment, child abuse, teen pregnancy, mental illness, and single-family households. Researchers suggest that these conditions are implicated in the enactment of problematic classroom behaviors (Dunbar, 2004; Yisrael, 2012). Yisrael argued that urban teachers face management problems that are unique to their context, which requires specific consideration of CM for urban schools.

SCIENTIFIC MANAGEMENT

A concern with CM pertains to the importation of the logic of the natural sciences to shape human behavior, which can be understood broadly as scientific management. The guiding assumption of scientific management is that there are laws of behavior that can be studied, known, and applied to produce particular behaviors and outcomes (Taylor, 1914; Tavares, 1996).

Psychology plays a significant role in this type of management, especially in schools (Kliebard, 1994; Tavares, 1996; Martin & McLellan, 2013). Psychology is broadly understood as the scientific study of human thought and behavior, with consideration of development, personality, learning, motivation, and adjustment (Martin & McLellan, 2013). These authors argue that people are enthralled by the possibilities of psychology to solve problems with personal and working life because of the efficacy of science to solve problems in other domains. In order to gain disciplinary legitimacy, psychologists have relied on the logic and methods of the natural sciences. The use of these methods is supposed to produce universal and generalizable laws of human conduct, ones that can be applied to improve individual and collective life.

In order to produce laws of human conduct, psychologists are committed to studying, naming, classifying, and calculating individuals, which have all become necessary for CM (Tavares, 1996). Studying populations to achieve management goals dates back to slavery and industrialization, and persists in modern CM discourse. For effective CM, teachers are expected to rely on the products of the scientific study of groups but also to practice such psycho-education themselves. The imperative to manage is tied inextricably to these practices and expectations. Kliebard (1994) argued that principles of scientific management coupled with the emergence of experimental psychology gave rise to the modern discourse on CM. Tavares (1996) made a slightly different point and argued that the rise of psychology is implicated in shifting the logic of management to psychology. She acknowledged that behavioral problems in schooling environments have always been an issue, but that psychology changed what it means to manage and the techniques for management. The integration of psychology into the classroom was supposed to enable teachers to diagnose deviant behaviors and prescribe interventions to change those behaviors. To do that, teachers had to rely on the concepts and measurements produced by psychologists, as well learn how to observe, measure, reform, and intervene to shape students' behaviors.

For both orientations and for nearly every CM management model, the intelligibility of people is essential. Management is fundamentally about examining, knowing, and using laws and rules underpinning human behavior to achieve an instructional goal. Knowledge of individuals is supposed to guide the interactions and structures that are responsible for developing particular behaviors, dispositions, habits, and knowledge. Psychology has played an instrumental role in the production of these laws and rules (Tavares, 1996; Kliebard, 2004). Psychologists have also provided teachers with the tools, concepts, and procedures to study students (Tavares, 1996). Although the application of psychology in schooling is often viewed as helpful and necessary, this author contended that this field contributes to a new logic for governing that is based on producing and protecting ideas about what is normal and pathological.

The more that is known about people and how they behave under certain conditions, the more vulnerable they are to subjugation. Knowledge can be used to render individuals amenable to institutional norms and structures. For example, if a child is "misbehaving" and it has been determined that the cause is the incongruence between the child's need for self-expression and the pedagogical structure, then an intervention can be developed to satisfy that need. The intervention can include a teacher and student interaction, an assignment, or a whole class activity. Through the careful application of psychological expertise, a proper intervention can be offered. Success is determined by the child's amenability to the classroom structure and pedagogical goals. Knowing developmental needs, natural proclivities, and cultural backgrounds can all serve a similar function. Although having and using this knowledge for CM may seem like sound pedagogy, it cannot be ignored that the function of this knowledge serves the purpose of rendering individuals amenable to classroom structures. If students are made intelligible through study and documentation, the achievement of instructional goals can be made efficient and productive, which are markers of good CM.

As do models based on operant theory, those that are based on students' needs also rely on observation and study to understand, monitor, and modify the behaviors of students. Taking into account the emotional, developmental, and cultural needs of students is still about modifying behavior for the purpose of rendering individuals amenable to instructional goals and contexts. This orientation relies heavily on using the psychology to formulate knowledge of students, especially in terms of natural proclivities, development, and culture. Although reflecting a humanistic approach to schooling broadly and CM in particular, this knowledge is dangerous. If the psychological construction of students is accurate, then school authorities may be better equipped to manage students' behaviors for the purpose of achieving instructional goals.

Critical theorists raise concern that the knowledge of persons, regardless of its accuracy, subjugates them to administrative control (Rose, 1999; Lesko, 2001). For this reason, Casey et al. (2013) argued that culturally responsive CM is ethically, pedagogically, and ideologically a problem. They are concerned that cultural knowledge of oneself, students, and curricula can provide school personnel with the tools to make minor pedagogical adjustments in order to achieve instructional goals. Casey et al. reasoned that the imperative to cultivate positive relationships with students, remain reflexive about cultural identity, view teaching as a social and moral vocation, and understand the cultural backgrounds of students are not in and of themselves problematic. However, they stated, "Once understanding one's students becomes a requirement to manage them, rather than a pedagogical imperative for authentic learning, we are caught in the dehumanizing rhetoric and practice(s) of neoliberalism: of structuring classrooms for the purposes of better serving the needs and demands of global capitalism rather than the needs and demands of students" (Casey et al., 2013, pp. 51–52). According to these authors, the function and context of CRCM is a problem. Casey et al. suggested that anti-oppressive schooling focuses on the needs of students, but not for the purpose of managing them. For them, framing teaching as management and posturing to manage is inherently a problem as it preserves teachers' authority to render students amenable to the ideological context of schooling. Concerned about an inherent contradiction, Casey et al. doubt that mobilizing CRCM to manage students can ever resemble authentic, humanistic, and problem-posing instructional contexts. The same concerns exist for developmentally appropriate practice and natural proclivities.

Conclusion

Educators are charged with organizing environments to ensure that students behave in ways that are viewed as necessary to achieve instructional goals. If that is done well, the assumption is that effective CM fosters student success and serves students' individual interests. Evertson and Weinstein (2006) contended that exposure to a wide range of CM approaches, models, and strategies can support teachers' ability to achieve these goals. Teachers can adapt a model that is congruent with their pedagogical philosophy, use an amalgam of approaches that is flexible, or develop a CM heuristic. Teachers can choose one management model with which to adhere or select features of a number of models to hold in their CM "tool kit." Regardless, the educational psychology discourse is dedicated to discerning and propagating CM strategies that work best given instructional goals.

Educational psychologists tend to endorse a balance of the two orientations introduced in this chapter, despite the reliance on operant conditioning. Regardless of one's management commitments, critical concerns underlie both orientations. Although operant conditioning certainly seems more problematic than managing the environment, the goals of management are to render individuals amenable to instructional goals by using scientific psychology. Although the mainstream discourse surrounding CM has been focused on creating ideal environments for student learning, as noted CM is rooted in oppressive ideologies based on order, control, racism and neo-liberalism. Schools were established based on the factory model, which equates both teaching and student learning to forms of capitalist production. In this context, CM has evolved into a powerful tool for student indoctrination and compliance. Even those models that appear democratic and seem to encourage autonomy can be tied to obedience and to the maintenance of educational, social, and economic order.

Focusing on fostering students' self-management as a CM strategy does not circumvent these dangers. Individuals must be coached on the development of behavioral and cognitive scripts for academic engagement. If teachers can get students to manage themselves by using these scripts, then there is no need to manage them. This type of CM is certainly appealing; students performing behaviors through their own monitoring and correction is much more efficient than a teacher monitoring every student. Even from this approach, the teacher is the silent manager; the goal is to shape cognitive, emotional, and behavioral states to ensure students act on themselves as the teacher might.

To critically engage with CM requires an interrogation of the goals of CM. Acknowledging and critiquing the dehumanizing and oppressive foundations of neoliberal American education are crucial steps to rethinking the ways in which schools could be structured to produce authentic student learning and growth. In this restructuring, teaching will not be framed, thought about, and performed as management. A critical interrogation also involves rethinking the notion of management. A central authority dictating and requiring norms for behavior reproduces asymmetrical power relationships and can contribute to oppressive educational practices. Although it may seem that accounting for culture, developmental needs, and natural proclivities addresses this concern, when that knowledge is mobilized to manage students, it is difficult to see that knowledge aligned with social justice and anti-oppressive educational commitments.

For this reason, critics have suggested that the very framing of teaching as management needs to be changed if one is committed to anti-oppressive education (McLaughlin, 1994; Casey et al., 2013). These critics reason that teachers are never truly managing children, but the imperative to try to do so nonetheless only encourages a teacher's stance of dominance and control. Casey et al. advocate constructing the role of the teacher around techniques of communication and collaboration—not around a management technique. They explained,

> As educators . . . we do not ever manage our students. We support them in their inquiry into their lived experiences, we connect them to materials and ideas, we scaffold concepts, we facilitate dialogue, we engage them on their own terms, we understand them as political subjects and teaching as a political act. And of course, at times we interrupt important conversations to shift the class or the discussion, we ask them to arrive and stay for certain amounts of time, and so on. But these practices are not a part of managing them, as if they were merely pawns to be pushed and moved in certain ways, but rather pedagogical efforts to better understand our reality and society in the struggle to transform it. (p. 54)

Thinking about teaching this way may be compatible with management models that are based on culture, development, and natural proclivities. However, in this representation, meeting development needs or "understanding" cultural differences using scientific reasoning may render individuals adaptable and amendable to a predetermined set of instructional goals.

Kohn (1996) suggested that educators should work to develop a democratic classroom community where students are cared about, valued, respected, and think in terms of *we* instead of *I* (Kohn, 1996). Students as active class members and students' perceptions of and reactions to teachers' actions also determine student engagement and learning (Cothran, Kulinna, & Garrahy, 2003). Rather than trying to control behavior by manipulating or attempting to change a student's personality, behavior, or thought process, teachers need to understand that they can define, shape, and adjust the parameters of the classroom situation in ways that are not mere adaptations to a static neoliberal goal (Lotan, 2006). Specifically, students can be involved in the decision-making process and included in making judgments, expressing their opinions, and working cooperatively toward solutions that benefit the class (Kohn, 1996). Framing the issue of CM in this way allows the educational community to move away from a focus on fixing individuals— be it the student or the teacher.

CHAPTER SIX

Attention

ATTENTION CAN BE ARGUED to be the essential for learning. If students are not attending to the information presented to them, it might be difficult to envision how they could possibly learn that information. Yet despite its ostensible importance for learning, it is not clear what attention is, how it works, and how to control it. Controversies persist about the degree to which attention is (1) passive or active; (2) willfully controlled or determined by physical reactions to stimuli; (3) rapid or slow; (4) a skill to be learned or a natural human capacity; (5) of the body; (6) shaped by experience in the world; (7) a stable, internal feature of persons; and (8) a capacity that is more or less deficient. Resolving these debates is considered important in a climate that is purportedly amid a crisis in attention. Given the "raising" of standards and the pressure to facilitate students' movement as efficiently and effectively as possible through the curriculum, schooling requires intense and sustained attention. However, arguably students' attentive capacities are decreasing. For this reason, research directed at understanding and controlling students' attention has burgeoned in the last two decades (Neufeld & Foy, 2006; Klein & Lawrence, 2012).

The goal of this chapter is not to offer insight on how to improve classrooms or condition students' attentive capacities so they can adapt to schooling demands, but rather to examine the philosophical assumptions that underpin contemporary thinking about attention. This examination begins with a consideration of the conceptualization of attention from three perspectives that are competing and complementary: information processing, statistical learning, and embodied cognition. These perspectives help to trouble a narrow and singular understanding of attention. The critical analysis also includes a discussion of the historical, ideological, and political contexts that surround the emergence of the modern view of attention, which can be traced back to industrial capitalism, the rise of scientific psychology, technological changes, and philosophical shifts that took place during the late nineteenth century (Crary, 2001).

Conceptualization

Attention is generally thought about as a cognitive process whereby a stimulus, either from the environment or in one's own mind, is brought to consciousness (James, 1895; Klein & Lawrence, 2012). The idea is that any number of things—what will be called objects of consciousness—can be in one's mind. Attention is responsible for those objects. This understanding was articulated by one of the founders of educational psychology, William James, who defined attention as the "taking possession by the mind, in clear and vivid form, of one out of what seem several simultaneously possible objects or trains of thought. Focalization, concentration, of consciousness are of its essence. It implies withdrawal from some things in order to deal effectively with others, and is a condition which has a real opposite in the confused, daze, scatterbrained state which in French is called *distraction*, and *Zerstreutheit* in German" (1895, p. 75). For James, attention is the selection and conscious recognition of a stimulus, idea, train of thought, or a memory that is selected among a myriad of possibilities.

One cannot know another's object of consciousness without a behavior, which includes proclaiming what one is attending to. Thus, attention can be defined behaviorally as directing a gaze, shifting eyes, turning an ear, sitting up straight, or providing verbal affirmations (e.g., repeating the last thing another person has said or explicitly proclaiming, "I am paying attention") (Samuels & Turnure, 1974; Piontkowski & Calfee, 1979). In fact, the criteria for diagnosis of attention disorders are behavioral. In the Diagnostic Statistical Manual IV (DSM IV), inattention is a problem when six or more symptoms persist for at least six months to a degree that is maladaptive and inconsistent with developmental expectations. By this index, symptoms of inattention are demonstrated by the student who (1) often fails to give close attention to details or makes careless mistakes in schoolwork, work or other activities; (2) often has difficulty sustaining attention in tasks or play activity; (3) often does not seem to listen when spoken to directly; (4) often does not follow through on instructions and fails to finish schoolwork, chores or duties in the workplace (not due to oppositional behavior or failure to understand instructions); (5) often has difficulty organizing tasks and activities; (6) often avoids, dislikes, or is reluctant to engage in tasks that require sustained mental effort (such as schoolwork or homework); (7) often loses things necessary for tasks or activities (e.g., toys, school assignments, pencils, books or tools); (8) is often easily distracted by extraneous stimuli; or (9) is often forgetful in daily activities. Note that these behaviors are said to signify problems with cognitive functions.

Although theorists have exhibited a reliance on behaviors for assessing and measuring attentive capacities, attention is generally understood as a cognitive process. As argued by Crary (2001), this foundational understanding emerged in the nineteenth century and continues to endure today. Contemporary psychologists have elaborated on this understanding, distinguishing between forms and functions of attention, including intellectual, sensorial, selective, distributed, voluntary, involuntary, divided, and sustained attention (Styles, 2006). For example, selective attention is the ability to focus on a certain object for a particular period of time, while concurrently ignoring seemingly irrelevant stimuli. Divided attention is the ability to successfully perform more than one action at a time, while paying attention to two or more sources of information. Voluntary attention is the selection of objects of consciousness that is controlled and intentional, whereas involuntary attention is outside of conscious control. These examples are among the many in which researchers conceptually divide attention in order to provide a "complete" picture of the phenomenon that rests on a cognitive explanation, as is exemplified in information processing theory (IPT).

INFORMATION PROCESSING THEORY

Associated with Atkinson and Shiffrin (1968), IPT emerged with the advent of computer technology. This model draws an analogy between human cognitive capacities and computer operations to explain memory, for which attention is a central process. IPT depicts a linear process to explain how information from an external world is formed into memories. In this model, attention is essential for learning as it moves information from the senses to the working memory, where that information is processed and then stored into long-term memory. From this perspective, attention is limited by natural human cognitive capacities and, although it operates quickly and efficiently, is considered to be under voluntary control, or at least capable of being controlled. This theory has been widely researched since the 1950s and tends to dominate contemporary thinking about attention in educational psychology.

Sensory Register

The first component in processing information involves what IPT theorists refer to as the sensory register or sensory memory. The idea is that humans have senses that act as receptors to stimuli. The senses remain in constant contact with stimuli and receive a plethora of information from the external world. The sensory memory is the preliminary storage of information. This component has a large capacity but with a short duration; the senses pick up on numerous stimuli, which are available for further processing for one to two seconds. The information that reaches the sensory register is unprocessed; most of it has to do with the physical aspects of stimuli (Galotti, 2004). Not all information received by the sensory registered moves into working memory, or in other words, becomes an object of consciousness. However, any information received by the registers has the potential to be attended to and processed. Only that which is attended to moves to the working memory. Attention is the process of moving information from the sensory register to the working memory, which is the place where information is processed and potentially stored into long-term memory.

Attention

For IPT, attention is the essential mechanism for creating memories, as it makes the movement of information possible. From this perspective, claiming that students must pay attention in order to learn makes sense. Without attending to sensory inputs related to curricular stimuli, there can be no processing and storing of information. Only that information that is attended to is processed and stored as memories. Attention not only moves information from the registers to working memory, but it is also responsible for retrieving information from long-term memory by moving memories back into the working memory. For IPT, attention is elevated to heightened importance. Like all components and mechanisms of the information processing system, attention has its limitations.

According to this model, humans cannot attend to all the information that their senses receive. If they did, they would become overstimulated and would not be able to process anything. Like later information processing theorists, James (1895) argued that individuals could only pay attention to one object, idea, or train of thought at a time. He explained, "The number of *things* we may attend to is altogether indefinite, depending on the power of the individual intellect, on the form of the apprehension, and on what the things are. When apprehended conceptually as a connected system, their number may be very large. But however numerous the things, they can only be known in a single pulse of consciousness for which they form one complex 'object,' so that properly speaking there is before the mind at no time a plurality of *ideas*, properly so called" (p. 405; emphases in original). James argued that although a network of ideas and objects may be encompassed in an object of consciousness, James argues that at any one moment, or "pulse," only one object or idea, or several objects grouped into one unit, is present in consciousness. So even if individuals are so-called multitasking, they are not paying attention simultaneously to multiple stimuli but rather quickly switching their attention among ideas, tasks, or trains of thought. In contemporary discourse, this cognitive process is called alternating attention (Kurland, 2011). Here, at any one pulse of consciousness, there is only one object of attention.

Conditions for Selecting Stimuli

Given the vast possibilities for sensory inputs and the mind's limited ability to attend simultaneously to them all, information processing theorists have attempted to articulate explanations for why certain stimuli are attended to over others. One explanation is that individuals have filters that distinguish between essential and nonessential information. This mechanism determines the level of importance, relevance, and interest, which depend on numerous dynamics such as context and personal meaning. As governed by filters, only those stimuli that have immediate relevance are attended to and processed. Filters protect persons from information overload by excluding stimuli that are deemed to have little interest or adaptive function. Constructing attention in this way speaks to the importance of making learning meaningful. Apperceptive attention means attending to stimuli that already have an association in mind. The idea is that individuals are likely to pay attention to stimuli that can be connected to an experience. Therefore, the better teachers that can assist students in associating new stimuli to something already in the mind, the more likely that students will pay attention to the stimuli.

Another condition for paying attention is a student's level of alertness and energy (Sylwester & Cho, 1992/1993 Galotti, 2004). At low levels of alertness, only extremely important messages are likely to secure attention. At higher levels of alertness, less important messages can be attended to and processed. The idea is that cognitive and physical fatigue shape attention. For this reason, Sylwester and Cho (1992/1993) suggested that activities that require rapt attention should be scheduled in the morning when cognitive resources are generally replete. Whereas, activities that are likely to be socially engaging and require less cognitive engagement should be conducted in the afternoon. The lowered level of alertness that is believed to occur in the afternoon requires high levels of interest in order to elevate attention.

Voluntary Control

Although attention is limited, information processing theorists have contended that individuals can overcome those limitations. Researchers and philosophers have long debated issues of control over attention. In schools, the expectation is that students exercise voluntary control over their attentive behaviors; hence, the common refrain to "pay attention." Although tending to emphasize personal control, information processing theorists also recognize that attention can be involuntary. Consider one of the conditions that shapes attention to sensory inputs. One assumption is that individuals are more likely to attend to an object that already has an association in their minds. According to Felkin and Felkin (1895), this apperceptive attention can be voluntary and involuntary. On the one hand, individuals can seek connections between new stimuli and what is in the mind. The desire to seek connections likely has some motivational conditions, such as interest and purpose. The point is that individuals can exercise voluntary control over their attention by actively trying to form associations between objects of attention and what is already in their minds.

Apperceptive attention is also involuntary. Information processing theorists have contended that this attention consists of a rapid and involuntary scanning of the environment for stimuli that have relevance and meaning. This meaning can relate to stimuli that are dangerous or rewarding, such as shiny objects, sudden movements, and pungent smells. James (1890) gave an example of a cat paying attention to a bell because of its association with the presentation of food. He reasoned that the cat involuntarily responds to the bell because of a previous association; however, other sounds may not capture the cat's attention if they were not previously associated with rewards or dangers. The involuntary dimension of apperceptive attention is what James (1890) classified as "passive immediate sensorial attention."

This form of attention involves the force of a congenital impulse to perceive an intense or sudden stimulus. James contended that people attend in this way to moving things, wild animals, bright objects, metallic objects, loud noises, and certain words. He argued that this kind of attention is characteristic of children, who have not yet formed interests or concepts to control attention. James argued that with the development of permanent interests, attention becomes selective, controlled (less impulsive), and intellectual. He stated that:

> Childhood is characterized by great active energy, and has few organized interests by which to meet new impressions and decide whether they are worthy of notice or not, and the consequence is that extreme mobility of the attention with which we are all familiar in children, and which makes their first lessons such rough affairs. Any strong sensation whatever produces accommodation of the organs which perceive it, and absolute oblivion, for

the time being, of the task in hand. This reflex and passive character of attention . . . makes the child seem to belong less to himself than to every object which happens to catch his notice, is the first thing which the teacher must overcome. It never is overcome in some people, whose work, to the end of life, gets done in the interstices of their mind-wandering. (p. 417)

We can glean several important points from this quotation. The first is that, like contemporary theorists (Higgins & Turnure 1984; Ruff & Capozzoli, 2003), James viewed attention as having a developmental component. The second point is that attention can be governed by the physical properties of the senses and stimuli. Individuals cannot always control the structure of their senses and the information that the senses receive. In addition, individuals cannot always control the contents of their prior knowledge, which is the foundation of apperceptive attention. This point is important for teaching.

The idea is that students are likely to attend to things that have a connection to something they know or that is meaningful. The more connections students can make, the more attentive they might be. The more those connections are featured in the environment, and not dependent on students' intentional efforts to connect to prior knowledge, the less cognitive burden is placed on students. For this reason, James (1890) identified teachers as important sources for supporting voluntary attention. And as James argued, involuntary attention renders individuals as belonging to properties of stimuli and not to themselves. Thus the goal is controlled attention as this form signified personal autonomy and movement toward self-actualization.

SHIFTS, DEPARTURES, AND A REEMERGING PARADIGM

Research on attention has been dominated by IPT for the last five decades. Given its prevalence, there is much more to this theory, such as the factors that shape filtering criteria, the control of filters and when filters operate, and the relationship between filtering and attention. Rather than providing an exhaustive account of this literature, the present discussion introduced fundamental assumptions of IPT to serve as a starting point for considering contemporary shifts in attention theorizing. Although dominant, the IPT has been critiqued (Cobb, 1990; Hardcastle, 2003). A consideration of notions such as statistical learning and embodied cognition can highlight some of the critical concerns with IPT.

Statistical Learning

The notion of statistical learning (SL) is not a distinct separate theory but a phenomenon that can trouble some of the assumptions of IPT. SL is the idea that individuals have rapid computing power to pick up on patterns in the environment and form associations based on the frequency of stimuli occurring together (Saffran, Aslin, & Newport, 1996; Kirkham, Slemmer, & Johnson, 2002). In other words, individuals form ideas and concepts based on how often information is paired in combinations. As the notion of SL captures, this processing of information happens quickly and often outside of conscious recognition. That is, the information that is processed in order to form concepts and shape behaviors is not always an object of consciousness.

To illustrate, consider that SL was used to explain infant language acquisition (Saffran et al., 1996). Language has numerous rules, uses, and structures that are not all explicitly taught. Researchers have wondered how young children so readily learn and apply language without lengthy, sustained, and explicitly pedagogical interventions. Chomsky (1965) believed that children had an innate ability for language acquisition. That is, they had the biological structures in place for grammar and syntax. Language acquisition was, therefore, merely learning and ordering words. Chomsky's universal grammar theory was a departure from the previous behaviorist explanation, which was that children acquired language by being reinforced or punished for their utterances. The idea of SL, however, is that children learn language by being able to process large amounts of information by discerning patterns in stimuli.

Although author Malcolm Gladwell, in his popular book *Blink: The Power of Thinking without Thinking,* did not use the term, he was essentially discussing statistical learning. Gladwell used the terms *adaptive unconscious* and *rapid cognition* to describe what researchers call SL. All these terms have the same connotation, namely that individuals compute large amounts of information and form patterns and associations based on the probability of things occurring together. Gladwell argued that individuals make snap decisions and judgments with relatively little information in their consciousness. He argued that the bases of snap judgments and decisions are not always part of consciousness and, therefore, might be categorized as intuition or hunches. However, Gladwell explained that ideas, concepts, and spontaneous sources of knowledge that are seemingly without reason or logic are in fact a result of the rapid discernment of patterns or lack of conformity to patterns in the environment. The major contribution of SL to the discussion of attention and learning is that a great deal of information can be processed, stored, retrieved, and utilized beyond what appears as objects of consciousness.

The implicit association test (IAT) arguably measures the outcomes of SL. The IAT is designed to measure the strength of associations between concepts (e.g., gender, sexual orientation, race, and weight) and evaluations (e.g., good or bad). Based on a five-phase task structure, participants receive ratings about their preferences based on their implicit associations (e.g., homosexual and bad, skinny and good). The IAT is not a determination of one's values, but a measurement of implicit associations that result from experience, which includes media exposure, family life, school curricula, and involvement in any number of institutional orders. For example, in curricula, white men are often presented as primarily responsible for societal advancements (Sizemore, 1990; Ladson-Billings, 1998). This repeated association can lead to the implicit pairing of White men with success, accomplishment, and achievement. As another example, children's literature is replete with messages that normalize white-middle-class linguistic practices and ways of knowing (Gorlewski, 2011). This pairing can lead one to associate certain linguistic practices with more value and legitimacy.

Associations are not only formed by what is present. For example, without being explicitly told that homosexuals are bad, abnormal, or wrong, young children may easily form this association. In some cases, of course, this association is explicitly promoted, but for others, this association is formed by omission. In children's literature, media, and curricula, heterosexual relationships are the norm—a phenomenon known as heteronormativity. School policies (e.g., prom king and queen) and pressure for teachers to conceal their gayness omit and exclude homosexuality from everyday consciousness and contribute to the construction of heterosexuality as a norm. Such omission can foster negative associations with homosexuality, which can lead to discrimination, bias, and ignorance. Whether one is repeatedly exposed to associations or learning them through omission, the point is that information is processed beyond that which appears in consciousness. That information can shape ideas, attitudes, behaviors, and dispositions.

Thought about broadly, the notion of SL is complementary to an information processing theory of attention. The mind is still considered an active, internal, computing machine that rapidly and efficiently sorts through information. SL, however, invites different ways of thinking about attention. Information processing theorists have contended that information that is processed and stored must be the objects of attention. The idea of SL, however, suggests that attention, as understood as bringing an object to consciousness, is not always required for memory and concept formation. Individuals do not need to attend, in the information processing sense, to stimuli in order to process and store information. We can draw at least two possible conclusions from this SL. The first is that there are further cognitive mechanisms, other than attention, that are responsible for processing, storing, and retrieving information. The second conclusion might be that attention is more than the objects of consciousness. If one assumes that only attention is responsible for memories, then attention is more than the objects of consciousness. The idea of the active interpreter of stimuli is called into question. Attention can be considered largely involuntary and beyond what appears as an object of consciousness.

Whereas IPT emphasizes the role of intentional and active use of attention, the notion of SL highlights the non-active, passive operations of attention. With that said, even though our minds are considered rapid computing mechanisms, at some point, that which has been computed can become an object of consciousness. Arguably, when the results of the patterns become objects of consciousness, those confronted with such patterns could exercise intention and control. This is tantamount to awareness. For example, white people may not recognize ways in which whiteness is privileged in media and how that contributes to conceptions of themselves, others, and social institutions. However, awareness of the associations of whiteness in media can invite attention to subsequent associations. The idea is that those concepts and behaviors that formed in relation to pairings of stimuli may go undetected and thus uncontrolled but at some point can be brought to consciousness. This bringing to consciousness can happen by external prompts or through a seemingly unprompted realization. But once brought into consciousness, then control becomes possible.

Embodied Cognition

Although its roots are in nineteenth-century philosophy of mind, embodied cognition has recently reemerged as an alternative paradigm that stands in contrast to IPT. Embodied theorists contest the computational view of learning and memory. Instead of formulating thinking in terms of the linear processing of stimuli, the brain as a computational device, and learning as the storage of abstract of symbols, this perspective is about how behavior and thought emerge as a result of the real-time interactions between a nervous system with particular capabilities and an environment. In other words, learning and cognition happen in environments, for practical purposes, and are inseparable from the body; cognition is an embodied and situated activity, and thinking beings are acting beings (Anderson, 2003). Proponents of embodied cognition take as their theoretical starting point not that the mind carves out a perceptual field to process and store information via attention, but rather that the body is situated in a context and shares the cognitive burden of processing information.

The role of the body and world in cognition has been acknowledged for decades. This acknowledgment has manifested in different ways: the nineteenth-century view that thoughts can be imageless; motor theories of perception such as those suggested by William James and others; Jean Piaget's developmental psychology, which underscored the appearance of cognitive abilities out of a foundation of sensitometer aptitude; and the ecological psychology of J. J. Gibson, who considered perception in terms of the exchanges with the environment (Wilson, 2002). Ever since these theories were developed, mounting allegiance has attached to the suggestion that the mind must be understood in terms of its relationship to a physical body that is inseparable from a context. The growing interest in embodied cognition has given rise to diverse ways of thinking about the relationship between mind, body, and world: (1) biological structures make thinking possible; (2) the body processes information; and (3) the body is situated. These strands are not mutually exclusive, but rather highlight different aspects of embodiment.

BIOLOGICAL STRUCTURES GIVE FORM TO THOUGHT Some embodied theorists contend that the body furnishes individuals with conceptual and logical structures (Lakoff & Johnson, 1999; Maturana & Varela, 1987; Wilson, 2002). Lakoff and Johnson (1999) stated, "The same neural and cognitive mechanisms that allow us to perceive and move around also create our conceptual systems and modes of reason. Thus, to understand reason we must understand the details of our visual system, our motor system, and the general mechanisms of neural binding . . . reason is not . . . a transcendent feature of the universe or of a disembodied mind" (p. 4). Lakoff and Johnson made the general argument that reasoning and conceptual systems are not inseparable from bodily structures. It is a body within a particular space that gives shape to thought. It is not just that the mind needs a body to house thought, but the body shapes possibilities for thinking. Given this understanding, Lakoff and Johnson contended that reason and thinking are not radically free. The dependency on the body renders thinking and cognition not always an autonomous and controlled process. Rizzolatti and colleagues (1987) have also captured this view of embodiment as they have argued that attention is a consequence of how eye movements are programmed in the brain. Maturana and Varela (1987) have also theorized from this strand of embodied cognition by associating the qualities of consciousness to the entire human biological system. The big idea is that cognitive processes such as attention are made possible and shaped by biological structures.

BODY PROCESSES INFORMATION Another strand of embodied theorizing is that the brain is not the sole cognitive resource and author for thinking and problem solving (Wilson, 2002). From this view, the body is a cognitive resource. The body has senses that serve as instruments of investigation that provide information about how to think and act. As Lobel (2014) argued, thoughts, behaviors, decisions, and emotions are influenced by physical sensations, such as things that are touched and observed. Often without awareness, the texture, smell, light, and colors of physical stimuli are processed and shape thinking and behavior. Several experiments highlight this phenomenon. In one, participants were asked to accompany a research assistant to a fourth floor laboratory. They took an elevator and while in motion the assistant asked each participant to hold her cup of coffee. Half the participants were given iced coffee, while the other half were given hot coffee. Upon leaving the elevator, the assistant took back the coffee and the participant proceeded to the laboratory where he/she was given a description of an unknown person and asked to judge that person. The experimenter found that those who held the hot coffee were more likely to judge the person as friendlier and kinder than those who held the iced coffee. The influences on these judgments were unnoticed, yet they influenced participants' perceptions. From this view of embodiment, bodily sensation shapes thoughts and behaviors.

THE BODY IS SITUATED This strand of embodied theorizing is rooted in the tradition of sociocultural theorizing known as situated cognition. The idea is that thought is inseparable from the context, actors, purpose, and task. There is a strong assertion that cognition is not an activity of the mind unaided but is instead dispersed across the entire network of situations, including mind, body, and environment. The forces that drive cognitive activity do not exist exclusively inside the head of the individual, but are dispersed across individuals and the situations. One manifestation of this perspective pertains to the phenomenon known as "distributed cognition." The idea is that thinking and problem solving are group phenomena that include tools, task, relationships, and dialogue. Therefore, a thought that might be attributed to one individual is made possible only in relation to others within a specific context. For example, when solving a problem, many persons can contribute to the evolution of ideas. If one person made a statement that had significance for solving the problem, that statement was made possible because of statements and acts from other persons, the structure of the task, and situational demands. Perhaps without certain conditions or under different conditions, ideas that are attributed to individual actors might not have otherwise emerged.

To understand cognition, one must consider it, with all its structures and actors, as an amalgamated system (Wilson, 2002). While a cognitive process is taking place, situational information continues to come in that shapes processing, and motor activity is carried out that affects the environment in task-relevant ways. One example is that of physically moving around a room in order to produce solutions for where to place furniture. Other examples consist of spreading out the pieces of something that requires assembly in approximately the order and spatial interaction that they will possess in the finished product, or giving directions for how to get somewhere by first turning one's self and one's listener in the appropriate direction (Wilson 2002, 629). Memories are not abstract symbols that are stored and retrieved. Rather, they are the prolonged engagement with an experience and its accompanying sensations. The assumption is that the thinking and remembering of past events projects one into those moments wherein they reexperience the emotions, and sensations of the situation.

EMBODIED ATTENTION Attention from an embodied perspective poses challenges to IPT and SL. According to Anderson (2003), attention is being, acting, and engaging, regardless of the activity. Context is not reduced to a perceptual field by which willfulness, along with senses, brings objects to consciousness. This way of thinking is underpinned by the separation between world and cognition. That is, there is a world that exists independent of consciousness and the only way to bring the world into consciousness is attending to it. However, embodied cognition is based on the idea that body, world, and cognition exist together and are inseparable. Perhaps attention can involve an accentuation of an object into consciousness, but attention is not a mechanism that brings an object into consciousness. Thought is embodied and bodies are inseparable from context. Therefore, one's consciousness is tied to that context. For that reason, embodied theorists argue that in order to bring an object to consciousness that is not part of the context, individuals have to suppress stimuli by either looking upward or closing eyes. An embodied view troubles the conventional understanding of attention as a cognitive process that is distinct from the body and being.

Different ways of thinking about attention extend beyond these perspectives. Furthermore, there are several more nuances to each perspective than what was discussed. The preceding discussion is a starting point for conceptualizing attention as contested. Notwithstanding, a common thread can be found across the theorizing; attention is reified as a concrete mechanism that exists and is observable and measurable. Although embodiment can support resistance to this reification, attention is generally used to signify a feature of a person's being, whether inseparable from the world or involved in carving out a perceptual field. Another potential unifying theme has to do with function. From an embodied or information processing perspective, attention is a normalized part of teaching and an assumed component of students' profiles of their personhood. In other words, whether of the mind or the body, controlled or involuntary, inseparable from context or a perceptual field, attention is used to make sense of students. Although embodiment tends to align with critical perspectives in educational psychology, attempts to reify attention regardless of the perspective can be complicated by administrative practices, as is discussed in the following sections.

The Crisis of Attention

Although there are diverse ways of thinking about attention, there seems to be a agreement that students are amid a crisis in attention. The thinking is that modern culture is saturated with technological stimuli, which include mobile phones, video games, mobile games, computers, television, and cinema. (Tindell & Bohlander, 2012; O'Bannon & Thomas, 2015; McCoy, 2016). Students are always connected to others via Facebook, Twitter, Snapchat, and Instagram, all of which require immediate and short durations of attention. The constant connectivity can invite individuals to frequently check their phones, send a Snapchat picture, or post and read tweets from Twitter. Technology is implicated in encouraging persons to shift focus frequently or disrupt attention from other stimuli. Furthermore, information today tends to be abbreviated and, therefore, requiring attention to small amounts of information for brief periods. The assumption is that exposure to these types of stimuli shapes dispositions for attention. As a result, students may attend better in overstimulating, novel, and rapidly changing environments that do not provide depth of information.

The concern is that persons' lives are saturated with disruptions associated with certain forms of technology. As Goleman (2013) argued, the more disruptions people experience during tasks, the worse they perform on those tasks. The constant disruptions and shifting focus are argued to condition attention capacities. That is, persons may come to normalize, require, and practice the frequent and rapid switching of attention. For this reason, researchers are concerned that technology saturation leads to the diminishing of students' capacity to attend in situations that require sustained attention, such as in schools (Goleman, 2013).

The conditioning of attention to rapidly shift is especially problematic in contemporary schooling. Teachers need students to pay attention to more information and be attentive for long durations. With curricular initiatives such as Common Core, students are expected to learn a good deal of information at a rapid pace. Success in schooling requires students to be ever more focused. However, in a cultural context saturated with stimuli that are vying for students' attention, "capturing" and maintaining attention is argued to be increasingly difficult. These challenges can result from being susceptible to visual and auditory distractions, failing to pay attention to details, making careless mistakes, rarely following instructions carefully and completely, losing or forgetting things such as pencils and books, blurting out answers before hearing the whole question, feeling restless, fidgeting with hands or feet, squirming, leaving a seat during inappropriate times, and having difficulty waiting for a turn. All of these behaviors and cognitive responses can get in the way of achieving schooling goals.

The underlying assumption for this way of thinking is environments shape students' attentive capacities. There is also a belief that during formative years, brains are more plastic and malleable than in adulthood. Therefore, young children are more susceptible to being effected by technology exposure. From the theory of neural plasticity, experiences form neural networks that shape the functioning of the body and thought. If students come to schools with particular attentive capacities, then teachers have to consider whether they try to reshape or teach in accordance with them. If the latter and assuming that attentive capacities are shortened, then it follows that teachers should structure pedagogy in ways that continuously produce a sense of novelty, abbreviate information, finds ways to stimulate the senses, and move rapidly to avoid boredom with tasks. Although this approach can be reasoned to have value, matching classrooms to resemble students' capacities may exacerbate the crisis of attention. Furthermore, it is challenging to make schooling resemble the types of stimulation, novelty, and brevity of technology.

Even if possible to structure schooling in these ways, there is debate about whether teachers should cater to students' attentive capacities and dispositions or actively try to reshape them. Schwartz (2013) stated, "By catering to diminished attention, we are making a colossal and unconscionable mistake. The world is a complex and subtle place, and efforts to understand it and improve it must match its complexity and subtlety" (paragraph 3). This author warned of a self-fulfilling prophecy whereby when assuming students cannot attend for long durations, nothing is done to develop attentive capacities and skills. Therefore, this author calls for an explicit focus on the cultivation of attention, arguing that such a curricular focus is as important as mathematics, biology, or literature.

This pedagogical focus may not necessarily involve directly cultivating attention. Problems with attention may not be conceived as deficiencies in capacity, but rather with self-regulation. A common misconception about children with attention problems is that they are not paying attention at all, but they may in fact be paying attention to many things. Therefore, interventions may center on improving and discerning important stimuli, impulse control, blocking out stimuli, and self-monitoring. Issues with regulating attention can result from cognitive fatigue, which can result from overuse of self-control, improper diet, pacing oneself too quickly, or sleep deprivation (Doran, Van Dongen, & Dinges, 2001; Boksem, Meijman, & Lorist, 2005). Diet, rest, and cognitive training can all be considered when trying to train students to attend to the accepted quantity of information for the expected amount of time. These strategies to address attention problems seem underused in favor of prescription medication. Although the modern world is implicated in shaping attention, psychologists are primarily interested in diagnosing individuals and implementing interventions to reform them.

Although researchers seldom question the reification of attention as a human process, debates certainly persist about whether deficits are real or socially constructed. This debate centers on whether attention problems are deficiencies in individuals or environments, which includes structures of assessments, norms for attention, exposure to technology, and pedagogical environments. There are several problems with this debate. First, it diverts attention away from the assumptions that make it possible to argue one side or the other. Second, what is considered "real" is not necessarily distinct from what is "socially constructed." Third, like all others, this debate invites binary thinking. Fourth, both positions on this binary can be responsible for propagating problematic thinking and practice. On the one hand, unequivocally assuming the objective reality of attention disorders ignores the role that technology, ideology, and classrooms play in the production of attentive behaviors. In so doing, individuals are branded with neurological or psychological pathologies for what amounts to social and economic problems. On the other hand, refuting the possibility of attention deficiencies might involve discounting students' experiences. To conclude that attention deficits are merely an arbitrary social construct can divert attention away from the real kinds of struggles students have in relation to their academic work. As a consequence, students may not get the support they need in order to meet the norms for attention that are required for school tasks.

Critical Analysis

Critical theorists tend to eschew the kind of binary thinking about whether or not phenomena are "real." Likewise, the present analysis is not about the reality of attention and the associated deficits. Rather, it is about the contexts that give form to a notion of attention, how shifting contexts change the understanding of attention, and the effects that this notion has on people. For this analysis, attention does not connote an objective inner state of mental focus and concentration that can be measured with the proper assessments. Rather it is a phenomenon that takes form in particular relationships and discursive practices. Crary (2001) conducted a genealogy of attention and used the term not to reify a cognitive mechanism that can be known with the right tools and theories. He stated, "I use the term attention not to hypostatize it as a substantive object, but to refer to the field of those statements and practices and to a network of effects they produced" (p. 23). This way of thinking is a shift from viewing students as attentive beings, to thinking of ways and reasons it is possible to construct students as attentive beings. Attention is constituted through the category of attention, systems of measurement, economic perspectives, institutional motivations, historical context, and philosophical frameworks (Crary, 2001; Neufeld & Foy, 2006; Sugarman, 2014).

THE RISE OF ATTENTION

Attention has become an important concept for teaching. In modern schooling, teachers must assume the role of psychological expert and fix their gaze on students in order to assess, measure, cultivate, and, if necessary, reform students' attention. This role for teachers is a modern product, emerging in the late nineteenth century (Sobe, 2004). It was at that time that attention became the crux of instruction and the source for solving problems with schooling (Sobe, 2004). However, attention as a feature of students' internal worlds that needed to measured, controlled, harnessed, and developed is a relatively modern construct that has its roots in a particular historical context.

Crary (2001) acknowledged that although the notion of attention has been in existence for centuries, dating back to the writings of St. Augustine of Hippo in the early fifth century AD, during the nineteenth century the idea of attention took a specific form. The rise of industrial capitalism, the emergence of psychological science, philosophical changes, and the existence of particular urban, social, and economic problems changed the discourse on attention. These changes were conceptual as well as administrative.

Conceptually, attention changed from a process that was embodied, physiological, and automatic to one that was voluntary and willful, thus requiring that it be measured, regulated, and controlled. Administratively, attention was, and arguably still is, used to regulate cognitive capacities for the purpose of achieving institutional objectives.

Philosophical Changes

Crary (2001) argued that certain philosophical developments about consciousness, vision, perception, and experience had to occur before attention could be understood the way it is today. In the eighteenth century, British philosophers viewed the mind as a passive receiver of sensation. Attention was considered a response to auditory and visual stimuli in the real world (Crary, 2001). Prior to the nineteenth century, attention was inseparable from physical effort, movement, or action. This conceptualization is not like that seen in the idea of embodied perspective described above. Crary described attentiveness as a full embodiment of an observer and attention as coinciding with physiological or motor activity. That is, action and being signified attention not the bringing of a stimulus to consciousness. Prior to the nineteenth century, theorists regarded attention as a reflex that was involuntary and automatic. Although some theorists at this time deliberated over voluntary and controllable attention, Crary argued that these theorists understood the ambiguity of this distinction. Today, such a distinction continues to be unclear, despite the fact its complexity has been forgotten. It is not always clear when attention is voluntary and intentional and when it is involuntary and stimulus-determined.

Rather than attempt to conceptualize this distinction, a critical question is, what makes it possible to construct the distinction and why is it difficult in the twenty-first century to conceive of attention as primarily or largely involuntary? Although many modern theorists recognize that attention can be both voluntary and involuntary, there tends to be emphasis on the former. Individuals are conceptualized as attentive beings who have the capacity to exercise control over the objects of consciousness. The prevalence of medications in addressing the crisis of attention suggests that individuals cannot control attention without introducing chemicals into the body. In any event, addressing the crisis via medication still locates attention and its deficits in individual functioning. As long as attention is thought about as an individual and internal mechanism, it can ostensibly be controlled—whether that be by diet, cognitive training, medication, exercise, planning, or self-regulation. A key feature of the paradigm shift is that attention went from an embodied state, to one in which individuals were agents of attention.

Sobe (2004) argued that the study of attention ultimately supported the fragmentation of the mind, the world, and the relationship between the two. In the modern view, the mind is conceptualized as having a distinct cognitive process, separate from all others, that carves out the world into possible perceptual objects. Whereas the information processing model is a clear representation of this view, an embodied perspective is a challenge to this type of fragmentation. However, the dominant conception is that attention is a distinct cognitive process that is responsible for selecting some objects in a perceptual field while ignoring others. This conception includes fragmentation of the mind, contexts, and individuals' relationship to the context. Attention to one stimulus involves ignoring others. If only that which is attended to is processed for memories, then there are several parts of the context that are absent from consciousness. Parsing contexts into objects of perception and attention limits the relationship to those objects that are selected for attention. As a perceiver, one who selects objects of consciousness, individuals are fragmented from the world; individuals became perceivers of objects, not those who are inseparable from those objects. Conceptualizing individuals as perceivers of the world deepens a separation between mind and world.

Crary (2001) pointed to the philosophical shifts needed for the modern understanding of attention. Moreover, he pointed to the debates and controversies that surrounded this shift, stating that "the 1880s and 1890s generated a sprawling diversity of often contradictory attempts to explain [attention]" (p. 23). According to this author, the modern conceptualization of attention that emerged during this historical moment was among a number of theories. So why did the view of attention that became foundational to IPT become prominent? Crary debunks a scientific explanation. He and other critical theorists raise doubt that changes in psychological knowledge results from scientific progress in knowing persons. To conclude that the way attention is understood today is a result of scientific progress ignores the role that history, power, and politics plays in the acceptance of knowledge. Crary argued that the paradigmatic shift in our understanding of attention cannot be understood as a type of ahistorical scientific progress, but rather a shift that occurred for historical, philosophical, economic, and technological reasons.

Capitalism

During the late nineteenth century, industrial capitalism shaped economic, social, philosophical, and political relationships (Crary, 2001). In conjunction, industrial capitalism contributed to the modern concept and administration of attention. One way to think about this influence pertains to the metaphor of attention that informs IPT. The flow of information and the ways it is processed resembles an assembly line. Information flows linearly to be processed by different cognitive mechanisms until there is an end product, which is a memory. However, the capitalist underpinning extends this metaphor. As Crary explained, capitalism works because of attention and distraction. Individuals have to shift attention away from old products to new ones, demanding an acceptance of the idea that rapid switches of attention are natural.

A capitalist system depends on the continuous production of novel objects. Markets are flooded with products that overstimulate and attempt to "grab" attention. The novelty of new products may invite sustained attention for a short period, but distraction must eventually prevail in order to attend to novel objects. If novel objects do not grab attention, they will be modified to be louder, brighter, faster, and shinier. If unsuccessful for distracting, there could be careful research to ascertain which objects are likely to be attended to. The point is that attention and distraction support the consumption of new products. To sell products continuously requires shifting attention whereby products are stimulating and attractive to as many people in the targeted group. For this reason, Crary argued that capitalism contributed to the now pervasive view that attention can be produced and managed by understanding the processes of stimulation and attraction.

The shifting attention required under capitalism created a problem for individuals, their schooling, and engagement in political life. Crary (2001) explained, "The changing configurations of capitalism continually push attention and distraction to new limits and thresholds, with an endless sequence of new products, sources of stimulation, and streams of information, and then respond with new methods of managing and regulating perception" (p. 14). He argued that throughout the progression of industrialization, new inventions created new distractions, and with these new distractions came new problems. With the invention of printed media, books could now capture our attention and create possibilities for inattentive behavior and distraction. Likewise, the invention of the phonograph, which provided an auditory stimulus, was something to attend to, be distracted by, or ignore. More recently, cinema, television, and computer technology are stimuli that supply people with countless objects to attend to. These objects became points of reference to judge and measure attention.

The production of "novel" objects and new technologies created new types of attention requirements. One of the effects was the emerging need for individuals to self-regulate the objects they focused on. With the abundance of stimuli to be attended to, individuals were confronted with requirements to choose and attempt to control their attention, creating a requirement and expectation for self-management and control. This requirement made it possible for attention deficits to be seen. The idea is that if individuals are unable to distract themselves from some stimuli in favor of those that are assigned a value within a particular context, they can be labeled as having a psychological deficiency.

Freedom from Determinism

Historians categorize nineteenth-century thought as primarily concerned with liberating people from all kinds of determination that was outside of individual control (Crary, 2001). For example, Crary (2001) stated, "Man was to become part of his own liberty, a self-possessed soul" (p. 45). Although for centuries, and continuing today, debates about free will and determinism have existed, during the nineteenth century scientific psychology provided grounds for conceptualizing freedom from determinism. The lack of intentionality that characterized early conceptualizations of attention was a problem because individuals were conceived of as governed by stimuli, not masters of their own consciousness. To exercise control over themselves, people cannot be conceived of as passive receivers of stimuli. For this liberation from stimuli and one's cognitive system, attention could not be automatic and involuntary. Rather, people needed to be treated as observers who carve out a perceptual field in order to select information to be processed.

In contemporary discourse, attention is largely viewed as an internal cognitive mechanism, discrete from others, that is controllable, discontinuous, fragmented, voluntary, and a key source for learning. In the paradigm shift, attention became a discrete and independent mechanism that fragments psychology into distinct and discrete parts, like those featured in the IP model. In this model, individuals are viewed as intentionally selecting among numerous stimuli to bring to consciousness. Observers express their will by parsing out a perceptual field—deciding what to attend to and ignore. In modern discourse, willful, intentional, and voluntary attentiveness, if not exercised already, can be cultivated and learned. This new attention was something that could be studied, measured, taught, and improved; it was one of the mechanisms that freed individuals from external control.

The scientific study of attention was essential for rendering attention voluntary and controllable. In 1879, Wilhelm Wundt established the first laboratory for psychological experimentation. Artificial stimuli were presented to participants in order to construct a picture of patterns, functions, duration, and features of attention. These experiments were part of the reformulation of attention and sensation into quantitative, discrete, and observable mechanisms. Crary has argued that such experiments changed the nature of subjective experience to something that is quantifiable and observable. The experiments were necessary for scientifically constructing knowledge of attention, which supports control by both individuals themselves and authorities who needed certain kinds of attentive beings. The underpinning logic is that the more that is known about human psychological capacities and capabilities, the more control can be exercised.

If this thinking is true, one must recognize that this control works in a paradoxical way. In attempting to free people from determinisms by scientifically constructing knowledge of humans, individuals are required to submit to the authority of scientific reasoning, use particular concepts to make sense of themselves, and risk having knowledge of psychological functions be used by others who have particular agendas. Crary (2001) argued that this last requirement was actually the goal of the science of attention. He stated that attention became the "means by which an individual observer can transcend those subjective limitations and make perception *its own*, and attention is at the same time a means by which a perceiver becomes open to control and annexation by external agencies" (p. 5). The tension to control attention and have it controlled plays out in a number of contexts including schools.

INSTITUTIONAL POWER

Assuming the notion of attention makes sense as a way to constitute students' psychology, it is fair to conclude that all individuals are in a perpetual state of attention and distraction. Crary (2001) described these states as "existing on a continuum in which the two ceaselessly flow into one another, as part of a social field in which the same imperatives and forces incite one and then the other" (p. 51). Attention to one thing means distractions from others, and vice versa. Attention deficits are not breaks in attention, but the inability to attend to certain stimuli for designated periods of time without distraction. Thought about this way, institutional norms and values shape the interpretation of the qualities of students' attention. Being able to attend in ways that are valued shapes whether that attention is adaptive and productive, rather than counterproductive and deficient. For this reason, Crary argued that attention that is adaptive and normal is based on performative norms: "Attentiveness was a critical feature of a productive and socially adaptive subject, but the border that separated a socially useful attentiveness and a dangerously absorbed or diverted attention was profoundly nebulous and could be described only in items of performative norms" (p. 47). Although the distinction between adaptive and counterproductive attention is a reification of individuals as attentive beings, Crary contended that this distinction by itself is nebulous and determined by norms. Those authorities, practices, statements, and policies that contribute to the production and maintenance of such norms give form to the categorization and evaluation of students as either adequately attentive or deficient.

Thus, important questions include (1) what kind of attentive beings are valued for schooling; (2) what qualities of attention are adaptive versus counterproductive; and (3) how does the structure of schools and normative values interact with individuals to give form to the evaluations of students' attentive capacities? Students who are easily distractible by attending to various stimuli may pose problems for modern classrooms while those students who can fix their attention and sustain it for long periods are, perhaps, ideal. On the other hand, there can be instances when intense and durable attention poses a problem for schooling. If a student is deeply engrossed in an activity or thought, it may be difficult to divert attention to something else. Schooling contexts tend to require divertible attention. With the array of subjects covered each day, adaptable and functional attentiveness is demonstrated in students' ability to switch efficiently and abruptly to and from scripted and timed tasks. Fixed, sustained attention that cannot be diverted may be counterproductive in many contemporary classrooms.

If students can fixate on objects presented during one moment, shift attention when instructed, maintain intensity and fixedness on the new object, and repeat the cycle, then it is assumed that they can be successful in schools. Adaptive and productive attention is relatively short, intense for a predetermined duration, instigated by the teacher, and divertible by the teacher, curriculum, peer, or school bell. If long attention spans with sharp focus are valued, then that would seem to contradict the ways schools are structured. Scripted, well-defined, time-determined classrooms could be implicated in contributing to the crisis in attention, which is so often blamed on technology. Such classrooms can communicate that it is completely normal to switch attention abruptly and to perhaps engage cursorily with objects of attention. If the goal is to cultivate long attention spans with intense focus, modern classrooms may present a challenge.

Certain classroom structures are explicitly intended to cultivate attention. For example, Maria Montessori's aim was to construct environments in ways that supported the expression of what she considered to be children's natural capacities. Sobe (2004) referred to Montessori's method as a pedagogy of attention. According to Sobe, Montessori believed that individuals have attentive capacities that must be trained through practice. Rather than relying on teacher directives, explicit cognitive training, bells, or attractive stimuli, Montessori believed that attentive capacities were developed in environments wherein individuals were left to engage in tasks autonomously and with self-direction. The logic is that students have natural proclivities and capacities to be attentive. However, early in life, attention can wander. According to Montessori, training and directing that attention is not achieved by teachers' explicit actions to shape attention, but rather by teachers' inaction to shape attention. With opportunities to engage autonomously in her classroom structure, Montessori believed that students will fix their attention on particular objects of interest and engage repetitiously with those objects until they have mastered them (Sobe, 2004).

The idea here is that neither teacher, peer, nor bell should break concentration on tasks, as such distractions will undermine the pursuit of task mastery and invite a cognitive orientation of distractibility. Rather, distraction from one task and attention to another must be a spontaneous maneuver directed by each individual student. Montessori believed that this shift in attention occurs when individuals after repeated efforts competently perform those tasks to their satisfaction (Sobe, 2004). She also believed that opportunities to engage autonomously not only help to train wandering attentiveness but also produce calmness, serenity, and internal resolve as well as encouraging self-mastery and pursuit of perfection (Sobe, 2004). Montessori questioned the degree to which students in scripted environments can fix their attention, engage repetitiously, pursue mastery of skills, and develop and train their attentiveness (Sobe, 2004). Her method certainly seems appealing for addressing a crisis in attention.

Montessori's method is especially relevant during a time when researchers, parents, and policy makers are interested in strategically and intentionally shaping pedagogical environments to target students' attention behaviors and patterns. More than other cognitive mechanisms, attention is viewed as formed, transformed, and misformed by sociocultural surroundings, such as exposure to technology, educational structures, diet, socioeconomic class background, and culture. Given its purported malleability, researchers are focused on understanding the particular relationship between sociocultural factors and attentive capacities. They are also focused on understanding the conditions that enable practitioners to cultivate certain forms of attention. Although Montessori provided a pedagogical format for the cultivation of attention, her approach is not widely adopted in preK–12 classrooms. For educators to adopt her method would require that the structure of schooling be dramatically reconfigured. The concern here, however, is not which pedagogical structures are best for cultivating adaptive attention. Rather, the concern is about the drive to know how best to cultivate students' attention.

This drive speaks to the role of institutional control for the cultivation of attention. As theorists have argued, the discourse on the pedagogy of attention is entangled in the operation of power and tied to the administration of populations (Crary, 2001; Sobe, 2004; Sugarman, 2014). The notion of attention has become a way to inscribe, discipline, and control subjectivities, which is made possible through categorization, description, and evaluations. There are ways to measure, monitor, and intervene to create a kind of attentiveness. The aim is to construct knowledge about what attention is and how it works so that teachers can use this knowledge to produce optimal attention—all for the purpose of achieving institutionally sanctioned learning goals. The study of attention and its importance for teaching is bound to efforts to produce particular types of people (Crary, 2001; Sobe, 2004; Sugarman, 2014). Cultivating particular qualities of attention is viewed as necessary for creating a particular type of person, one who can perform in ways that are valued within institutional settings.

The pedagogy of attention is about figuring out how to shape attentive capacities in specific ways that align with an institutional, social, and political aim. For this reason, Sobe (2004) argued, "Attention is related to the organization and management of individuals; in the exercise and selection of what one is attuned to and how one is attuned to it, attention becomes a knowledge of the self that embodies regulatory practices" (p. 281). A key part of the regulation of attention is attending to objects that have value within a particular context. Those owners of the means of production want attention to their objects for consumption. Teachers wanted attention to the curriculum. Cultural critics want attention to politics and the workings of government. The governing of individuals is tied to their attention. While various sources vie for one's attention, there is simultaneously the self-evaluation, monitoring, and judgment of that attention. In modern discourse, individuals are increasingly viewed as responsible for their attention and must, therefore, exercise the self-regulation of their attention. The pedagogy of attention is not just how to shape attention, but how to shape individuals into those who can monitor, cultivate, and judge their own attention.

Conclusion

As we have seen, consideration of different perspectives on attention—as information processing, as statistical learning, and as embodied—illustrates competing ideas about what attention is and how it operates. Other theories can be considered to further complicate this landscape, but the purpose of the present analysis is not to exhaust all these different possibilities but rather to show that controversies and debates have always and continue to accompany the notion of attention. Although the subject is surrounded by contradictions and contentions, much of this turmoil has been laid to rest. In contemporary discourse, the information processing view tends to inform thinking about attention. The prevalence of this perspective is buttressed by its alignment with some of the dominant ways of thinking about human psychology, such as the separation between internal and external, a constructivist conception of sensory experience, the fragmentation of psychology, and the persistent belief in personal control.

Regardless of the perspective from which it is considered, attention is a normalized and naturalized part of education discourse and education psychology. Attention is studied as a cognitive mechanism that is studied and taken for granted as responsible for learning. Therefore, the discourse of attention is about how to develop, train, and sharpen this process. The purpose is to support specific institutional aims for the production of particular types of attentive persons; hence, the prevalence of the pedagogy of attention. Psychologists, parents, and teachers want to understand the causes and solutions of attention problems, often at the level of the individual, so they can be fixed. Attention problems, however, are not solely attributable to individual deficits.

This chapter's analysis invites the possibility of thinking about and engaging with the notion of attention in a different way. Rather than define the properties of attention in order to construct or validate a pedagogy of attention or empirically declare mental or neurological capacities of attention, one can consider why attention is understood in a particular way and why that understanding shapes administrative practices to create persons with particular attentive capacities. The way attention is understood today is not arbitrary or necessarily the result of the objective scientific progress on human functioning and capabilities but rather situated within a particular historical, economic, and philosophical context. Critical analysis evokes questions about the certainty of ideas about attention, and such analysis shows how certain conceptions of attention have been mobilized to achieve specific institutional, ideological, political, and social aims.

Practitioners should continue to ask the following questions: (1) what are the values, norms, practices, policies that contribute to forming a particular understanding of students' attention; (2) what forces underpin the production of such an understanding; and (3) how does this understanding effect the understanding of teaching and students? These questions can serve both to challenge the epistemological certainty of attention and avoid ideological individualism, which in this case manifests in pathologizing individuals for attention problems.

CHAPTER SEVEN

Assessment and Measurement

CONTEMPORARY EDUCATION DISCOURSE places a high premium on assessing and measuring all facets of schooling, including teacher preparation programs, teacher performance, student outcomes, and district, state, and nation-wide performance. Informed by neoliberal rhetoric, a prevailing assumption in policy reform discussions is that schools are in crisis. Researchers and policy makers, such as Secretary of Education Arne Duncan, tend to believe any problems with schooling in the United States can be understood and fixed with "high quality" assessment and measurement (AM) (Pellegrino, Chudowsky & Glaser, 2001; Duncan, 2010). AM is assumed to provide information about (1) students' learning, potential, attributes, and capacities; (2) teachers' achievement of curricula goals; (3) individual school performance; and (4) district, state, and the country-wide academic performance. The ostensible purpose of collecting this information is to guide interventions and reforms in order to improve student academic performance. Over the past three decades, the imperative to assess and measure all facets of schooling has become so dominant in policy and practice that it appears both necessary and unavoidable, if not inevitable (Hursh, 2007).

Thought to be the best mechanism for revealing where problems exist, the use of AM is lauded by scholars and policy makers alike as serving as an educational compass directing where educational interventions are best implemented. Although AM is used at multiple levels of education, the focus of this chapter is on assessing and measuring students. In contemporary discourse, teachers are expected both frequently and systematically to implement AM that represents their effectiveness at moving students' toward state-mandated curricula goals in a particular time frame. In the classroom,

AM is about gathering as much information as possible about students in order to guide interventions and justify pedagogy as evidenced-based.

Despite these purposes, AM are highly controversial. Critique of the assessment and measurement of students identifies numerous dangers, with AM shown to be culpable in the reproduction of inequality, support of a neoliberal agenda, narrowing of students' ontology, and endorsement of a problematic ethic of selfhood. These concerns relate not only to standardized tests, which will be scrutinized in the following discussion, but rather can be broadly applied to a variety of AM practices.

Background
NEOLIBERAL UNDERPINNING

Over three decades ago, public education in the United States was determined to be in a state of crisis. When the Department of Education published its analysis of the issues plaguing public education in a report titled *A Nation at Risk* in 1983, during the Reagan administration, the report served as a wake-up call on the failure of public schools to prepare students for the competitive, global workforce. "If an unfriendly foreign power had attempted to impose on America the mediocre educational performance that exists today," wrote the authors, "we might well have viewed it as an act of war" (Gardner, 1983, p. 13). The report proclaimed that the poor quality of public education in the United States guaranteed the nation's inevitable decline as a world power. Igniting a nation-wide panic about the perceived threat of America's failing schools, the narrative underpinning the purpose of public education was reconceptualized to endorse values such as competition and accountability (Hursh, 2007).

Gradually, AM was written into laws and policies, and as such, the narrative of public education was rewritten to reflect a commitment to improving educational outcomes for all students reinforced by the belief that the issues that plagued US education could be better understood, and potentially alleviated, with the development and implementation of better AM (Pellegrino et al., 2001; Duncan, 2010). The goals of these initiatives are underpinned by a belief that AM can accurately measure students' content knowledge at the time in which the AM is administered. The assumption is that a student's performance reveals potential sources for concern or a need for improvement while also providing a means to hold teachers and schools accountable. From there it becomes possible to isolate key features of "successful" schools, as well as making it possible to identify and address those areas that fail to meet state and federal standards (Norris, 1990). Essentially, the goal is to be able to clearly analyze student and teacher performance on both a micro and macro level, in turn enhancing schools' performances across the board. However, many scholars are concerned by the political and economic underpinnings guiding this philosophy, which is undeniably tied to specific neoliberal assumptions about the purpose of public education and of society itself (Hursh, 2007).

Standardized tests play a major role in supporting a neoliberal agenda in schools. To accommodate the demands of the competitive marketplace, contemporary educational discourse and policy makers place a high premium on the efficient and reliable collection of educational data, placing particular emphasis on teacher performance and student achievement (Stiggins, 2002; De Lissovoy, 2013). In the effort to gain a comprehensive understanding of the state of public education in the United States, the ability to collect large amounts of data on student and teacher performance has become an invaluable asset in assuring both politicians and the general public that resources are not being wasted. Furthermore, standardized tests help to ascribe value to schools so that parents can make informed consumer choices. These tests are also implicated in competition to determine funding allocation, supporting a neoliberal type of accountability (which has led to firing teachers and closing schools) and economic instrumentalism. Another way standardized tests are implicated in neoliberalism relates to content, as these tests are argued to measure the knowledge and skills that are required for students to be twenty-first-century workers. Finally, standardized tests are punitive, which Mathison (2009) argued is required for justifying corporate and state control over schools, the privatization of public education, and the dismantling of teachers' unions.

Typical concerns with standardized tests are that they are homogeneous and test a universal way of thinking and reasoning. However, standardized tests of students' academic performance are troublesome far beyond this concern. In order to explore the ideological underpinnings of any type of AM, it is important to move beyond critiques that are based on concerns with universalism and individualism. Even AM that is ostensibly personalized, differentiated, and adapted can serve neoliberal purposes.

Neoliberal influences extend beyond the ubiquity of and value for standardized AM, over which teachers generally have no control. Teachers' accountability to achieve state-mandated curricular goals has led to increased pressures to use everyday AM in order to systematically collect, document, and chart students' performance and progress. Teachers are pressured to adopt, create, implement, and center their teaching on AM. The consequences of not achieving mandated curricula goals could be termination of employment, closing of schools, and the privatization of schools. Given that neoliberal forces are implicated in the shaping of curricula goals, AM can be viewed as a tool to garner compliance to and maintenance of neoliberal values (Bonal, 2003; Hursh, 2007). In essence, teachers are required to use AM in accordance with the schooling goals that are informed by neoliberal ideology.

Whatever is assessed and measured, be it a teacher, student, a school, or a system of schools, the common assumption is that the more efficiently information can be accumulated via valid and reliable measurements, the better schooling can be shaped to support student success. Pellegrino et al. (2001) stated, "Needed are classroom and large-scale assessments that help all students learn and succeed in school by making as clear as possible to them, their teachers, and other education stakeholders the nature of their accomplishments and the progress of their learning" (pp. 1–2). These authors speak to the importance of large-scale AM, such as standardized tests, as well as the everyday AM administered by teachers to provide knowledge of students' achievement of curricular goals. The assumption is that if educators unequivocally and objectively know what students know, and use that information to inform interventions, then problems with educational disparities can be addressed. From this line of reasoning, disparities persist because teaching and learning are not adequately assessed and measured. Problems with AM tend to be explored in terms of reliability and validity.

PROBLEMATIZING VALIDITY AND RELIABILITY

Researchers and policy makers tend to believe in the value of AM, despite disagreement regarding which assessments and measurements are best for the classroom. Yet rather than question the value, function, and consequences of AM, debate persists about accuracy, which refers to validity (i.e., do assessments and measurements actually measure what they purport to measure?) and reliability (i.e., do assessments and measurements produce the same result across a range of implementation?). The concept of validity is about the degree to which instruments measure what they purport to measure. For example, questions of validity might include, do intelligence tests measure intelligence; do creativity scales measure creativity; and do grit scales measure grit? Reliability is about whether instruments will produce the same results across different applications, that is, across persons and times of administration? The terms *validity* and *reliability* are related, and together speak to the issues about the scientific objectivity of AM. The goal of social science researchers, and the hope of policy makers and teachers, is that the instruments used to assess and measure students will actually represent them.

Issues with validity and reliability are scientific problems that are addressed through scientific thinking and rationalized through a narrative of scientific progress. Although some researchers and policy makers are likely to agree that current AM is imperfect,* they are also likely to agree that there is progress in the development of scientifically valid and reliable representations of students, teaching, and learning. For example, the Obama administration held a competition for companies to vie for federal money to improve standardized assessments (Duncan, 2010). As a result, two companies were awarded $300 million to develop what Duncan (2010) referred to as "21st century assessments." These new standardized tests include various types of test items other than multiple choice. Commenting on the new tests, Duncan (2010) stated, "I am convinced that this new generation of state assessments will be an absolute game-changer in public education. For the first time, millions of schoolchildren, parents, and teachers will know if students are on-track for colleges and careers—and if they are ready to enter college without the need for remedial instruction" (paragraph 4). As if it had never happened before, ostensibly because of the quality of AM, Duncan believed that what he referred to as the "new generation" of assessments would provide valid and reliable information about whether students are on track for college and career readiness; the time had come with this massive investment that AM could provide valid, reliable, objective information that could be used to justifiably sort students, design interventions, and improve learning.

The problems of representing students, however, are not likely to be solved with modifying standardized tests from strictly multiple choice to a combination of short answer, multiple-choice, and fill-in-the-blank questions. Work on validity and reliability has been directed at a number of classroom assessments and measurements. This work asks, what are the best instruments to represent what students know, have learned, and can?

* The notion of the perfect AM is of the AM that objectively, unequivocally, and ahistorically represents something. From a critical perspective, the achievement of perfection in this context is not possible as it assumes that a phenomenon exists independent of its measurement and classification. The binary between perfection and imperfection assumes that the latter is possible given scientific improvements. The notion of the perfect AM, or that there is movement toward perfection, is underpinned by a number of problematic assumptions about persons, and it ignores the role of AM in the construction of persons.

Given the strong scientific rationality that underpins the contemporary discourse on AM, educational psychologists have a great deal to contribute to the conversation. Coinciding with the massive federal efforts to develop standardized assessment, a great deal of work has gone into developing valid and reliable AM for everyday classroom application. Educational psychologists take a keen interest in AM and work to develop instruments to collect and interpret student data as well as help teachers develop their own instruments. They pursue these objectives by promoting scientifically valid measures of students' development, learning, attitudes, attributes, capacities, emotions, and self.

The merger between science, educational assessment, and educational psychology was the motivation behind the National Academies' Committee on the Foundations of Assessment book titled *Knowing What Students Know: The Science and Design of Educational Assessment*, by Pellegrino et al. (2001). The authors, two of whom, Pellegrino and Glaser, are prominent educational psychologists, set out to rethink and reform educational assessment by highlighting advances in what they called cognitive and measurement sciences. They raised concern that educational assessments may not have reflected advances in these sciences and, therefore, may not accurately represent what students know and can do. Although there are concerns, some of which will be addressed in this chapter, with assumptions about students' cognition and its measurability, these authors, like other researchers and policymakers, believe in the efficacy of science for improving AM on all levels of administration. Given the ubiquity and expectations for AM in everyday classroom application, it is important to understand what these terms mean.

Conceptualization

Despite commonly being discussed jointly, the terms *assessment* and *measurement* connote different things. Assessment can be understood as the appraisal of thinking, behavior, and performance (Sadler, 1989; Palomba & Banta, 1999; Huba & Freed, 2000). Huba and Freed (2000) defined assessment as a process of gathering information from multiple and diverse sources in order to develop an understanding of the target phenomenon, such as student learning, student potential, psychological states, teacher performance, principal effectiveness, and school-wide performance. Assessment does not necessarily have to involve multiple and diverse sources.

However, the authors are speaking to an often-cited concern about the validity of singular assessments in reliably representing target phenomena. For example, standardized tests may not be perceived as the best representation of students' knowledge and capacity, as anxiety, test structure, and arbitrary time constraints can affect performance.

Palomba and Banta (1999) added to the definition of assessment by taking into account function. They described assessment as the systematic collection, review, and use of information for purposes of improving teaching and learning. In fact, Pellegrino et al. (2001) argued that AM should be judged by the extent to which it promotes student learning: "People should gain important and useful information from every assessment situation. In education, as in other professions, good decision making depends on access to relevant, accurate, and timely information. Furthermore, the information gained should be put to good use by informing decisions about curriculum and instruction and ultimately improving student learning" (p. 222). These authors believed that if designed and implemented well, information about students that is accurate, relevant, and timely could be ascertained to inform policies and practices that benefit students' learning. In modern discourse, there is emphasis on the systematic collection of student data. There is a growing practice and expectation for teachers to keep data books on all students that contain performance on assessments administered throughout a particular time period. The purpose of collecting and interpreting information is to support learning by informing interventions, which should also be assessed and altered based on students' performance. Assessments are supposed to enable educators to evaluate whether or not objectives and standards are met.

Given the purported function of everyday classroom assessment, Butler and McMunn (2006) contended, "Assessment is not a thing that is done to students but a process that can lead to improved learning" (p. 2). Rhetorically, this understanding is appealing but there is a great deal about which to be critical. Whether one perceives AM as something that is not done to students, there is good chance that those students do not feel that way. AM may very well be conceptualized as "a thing done to students" for the purpose of improving learning, but nonetheless they are done to students. To rhetorically call it otherwise is an attempt to make AM more palatable and less an instance of violence. Another concern has to do with the improvement of learning. Although an important goal to pursue as teachers, the improvement of learning cannot be understood abstractly. That is, the improvement of learning is specific to the content to be learned, the pace for learning, and the determination that the content has been learned.

The term *measurement* tends to connote quantification using standard units of analysis, such as distance, speed, and volume (Martin & McLellan, 2013). Measuring is collecting information in accordance to a rule or standard. Some measuring devices include rulers, meters, weight scales, and thermometers. A standard device is used to measure something else in relation to that device. Given this understanding, Martin and McLellan (2013) problematized the notion of measurement as applied to students' learning and psychology. They stated, "The vast majority of psychological phenomena having to do with experience, intentional action, mind and selfhood do not lend themselves to being measured in anything like the conventional meanings of *measuring* or *measurement*" (2014, p. 163; emphases in original). They reason that there is no standard metric with which to measure students' thinking. Despite educational psychologists' best efforts to create these standards, Martin and McLellan argued that students' learning and psychology cannot be understood the same way as physical objects. Yet, the authors argued, schooling practices are underpinned by a commitment to measure students buttressed by a belief that instruments are in fact measuring them. Regardless if one entirely rejects the notion of measurement in favor of assessment, the underlying commitment to objectively and scientifically represent students using instruments remains the same.

Types of Assessments and Measurements

AM is nothing new to teachers and teaching. The assessments and measurements used in schools range from informal, everyday observations of students to state standardized tests. Everyday AM includes homework, reports, discussions, and observations to assess and measure students' learning. Organically, these instruments provide information about students' learning, assessments of progress toward objectives, and knowledge regarding areas in need of improvement. There is growing acceptance that students' learning should be represented using multiple instruments and not be reflected in any singular source. Advocates of this multidimensional approach are concerned about the reliability of any one instrument to represent what students know, learned, and are capable of doing (Darling-Hammond, 1994; Pellegrino et al., 2001; Kim & Sunderman, 2005). However, not all compilations of instruments will be appropriate with every student and in every context. Researchers have raised concern about using the same instruments for all students.

Pellegrino et al. (2001) warn of adopting a one-size-fits-all approach to AM. The assumption is that individual learning differences can impact performance on assessments and measurement. The mismatch between students' cognitive processes and the cognitive processes required for the AM may lead to poor performance that is a result of that mismatch. Therefore, teachers must find the combination of AM that is most appropriate for their students. When assessing and measuring students, teachers need to consider three things: instruments to collect information (e.g., exams, journals, and projects), norms for evaluation of that information (e.g., standards or benchmarks), and ways of representing the evaluation (e.g., grades). These considerations may lead teachers to select different types, approaches, and instruments for AM. The following, rather than attempting an exhaustive list of the ways that student performance is assessed and measured, provides a brief overview distinguishing between basic types of AM.

The first major distinction that researchers make is between formal and informal AM. The former connotes data-driven AM, such as quizzes, periodical examinations, long and short answer tests, multiple-choice examinations, observational protocols, monitoring (a running record), and/or an oral examination. Formal assessments typically entail student comparison(s), as well as a normalized or "standardized" tool. Standardized tests are good examples of formal AM. These tests require all students to answer the same questions, in the same manner, and with the same time limit. Scoring is conducted in a standard manner and aggregated to compare students. When a standardized test is administered, it adheres to particular rules and specifications so that the testing conditions and environments are the same for all individuals. Standardized testing is used predominantly to compare a student's knowledge and skills in a particular area to those of other students. Some examples of a standardized test include the SAT, the ACT, Virginia's SOL (Standard of Learning), other state achievement tests, and the NAEP (National Assessment of Educational Progress).

An informal assessment, on the other hand, is not necessarily data driven, but rather content and performance driven. Examples of informal assessments include homework, journals, presentations, debates, and portfolios. Some researchers and policy makers emphasize the value of portfolios, in particular, for representing students' knowledge and capabilities. Portfolios are defined as "a purposeful, integrated collection of student work showing effort, progress or a degree of proficiency" (Butler & McMunn, 2006, p. 66). This type of assessment is multidimensional and ongoing, which are two key features of effective AM. Portfolios allow students to showcase their creations and compositions, as well as provide physical documentation that can serve as evidence of growth and development throughout the learning process. Although portfolios require some type of comparison and standardization, both in composition by students and evaluation by educators, they can include different artifacts, works, and conditions for completion that distinguish this AM from formal ones. In general, informal assessments are standardized in different ways from formal AM.

Another common distinction is between summative and formative assessments, either of which may be formal or informal. Formative assessments are those that are ongoing throughout learning that give a sense of progress toward a learning goal. These assessments are typically not graded and are intended to provide information about students' understanding, as well as ideas about what pedagogical interventions are needed. Teachers and students alike can use this information in order to ensure progress is made toward learning objectives. Examples of formative assessments include logs, journals, projects, quizzes, concept maps, and Venn diagrams. As an example, student logs can provide documentary evidence of events and thought processes related to those events. Logs can show progression of students' thought and reveal gaps, inconsistencies, or misconceptions in their thinking. Summative assessments, on the other hand, are administered at the conclusion of a learning goal in order to evaluate the learning of an objective. These types of assessments include midterms, finals, reports, and presentations. Summative assessments can also be formative if used to guide instruction.

A third category of AM distinguishes between norm-referenced and criterion-referenced. Norm-referenced AM is designed to determine student performance in relation to a group. For example, this type of assessment can determine "high" and "low" achievers. These types of assessments help to categorize and sort students by how well they perform in relation to each other. Criterion-referenced assessments and measurements are those that categorize students in relation to a particular learning objective. Such assessments and measurements are supposed to reveal how well students have learned curricula objectives.

Regardless of type, approach, instrument, or purpose, researchers generally agree that AM must be multidimensional, ongoing, and iterative. Debates persist about which kinds of AM are best to evaluate and represent students' learning. Should teachers rely on formal, summative, and criterion-referenced assessments, such as standardized tests? Or should teachers rely on formal, formative, and norm-referenced assessments, such as portfolios? The debates are essentially about the best way to represent students' learning, capacities, progress, and potential. Of course, educators can use all tools to achieve this purpose. The aim then is to figure out which combination of assessments and measurements can most validly represent students. Achieving this goal is no easy task and well beyond the scope of this chapter. Rather, the focus is on the critical analysis of the ethics and philosophical assumptions that underpin efforts to represent students.

The Ethics of Assessment and Measurement

Schooling is replete with initiatives to improve and implement AM. Some researchers and policy makers contend that such initiatives serve a goal to achieve educational equity (Darling-Hammond, 1994; Pellegrino et al., 2001). The assumption is (1) that knowing what students know, can do, and the qualities of their character can enable educators to contemplate, and change if necessary, pedagogical interventions so that school success can be attained by all; and (2) that AM can provide educators with key academic information related to students' intelligence, noncognitive skills, and cognitive skills. This information is supposed to reveal if students are progressing at a designated pace as determined in relation to a well-defined learning goal. One might argue that without the ability to accurately assess and measure students it would be difficult to design pedagogical interventions to ensure that students are adequately progressing.

Although AM is rhetorically associated with educational equity and students' well-being, contemporary discourse on AM, as suggested, presents several concerns. Critical exploration begins with presenting a different narrative about the purposes of AM. This story centers on the role that AM plays in supporting human capital accumulation, pedagogical control, sorting, accountability, and an ethic of perpetual self-improvement—all of which align with neoliberal thinking. Although part of schooling for decades and not necessarily a product of neoliberalism, AM takes on a particular role and has particular features within a neoliberal context. The analysis then shifts to concerns with validity. The argument in this section is that AM does not necessarily and unequivocally represent students as they naturally and objectively exist but contributes to the formation of them. To engage in a debate about which types of AM are valid or invalid may preserve the idea that students have natural qualities and quantities that can be, but have yet to be, objectively measured. This idea can invite an orientation to improve AM through rigorous scientific methods to justifiably represent students. However, the questioning of validity in this section moves beyond this aim. AM contributes to the formation of persons, not the representation of them.

PURPOSES OF EXAMINATION

An examination of the purposes of AM is not about scientific validity, which is bracketed for this component of the analysis. Rather, an alternative narrative of AM is presented that rereads the purposes of contemporary AM, and not just for standardized assessments within a neoliberal context. It has been well argued that standardized assessments serve a neoliberal agenda (Broom, 2007; Hursh, 2007; Mathison, 2009). However, neoliberal thinking can be connected to a broad range of AM, not just standardized tests. As Brown (2003) argued, neoliberalism brought metrics to all spheres of public and private life in order to serve a particular agenda. Neoliberalism is associated with the belief that anything that has value for the economy is worth assessing and measuring. That which has value for the economy shapes policy and practices regarding student outcomes. Within such a context, the purpose of AM is to identify, measure, and cultivate knowledge, skills, and dispositions that have value. Regardless if it is associated with equity or with economic instrumentalism, this purpose is underpinned by the imperative of control, which comes in the form of identification, categorization, and reformation. AM can be used to mark those who have those qualities and quantities of value and who, therefore, should have access to certain opportunities. In other words, AM serves a sorting function by ascribing qualities and quantities to students that have particular economic value.

Assessments and measurements are shaped and informed by the pursuit of certain outcomes. People have ideas about what students should be, know, and be able to do. Thoughout history, these outcomes have changed. Contemporary discourse includes emphases on higher order thinking (HOT) and noncognitive skills (NCS), which are key features of the twenty-first-century worker (Gewertz, 2008; Silva, 2009). Thus, AM will ostensibly measure students' HOT and NCS as well as teachers' effectiveness for fostering these so-called skills. Teachers and policy makers assume an authoritative role in categorizing, measuring, and marking students in accordance with these outcomes. While not thought about rhetorically as something that is done to students, AM is largely implemented unilaterally from an authority figure to students. However, in a neoliberal context, AM also involves students' internalizing the imperative to assess and measure themselves. Given the neoliberal value of the self-management of human capital accumulation, students must learn to internalize the representations of AM as well as to self-administer them in order to evaluate choices, academic progress, accumulation of credentials, and marketability. This requirement and expectation is couched in terms of self-improvement and the realization of potential. Students must learn to use AM themselves and interpret data to make strategic choices that are going to support the maximization of their value and competitiveness in the economy. The neoliberal narrative of AM centers on value, control, sorting, perpetual improvement, and accountability.

IS IT WORTH MEASURING?

Although the author does not endorse this statement, Mathison (2008) noted, "There is a predominant view that we truly know something is valuable when it can be objectively measured and statistically manipulated" (p. 534). Here Mathison speaks to a relationship in which value is ascribed to that which can be objectively measured. Not only is something given value when it can be objectively measured, when something has value, it will be subject to objective measurement. Either way, in contemporary education discourse, objectivity and value are the standards against which schooling policies and practices are determined and judged. If something does not have value, which means supporting the improvement of schooling goals, it is not worth assessing and measuring. If something cannot be assessed or measured objectively, then it is not worth considering for educational policy and practice. Although researchers and policy makers may not always explicitly state this belief, this type of thinking informs the modern discourse.

Researchers and policy makers seem to care most about that which can be assessed and measured, and the degree to which AM can be used to facilitate the achievement of specific academic goals. This commitment is clearly seen in the growing interest in noncognitive skills (NCS) as a composite of beliefs, character traits, values, aspirations, mind-set, and personality that are associated with academic success. Typically included in NCS are grit, zeal, optimism, self-control, and dependability (Duckworth & Yeager, 2015). NCS are identified as a key feature of human capital that various stakeholders argue predict school performance and success within modern work environments (Pinquart, Juang, & Silbereisen, 2003; Hoy, Tarter, & Hoy, 2006; Duckworth & Yeager, 2015). For that reason, a great deal of discourse has centered on the most valid and reliable ways to assess and measure NCS (Pintrich, 2004; Duckworth & Quinn, 2009; Duckworth & Yeager, 2015). The ostensible economic importance of NCS has now prompted researchers and policy makers to care about objectively measuring these features of students and teachers' efficacy for cultivating them.

The National Assessment of Educational Progress (NAEP), which is a federal center charged with gathering data on what students know and can do, is working on developing metrics for NCS, such as grit. The assumption is that AM can serve students' interests by helping identify those who have and do not have the qualities and quantities of NCS that are associated with academic success and twenty-first-century competence. Those who have the right qualities and quantities of NCS can be identified as suitable for certain opportunities and those who do not can be identified for interventions to develop them. If NCS predict success in and outside of school, then assessing and measuring these skills for the purpose of cultivating them can support the leveling of the playing field by targeting those who lack this type of human capital. Given the overstatement of control that teachers have on shaping all aspects of students, measuring teachers' efficacy for cultivating NCS is also part of this discussion.

It may seem as though the attention to NCS is driven by liberal-democratic values for understanding and teaching the whole child (Elias, 2009). The thinking is that students are more than their performance on cognitive tasks. However, it stands to reason that if this particular conception of the whole child were not associated with academic achievement as it is contemporarily constructed, or with economic instrumentalism, it is doubtful that researchers and policy makers would give the same priority to objectively assessing and measuring students' NCS. In a neoliberal climate, it is difficult to advocate and push for policies and practices that do not serve an economic goal. It seems that many policy makers and researchers care most about what can be objectively measured and what has value for achieving state-mandated goals, which are informed by neoliberalism.

Although a number of methodological, conceptual, philosophical, and pedagogical complexities surround the measurement of NCS, the purpose of discussing this subject here is to point to the ideological underpinnings of the initiative. Similar underpinnings are discernable in the discourse of higher order thinking (HOT). The motivation to assess and measure creativity, problem solving, and critical thinking is driven in part by what has value for the twenty-first century economy, as depicted by business leaders. So rather than asking if NCS and HOT, as examples, can be validly measured and if they are predictable of academic success, though these are essential questions, critical inquiry is guided by an examination of why certain knowledge, skills, and dispositions are the subject of AM. This inquiry can be applied to all that is assessed and measured in schooling. It is important to reflect on and create a multidimensional narrative about why certain things are assessed and measured in contemporary discourse.

Uses in Control and Authority

AM is about control. This purpose is usually not explicitly acknowledged because control has negative connotations, especially in a cultural context that celebrates individual freedom, free will, autonomy, and self-governance.

However, all types of AM are about control; they are about representing qualities and quantities of students' knowledge, potential, and skills at a particular moment for the purposes of using that information to structure pedagogical interventions to achieve a particular outcome. AM is necessary for ensuring students are learning what they are supposed to at the acceptable pace. Interventions can be implemented for those students who deviate from norms and expectations. AM is about representing qualities and quantities of students in order to guide change toward a particular endpoint. Duckworth and Yeager (2015) contended that "intentionally changing something is dramatically easier when one can quantify with precision how much or how little of it there is" (p. 237). Although the authors emphasize the quantification of students, this thinking informs all initiatives to assess and measure, including qualitative instruments. Regardless of the method, AM is supposed to guide pedagogical interventions in order to intentionally foster particular changes in students. Although there is debate about what methods generate the most "accurate" information, students are rendered calculable and knowable for the purposes of evaluation, judgment, and discipline.

One might reason this control is for students' own good. For example, if NCS predict academic outcomes and are necessary for twenty-first-century employment, then implementing interventions to ensure students develop the targeted quantities and qualities of NCS is necessary to support academic performance and employability. Although NCS are not new considerations for teachers, the association with academic achievement and twenty-first-century employment contributes to the institutionalization of these so-called skills. From this association, assessing and measuring NCS can ensure that teachers are fostering students' human capital accumulation.

The attention to NCS in contemporary policy discussions has generated moral, philosophical, psychological, and psychometric questions, such as (1) what are the right quantities and qualities of NCS; (2) what is the most valid way to assess and measure NCS; (3) should the goal of AM be to support one's place in the economy; and (4) what does academic success look like and how do NCS help realize that vision? Defining these skills and measuring them is no simple task. However, any resolution of the argument does little to alter the legislative function of AM. Whether measuring intelligence, NCS, cognitive skills, self-esteem, or personality, the psychological measurement of students is about rendering them knowable and calculable for the purposes of achieving a particular objective, which for NCS has its roots in neoliberal ideology.

Given this purpose and function of AM, Mathison (2009) used the phrase "Evaluator as Technician" to describe the contemporary role of those who create and implement AM. She argued that this role aligns with neoliberal governance, which is carried out by experts of the human soul. Mathison stated, "Educational evaluators become technicians in this [neoliberal] environment, carrying out the tasks associated with managing, administering, and reporting student assessment data" (2009, p. 531). Regardless if AM is created by private companies and sanctioned by the federal government or if AM is local, the emphasis on collecting student data positions educators as experts on the marking and ascribing of properties to students. Such marking is about calculating students and informing interventions so that institutional goals can be achieved.

AM has functioned this way for decades. As Rose (1999) argued, psychometrics were important instruments for governance in the early 1900s, with intelligence tests as a prominent tool. Psychometrics are tools for calibrating students' learning, thinking, emotions, attitudes, aspirations, and relationships. Institutions, such as schools and hospitals, gathered people and rendered them visible for the purpose of eliminating certain habits, propensities, aptitudes, and morals while inculcating others. He called the formal and systematic calibration of individuals a regime of visibility. The goal was to make all facets of students known through measurements of psychological qualities and quantities, which are evaluated against a continuum of normalcy. One's placement on this continuum provides a rationale and justification for intervention and discipline.

By highlighting this function of AM, Rose (1999) was not engaging in an argument about the reliability and validity of psychometrics. Rather, Rose was concerned with the role that psychological measurement played in marking persons' differences along a normalized continuum. Furthermore, he pointed out that this marking was necessary to sort individuals and implement interventions for those whose performance did not reflect a norm. Regardless if viewed as positive or negative, the regime of visibility is intended to know persons in all their minute particulars in order to identify those who embodied normalized values and those who needed reformation. Rose argued that psychometrics functioned this way in order to render people manageable by maximizing their utility and minimizing dangers associated with their difference: "With psychometrics, psychology had begun to establish its claim as the appropriate authority to adjudicate upon the lives of individuals, to administer them in such a way that would maximize their social utility and minimize the social danger their difference might represent. . . . Psychometrics rendered the intellect manageable (1999, p. 144)." The fact that AM is explicitly justified as helping to support students' adaptation to twenty-first-century economic environments, as well as adaptation to school demands, is a testament to the persistence of this function.

Use in Sorting and Meritocracy

Although it is not always their explicit purpose, schools operate as sorting machines that mark and brand students with credentials and qualifications. Schools are supposed to operate as meritocracies, and one's performance in school is to signify the potential to fill certain societal functions. The hope is that all students have an opportunity to develop the knowledge, skills, and dispositions to fill any rung on the socioeconomic hierarchy. AM provides the knowledge of who has what skills for what position. In this regard, AM provides the justification for denying and granting opportunity. Sacks (1997) made this point in relation to standardized test scores: "Test scores have told the gatekeepers of American's meritocracy—educators, academic institutions, and employers—that one student is bright, the other is not bright, that one is worthy academically, the other less so. Some, with luck, are able to overcome the stigma of poor performance on mental tests. But others will not. Indeed, not only is it a stigma, but one that is largely unrecognized in our culture. Meritocracy's gatekeepers brand those who score poorly on standardized tests as somehow deficient, incapable" (p. 25). Sacks made this point to problematize the effects that standardized tests have on the social reproduction of class status. He pointed out that there is a correlation between socioeconomic class and standardized test performance. The higher one's class status, the higher his or her performance on standardized tests. If standardized measures serve as a tool for sorting—those who do well get access and opportunities to obtain more and more credentials—then students from economically disadvantaged backgrounds may have limited opportunities.

Although AM in the classroom is becoming more diverse and multiple, potentially giving students more opportunities to "validly" display their knowledge and skills, AM is still implicated in sorting and the (re)production of a hierarchy. Developing AM that appears valid may not help to mitigate inequality but serve as a strong basis for justifying it. If assessments and measurements are deemed scientifically valid—meaning they accurately represent students—and they measure competencies for certain opportunities, then those who are marked as capable, intelligent, dependable, and gritty will deservedly get access to those opportunities. Thus AM is used for ranking, comparing, credentialing, and justifying access to opportunity. Although this dimension of AM is problematic, Pellegrino et al. (2001) argued that this function actually determines the quality of AM, which may not necessarily be a problem if one assumes that (1) assessments and measurements are valid; (2) all students have equal opportunity to perform well on assessments and measurements; (3) performance on assessments and measurements is used to inform pedagogical interventions; (4) interventions are effective; and (5) assessments and measurements accurately measure effectiveness of the interventions. Contradictions with any of these assumptions may contribute to unfairly ranking and sorting students.

When evaluating the validity of AM for sorting, it becomes crucial to consider the justifications provided, as well as the various historical and political underpinnings that guide and shape which outcomes to pursue, assess, and measure. In contemporary discourse, educational researchers and policy makers cite business leaders when advocating for what academic outcomes to pursue (Robinson, 2013; Stiggins, 1995). For that reason, student outcomes are being shaped by representations of the twenty-first-century worker, for which AM is being developed and implemented to determine which students best embody the features of this worker. AM is inextricably tied to predetermined norms and expected outcomes, which are determined and legitimized by the interests of corporate and state initiatives to maintain and manage the production of human capital (Bonal, 2003). Those who can show that they embody ideals of the twenty-first-century worker can be sorted accordingly.

Accountability

Accountability is a notion that appears a great deal in education discourse, especially in relation to AM. Rhetorically, the goal of accountability is to improve the quality of schooling outcomes. For ideological reasons, accountability falls heavily on teachers and principals, and certainly to a lesser degree reaches school superintendents, parents, teachers, university teacher preparation programs, and state and federal legislators. Although the notion of accountability is highly controversial, Mathison (2012) argued that accountability by itself is not a problem. However, when teachers are rendered accountable for students' outcomes, a particular narrative is reproduced about inequality.

This narrative locates inequality in the choices and efforts people make, not the systemic inequalities inherent in income distribution, access to opportunity, and structural barriers. In this narrative, schools are a meritocracy and teachers can control students' outcomes to ensure they develop the human capital to compete for any social and economic position. Failure to create a level playing field is the culpability of teachers. Holding teachers accountable not only conceals the way power operates but can serve as a justification for dismantling teachers' unions, which are charged with protecting "bad teachers." In neoliberal discourse, unions are viewed as hindrances of the free market and as targets for destruction. Branding teachers as good or bad and schools as succeeding or failing is made possible only by AM.

The notion of accountability has become a normalized part of education conversations. Yet its conceptualization can vary. Wagner (2013) explored the meaning of this notion by pointing to its root word, which is "account." In its verb form, account can mean to explain and rationalize activity. It is not any particular activity that needs rationalization. In schooling, the activity that must be rationalized is that which supports the achievement of top-down schooling goals. This rationalization, however, does not come from teachers but from AM that are administered by others. These AM can be in the form of teaching evaluation protocols and students' standardized assessments. These AM stand as rationalizations and justifications of teaching activity. Teachers' performance in relation to evaluative protocols and students' test performance stand as their accounting, as the justification, rationalization, and testament to pedagogical activity.

In this regard, it is possible to see how AM serves a neoliberal form of governance. Mathison (2009) argued that neoliberal governance is not freedom and liberation from government, but tighter control by states and corporations, stating, "It is important to understand that neoliberalism defines a role for government—it is not an ideology that rejects governmental intervention. Whereas classical liberalism simply rejects the state, neoliberalism accepts and fosters a role for the state. Corporate CEOs, politicians, and bureaucrats work together to promote and sustain the ideology's core values" (p. 530). It has been well argued, and I argue throughout this book, that neoliberal values are embedded in and inform curricula and policy. Accountability is to ensure that teachers are helping to achieve neoliberal-informed objectives and propagate neoliberal values. Rendering teachers accountable for students' NCS development and HOT are examples of this effort. Accountability measures are used to ensure that teachers orient their activity to support specific curricular objectives, which tend to be underpinned by neoliberal values. AM is used to hold teachers accountable to neoliberal standards. This accountability is about the legislation of teaching and the justification for firing teachers and closing schools that are deemed as failing to meet standards.

An Ethic of Perpetual Self-Improvement

The rhetorical conceptualization of assessment being not as something that is done to students but as a process that can lead to improved learning frames AM as innocuous. But when evaluator technicians use tools and instruments to assess and measure students, even when it is rationalized as improving learning, it is something that is done to students. Those with institutional authority use tools, which can be created by other authorities that students are required to engage with. Performance is interpreted as and stands as a representation of students. The evaluations that occur in schooling can be significant markers of identity as schools are places of authority for calculating and disciplining persons. This process can be subjugating and involves imposing control on students, even when it is administered with a moral purpose for improvement.

One ostensible way to circumvent the operation of this type of power is to shift the responsibility of AM to students. Rather than teachers administering assessments and measurements, students can learn to administer them without an immediate external prompt. The goal is to help students develop the self-regulatory knowledge and skills to guide their own AM, and ultimately steer their own reformation. This pedagogical goal is also foundational to neoliberalism, which is underpinned by a radically responsibilized subject (Davies & Bansel, 2007; Hursh, 2007). The neoliberal subject assumes responsibility for life outcomes and is an autonomous entrepreneur charged with seeing to personal development, which means human capital accumulation and marketability. When translated into an educational space, this means that students are responsible for their learning outcomes by virtue of their choices. However, to make good choices that optimize human capital accumulation and improve marketability, students must set particular goals and strategically manage their lives to achieve those goals. This ethic requires perpetual and iterative monitoring, evaluation, and adjustment.

Martin (2004) used the notion of the scientific self to capture contemporary values for this brand of selfhood. The scientific self captures an orientation to oneself as knowable and manageable through systematic evaluation and calculation. The better individuals assess and measure features of selfhood, the more they can influence their choices and life outcomes to produce the effects they want. This commitment is reminiscent of the maxim "know thyself." In neoliberal discourse, this ethical commitment involves the self-administration of AM in order to make oneself calculable and manageable. This goal itself is tied to neoliberal governance, but when considering the expected outcomes of self-management, the neoliberal connection gets stronger. Students are expected to manage themselves to pursue perpetual improvement so that they can maximize their value and be efficient and productive. Thus AM has the same function whether it is self-administered or administered by others. While the self-administration of AM might produce the perception of autonomy, it nonetheless requires a commitment to neoliberal selfhood.

Up to this point, the critical analysis of this chapter has centered on a different narrative of the purpose and function of AM, one that is entangled in economic value, control, sorting and credentialing, supporting an ethic of self-improvement, and justifying and rationalizing accountability. It is reasonable to wonder whether if used for a different purpose AM could serve alternative ideologies. Perhaps one might conclude that AM is not inherently neoliberal but rather its function and use renders it as such. If AM were not high stakes, used to sort students, used to discipline students' differences in accordance with institutional norms, instrumentally tied to economic reasoning, or centered on perpetual self-improvement, then maybe it could be disentangled from neoliberalism. This disentanglement must be considered possible, as critical inquiry is underpinned by hope and optimism for resisting oppressive ideologies. However, one must be careful not to assume that AM unequivocally supports or resists a particular ideology.

ONTOLOGY AND PSYCHOLOGICAL MEASUREMENT
Constructing Students

A different critical angle of AM involves a consideration of ontology, or the study of the nature of being, existence, and reality. The ontological question is, when AM is administered, do the results represent a phenomenon that already exists? This question captures an ongoing debate about the origination and objectivity of psychological phenomena. AM includes a range of techniques of representation that are intended to signify qualities, capabilities, and potentials of persons that exist at a particular moment. The underlying assumption is that persons have inner worlds that can be known using valid and reliable measurements. This view is underpinned by the efficacy of science to reveal the qualities and quantities of persons. Those who endorse this view may recognize that assessments and measurements are imperfect, but that does not discount the existence of an inner natural psychological world that merely requires the right instruments to represent it. From this side of the issue, progress means developing scientific instruments that unequivocally and objectively represent that internal life, which some might believe exists prior to any tool or instrument to assess and measure it.

Take, for example, the notion of self-regulated learning (SRL). This notion emerged as a formal object of study in the late 1970s and early 1980s. From a review of the educational psychology literature, Martin (2004) showed that prior to SRL, notions such as self-management and self-control were used to capture psychological phenomena that resembled SRL. Although SRL has conceptual overlaps with related terms, SRL signifies different psychological qualities and processes that are not as widely used in contemporary discourse as they were prior to the 1980s. One way to interpret these changes is that researchers are improving their conceptual tools and instruments to objectively represent and measure psychological phenomenon. The corollary assumption is that persons have always been self-regulated, but researchers did not have the concepts or instruments to recognize and measure it. This line of thinking can be applied to all psychological phenomena such as NCS, self-efficacy, development, and attention. For any attention deficit disorder, one might conclude that researchers are just now developing the tools to recognize, diagnose, and reform attention. The ontological assumption is that deficiencies in persons have been present throughout time, just not recognizable and measurable as such.

Critical theorists tend to question this ontological position (e.g., Danziger, 1990; Hacking, 2002; Sugarman, 2009). Rather than view psychological phenomena as a priori, a critical perspective is informed by the assumption that concepts, instruments, styles of reasoning, cultural norms, politics, and ideology are implicated in giving form to psychological phenomena. Danziger (1990) captured this view when he noted that psychology "deals in test scores, rating scales, response distributions, serial lists, and innumerable other items that the investigator does not just find but constructs with great care. Whatever guesses are made about the natural world are totally constrained by this world of artifacts. The same holds true for the immediate human sources of the psychologist's information. The psychologist's interaction with such sources takes place within a well-regulated social role system. . . . In talking about a field of scientific psychology we are talking about a domain of constructions" (p. 2). This theorist is not necessarily endorsing the view that psychological phenomena do not exist. His comment that artifacts constrain guesses about the natural world (i.e., psychological characteristics of persons independent of their naming and classification) reifies a distinction between a natural and constructed world. Although some critical theorists may go further to question the existence of a natural world, they agree, nonetheless, that the tools and instruments used in relation to persons occur within a context that shapes possibilities for making sense of persons.

This position reflects a commitment to historical ontology, which is typically featured in critical educational psychology theorizing (Burman, 2008; Sugarman, 2009). Either for one's research or for assessing and measuring students in the classroom, the context and tools used to investigate phenomena give form to those phenomena. This formation happens in a historical moment, in relation to persons, and relying on particular instruments, categories, descriptions, and norms. From a historical ontological view, assessments and measurements are not tools to discover what is firmly within a student, but tools that give form to phenomena and contribute to the making of students as particular types of beings. For this reason, assessments and measurements are both constructive and destructive, leading to (re)organization and inscription of selfhood. Identity, meaning, and purpose are forged in relationship to AM. For this reason, Stobart (2008) described assessment as a value-laden social activity that does not objectively measure what exists but rather creates and shapes what is measured.

It is important to understand that conceptualizing AM as constructive is not about the validity of representation. This way of thinking is not about progressing toward a more accurate and truthful representation of students. Rather, this perspective is about understanding how it is possible to form such representations. The major assumption is that any type of AM, whether implemented by teachers, researchers, or students themselves, is not measuring phenomena that are already present but giving form to them. Available concepts, instruments, cultural norms, politics, and ideology shape this formation.

Direct and Indirect Measurements

Another ontological concern with AM in schooling can be understood by considering Lindquist's (1951) distinction between direct and indirect measurements. He defined the former as the measurement of a behavior series that is directly related to an educational objective. Lindquist gave an example for high school social studies. If the goal was to predispose students to vote in elections, he argued that a "perfectly valid" measure of the effectiveness of instruction to foster this predisposition requires a tabulation of the number of times individuals had opportunities to vote in elections and the number of times they took advantage of those opportunities. In another example, if students are instructed in regard to sight words, Lindquist (1951) might argue that a perfectly valid measurement would be children's ability to identify those words in all situations in which they encountered them. However, identifying sight words within a well-structured situation is still only a measure of a student's ability to recognize these words in a well-structured situation. Although one can objectively represent performance on these types of assessments, they may not reveal much about students' reading ability and potential.

Indirect measurements are based on behaviors that are not part of, but that presumably relate to, an educational objective, criterion, or standard.

For example, to measure high school students' predisposition to vote in elections as adults, an indirect measurement involves observations of those students' propensity to vote in school elections. For these measurements, the behavior and the outcome associated with the assessment are believed to indicate something that was not immediately measured. Lindquist argued that educational measurement seldom involves direct measurements and mostly involves indirect ones. Lindquist argued, however, that the only perfectly valid measures of students' dispositions, knowledge, and skills require direct measurement. That is, they require one to observe students in any and all situations in which the intended learning objective can be observed in students' behavior. Of course, these types of AM are not feasible. Therefore, numbers, quantities, and categories are used to stand as representations of students that ostensibly indicate the likelihood that certain learned behaviors will be performed when in a particular situation.

An example of this issue relates to the AM of creativity. Business leaders and politicians explain the importance of fostering creativity because the twenty-first-century environment requires people to be innovative and entrepreneurial. Assessments and measurements of creativity are supposed to indicate students' capacity for being innovative and entrepreneurial. However, these measures merely stand as indirect indicators of this capacity. There is no way of directly measuring the potential for creativity in twenty-first-century work environments, unless one assesses and measures students in all situations in which they are expected to engage creatively. Herein lies a key point. In any AM, a certain number or qualitative analysis stands as a representation of students that is intended to signify their qualities, potentials, capacities, and propensities. However, if scientific objectivity is the goal standard, then school assessments and measurements cannot unequivocally stand as depictions of what students learned, can do, or will do outside of the classroom.

Conclusion

In his 1996 book *The Mismeasure of Man*, Stephen Jay Gould discussed the now debunked practice of craniometry, or the representations of persons' intelligence based on cranial measurements. It is easy to look back in history and recognize the problems with this type of measurement, what it signified, and how it was used to justify racial and social hierarchy. It is challenging to look at contemporary AM, those instances accepted as objectively and validly representing students, in order to discern the cultural, political, and ideological norms that underpin them. Although it seems progress has been made with developing AM to represent students validly, Gould invited his readers to reflect on the assumptions, beliefs, and practices on which all assessments and measurements rest. Further, critical psychologists have argued that we should explore not the underpinnings of AM, but also how assessments and measurements contribute to constructing the phenomenon that it is intended to objectively measure. In other words, the phenomena that assessments and measurements are intended to measure are a result of the interaction between the person being assessed and the instrument, research context, and analysis. A shift in any of these factors can change how persons are constructed. If AM is treated as depicting students as they objectively are, then the risk of constructing them in normative ways that are driven by particular ideological and political purposes is ever present.

Conclusion

IDEAS ABOUT STUDENT LEARNING and development implicitly and explicitly inform teaching, policy, and curriculum. The argument about how and why students think the ways they do, what they are and what they are supposed to be, how they change, and what teachers can do to facilitate that change is a highly contested discourse that is complicated by ideological, philosophical, cultural, and political contexts. Yet teachers are expected to know, understand, and apply either singular or composite sets of theories of learning and development in their classrooms without a consideration of these underlying contexts. This expectation manifests in the teaching of educational psychology to teachers in a variety of ways. To be certified, it is not uncommon for teachers to be required to (1) articulate a philosophy of learning and development; (2) demonstrate knowledge of educational psychology on licensure exams; and (3) demonstrate an ability to apply educational psychology to the analysis of classroom artifacts. Teachers are implicitly and explicitly promised that mastering educational psychology can support efforts to carefully and strategically structure classrooms to achieve teaching goals. For that reason, educational psychology texts tend to be declarative and prescriptive. They introduce concepts, theories, and imperatives related to learning that are coupled with suggestions for classroom application. The underlying assumption is that if applied well, educational psychology can be used to achieve teaching goals while supporting student well-being.

The discussions in this book have addressed prominent topics in the dominant discourse of education psychology for teaching. Review of the topics provides evidence of the concepts that are valued in education while also setting the context for critique. The analyses offered here, unlike those in conventional educational psychology texts, are not intended to provide a clear set of directions for how to use psychology most effectively in the classroom. Nor is the critique intended to dismiss the place of educational psychology in teaching, though, as noted, some critical theorists have argued as much. Rather, it is intended to bring to the forefront critical analyses of the theories, principles, concepts, and models that teachers are likely to be confronted within their professional lives. This commitment is called critical educational psychology, which involves operating within the traditional boundaries of educational psychology but with attention to the ways philosophy, ideology, culture, and politics complicate the field.

In presenting a different narrative of educational psychology in this book, perceptions about the efficacy of the field to support teaching and learning via scientific investigation have been replaced with questions about the assumptions and implications of applying educational psychology to teaching. The foundational commitment of this narrative is that educational psychology cannot operate under the cloak of scientific objectivity. Failing to consider this critical narrative encourages faith in psychological knowledge to objectively represent students, learning, development, and teaching. As a consequence, ideas, principles, imperatives, and theories are applied as objective representations. However, as the analyses in this book reveal, an awareness of the political, historical, cultural, and ideological features that are foundational to educational psychology can help teachers make ethical decisions about their application of psychology in the classroom.

Given the mainstream and dominant application of psychology to limit, constrain, normalize, and pathologize, the critical project in psychology is to work within the field to illuminate these effects, which could either lead one to reject the knowledge of the field or apply it a way that is more palatable, ethical, and just. In order to get to this ethical place, there must be an understanding of where educational psychology ideas came from, why certain ideas are believed to be true, and the consequences of applying those ideas. Considering these possibilities can support teachers' ethical decision-making surrounding the application of educational psychology knowledge.

This work has argued that educational psychology discourse is entangled in neoliberal ideology. We have seen how the rise, acceptance, and conceptualization of the notion of higher order thinking is linked to the production of twenty-first-century workers, and how Vygotsky's developmental theory can be interpreted and employed to support competition and perpetual self-improvement. Assessment and measurement are used for visions of accountability and sorting that serve a neoliberal agenda. The phenomenon of teaching as management entails remnants of Taylor's efforts—described in the chapter on classroom management—to efficiently and effectively mobilize human resources to maximize worker productivity.

Beyond the identification of a neoliberal influences, each of the topics discussed includes specific philosophical, cultural, and political under-pinnings. Narratives of development are cultural and do not reflect universal frameworks for change. Knowing students can be tied to rendering them amenable and adaptable to institutional settings. Teaching the "whole child" means ensuring that no aspect of the child remains untouched by institutional power. The whole child is also used to endorse the importance of teaching and learning grit, which is identified as a discourse that aligns with problematic views of schooling and sources of inequality. A modern view of attention is embedded in philosophical shifts in how subjectivity and experience are understood. Certain classroom management approaches can be specifically tied to the militarization of schooling for African-American students. The analyses illuminate ways that the discourse of educational psychology is inseparable from culture, politics, ideology, and philosophy. Telling this narrative is not about rejecting the discourse in hopes to find better and more objective representations of students, learning, teaching, and development. Rather, the starting position of critical educational psychology is that all knowledge is embedded in some context.

The tendency to ignore these contexts is understandable, as numerous concepts, imperatives, and principles of educational psychology are seductive because they may align with specific teaching philosophies. Developmentally appropriate practice, higher order thinking, knowing students, teaching the whole child, noncognitive skills, managing the classroom, optimizing attention, motivating students, and accurately assessing learning are arguably all ideas that underpin good teaching. Teachers, policy makers, researchers, and parents are unlikely to endorse not knowing students, fragmenting and isolating them, focusing only on cognitive skills, only teaching lower order thinking, promoting chaos, optimizing distraction, and inaccurately assessing students. Yet as has been demonstrated the seemingly better options are grounded in semantics and practice that are in no way neutral, value-free, and unequivocally beneficial to teaching.

Thus the caution to avoid binary thinking. Recall several binaries that have featured implicitly and explicitly in this book: knowing students/not knowing students, developmentally appropriate/developmentally inappropriate, lower order thinking/higher order thinking, managing students/permitting chaos, cognitive skills/noncognitive skills, objective assessments/subjective assessments, and whole child/fragmented child. Despite the limits of binary thinking, at times it can be a helpful starting point for recognizing alternative views. However, if binary thinking is to govern psychological commitments in teaching, then it would make sense to adopt, endorse, and unequivocally value certain concepts and imperatives. If choices for psychological commitments were limited to only two options, then it would make sense to adopt without question the imperatives and concepts that are critiqued in this book. However, concern for identifying alternatives should not be the impetus to accept certain truths and practices.

So the critical analyses offered here have been intended to discourage a commitment to binary thinking, however natural such thinking might seem to be. Binary thinking limits the possibilities for constructing students by situating them on a spectrum. Exemplary representations inform opposite sides of the spectrum, while others are evaluated in terms of their proximity to those points. The phenomenon and instruments used to situate students and ascribe value to them are concerning. Higher order thinking provides a great example. Now that self-regulation, creativity, critical thinking, and problem solving are becoming institutionalized, assessments and measurements are used to locate students relative to exemplars on opposite sides of the spectrum. Students are thought about in terms of their qualities of higher order thinking. With evaluations of self-regulated learning students can be branded as either exemplary or poor self-regulated learners. Trying to locate students on this spectrum validates, normalizes, and reifies self-regulated learning as an identity marker, as a quality of students. The analyses throughout this book have shown that such practices contribute to constituting students' in specific ways that have negative cultural and ideological underpinnings.

A foundational commitment for critical educational psychology is not to engage in binary polemics of objectivity/subjectivity, real/socially constructed phenomena, whole/partial child, grit/giving up, self-regulated/dependent, creative/uncreative, and knowing/not knowing students. Engaging in these polemics merely reifies the existence of psychological categories, imperatives, and concepts. This danger was alluded to in a few chapters but was made explicit in the chapter on attention. Rather than engage in an argument about whether or not attention deficits exist, critical analysis is about exploring what made it possible to construct the distinction between those who were deficient and those who were not. This construction of attention deficits was made possible because of a new way of conceptualizing human subjectivity that emerged in a particular historical moment. However, engaging in a polemic about whether or not deficits exist can lead to the acceptance that attention is a specific process and capacity that can be identified as acceptable or defective.

The argument that attention deficits are socially constructed reifies the existence of attention as a distinct cognitive process that is ascribed value within an institutional setting. If one changes the institutional setting, then perhaps deficiencies might not exist. While this ethical commitment has merit, attention is reified as a cognitive process and mechanism. However, a sociohistorical perspective helps to show that the underlying view of attention in contemporary debates about deficits came into existence in relation to specific economic, technological, scientific, and administrative contexts. Critical analysis can help to denaturalize, problematize, and rethink ideas about persons. Such analyses are not just intended to problematize the understanding of, or narrative surrounding, certain concepts but to make problematic the concepts themselves. For example, critiquing narratives of development is important, but it is also important to critique the idea of framing students as developmental beings. Critical educational psychology helps to invite such possibilities.

To adequately support a critical agenda requires (1) recognition that educational psychology is bound to a specific set of beliefs and assumptions that are culturally, historically, and philosophically bound; (2) critical interrogation of these assumptions; (3) conversations about power and opportunity; and (4) explorations of potential consequences related to the discourse of educational psychology. Given the place of educational psychology in teaching, as well as the presence of psychology-based interventions and reforms in schooling, critical analyses are essential and must extend beyond the topics and critical angles explored in this book, which is a starting point.

REFERENCES

Agostinone-Wilson, F. (2006). Downsized discourse: Classroom management, neoliberalism, and the shaping of correct workplace attitude. *Journal for Critical Education Policy Studies*, 4. http://doi.org/Retrieved from http://www.jceps.com/archives/523

Alderman, M. K. (2013). *Motivation for achievement: Possibilities for teaching and learning*. New York, NY: Routledge.

Amabile, T., & Kramer, S. (2011). *The progress principle: Using small wins to ignite joy, engagement, and creativity at work*. Boston, MA: Harvard Business School Press.

Amsel, E. (2015). Conceptual and pedagogical challenges in understanding the whole person. *New Ideas in Psychology*, *38*, 1–3.

Ananiadou, K., & Claro, M. (2009). *21st century skills and competences for new millennium learners in OECD countries*. Organisation for Economic Co-operation and Development. Retrieved from www.oecd.org/

Anderson, J. (1974). Retrieval of propositional information from long-term memory. *Cognitive Psychology*, *6*, 451–474.

Anderson, J. R., & Reder, L. M. (1999). The fan effect: New results and new theories. *Journal of Experimental Psychology*, *128*, 186–197.

Anderson, M. L. (2003). Embodied Cognition: A field guide. *Artificial Intelligence*, *149*, 90–130. http://doi.org/doi:10.1016/S0004-3702(03)00054-7

Apple, M. (2002). Does education have independent power? Bernstein and the question of relative autonomy. *British Journal of Sociology of Education*, *23*, 607–616. http://doi.org/10.1080/0142569022000038459

———. (2004). *Ideology and curriculum* (3rd ed.). New York, NY: Routledge Falmer.

———. (2006). Understanding and interrupting neoliberalism and neoconservatism in education. *Pedagogies*, *1*, 21–26. http://doi.org/10.1207/s15544818pedo101_4

Arfken, M. (2014). Creativity. In T. Teo (Ed.), *Encyclopedia of critical psychology*. New York, NY: Springer-Verlag.

Arum, R., Ford, K., & Beattie, I. (2014). *The structure of schooling: Readings in the sociology of education*. Los Angeles, CA: Sage.

Ashton, H., Gallagher, P., & Moore, B. (2006). The adult psychiatrist's dilemma: Psychostimulant use in attention deficit/hyperactivity disorder. *Journal of Psychopharmacology*, *20*, 602–610. http://doi.org/10.1177/0269881106061710

Atkinson, J. W. (1964). *An introduction to motivation*. Oxford, UK: Van Nostrand.

Atkinson, R. C., & Shiffrin, R. M. (1968). Human memory: A proposed system and its control processes. In K. W. Spence & J. T. Spence (Eds.), *The psychology of learning and motivation: Advances in research and theory* (Vol. 2, pp. 89–195). New York, NY: Academic Press, Inc.

Auerbach, S. (2007). From moral supporters to struggling advocates reconceptualizing parent roles in education through the experience of working-class families of color. *Urban Education, 42*, 250–283.

Ayres, I. (2010). *Carrots and sticks: Unlock the power of incentives to get things done*. New York, NY: Bantam.

Ayers, W. (1993). *To teach: The journey of a teacher*. New York, NY: Teachers College Press.

Azer, S. A. (2001). Problem-based learning: Challenges, barriers and outcome issues. *Saudi Medical Journal, 22*, 389–397.

Azevedo, R., Johnson, A., Chauncey, A., & Graesser, A. (2011). Use of hypermedia to assess and convey self-regulated learning. In B. J. Zimmerman & D. H. Schunk (Eds.), *Handbook of self-regulation of learning and performance* (pp. 102–121). New York, NY: Routledge.

Azzam, A. M. (2009). Why creativity now? A conversation with Sir Ken Robinson. *Educational Leadership, 67*, 22–26.

———. (2014). Motivated to learn: A conversation with Daniel Pink. *Educational Leadership, 72*, 12–17.

Baddeley, A. D. (1966). The influence of acoustic and semantic similarity on long-term memory for word sequences. *Quarterly Journal of Experimental Psychology, 18*, 302–309.

———. (1981). The concept of working memory: A view of its current state and probable future development. *Cognition, 10*, 17–23.

———. (1986). *Working memory*. New York: Oxford University Press.

———. (1990). *Human memory: Theory and practice*. Boston, MA: Allyn & Bacon.

Baer, J., & Kaufman, J. (2012). *Being creative inside and outside the classroom: How to boost your students' creativity—and your own*. Rotterdam, NL: Sense.

Bagley, W. (1907). *Classroom management*. New York, NY: Macmillan.

Ball, C. (1989). *Towards an "enterprising" culture: A challenge for education and training*. Organisation for Economic Co-operation and Development Centre for Educational Research and Innovation.

Ball, D. L., Thames, M. H., & Phelps, G. (2008). Content knowledge for teaching what makes it special? *Journal of Teacher Education, 59*, 389–407.

Baltes, P., Reese, R., & Lipsitt, L. (1980). Life-span developmental psychology. *Annual Review of Psychology, 31*, 65–110. http://doi.org/10.1146/annurev.ps.31.020180.000433

Bandura, A. (1989). Human agency in social cognitive theory. *American Psychologist, 44*, 1175–1183. http://doi.org/10.1037/a0018378

————. (1996). Failures in self-regulation: Energy depletion or selective disengagement? *Psychological Inquiry, 7,* 20–24.

————. (1997). *Self-efficacy: The exercise of control.* New York, NY: Freeman.

————. (2001). Social cognitive theory: An agentic perspective. *Annual Review of Psychology, 52,* 1–26. http://doi.org/10.1146/annurev.psych.53.100901.135114

Bansel, P. (2007). Subjects of choice and lifelong learning. *International Journal of Qualitative Studies in Education, 20,* 283–300. http://doi.org/10.1080/09518390701281884

Barnes, J. M., & Underwood, B. J. (1959). "Fate" of first-list associations in transfer theory. *Journal of Experimental Psychology,* 97–105.

Barrows, H. S. (1980). *Problem-based learning: An approach to medical education.* New York, NY: Springer.

Bart, W., & Vong, M. (Eds.). (1974). *Psychology of school learning: Views of the learner* (2nd ed.). New York, NY: MSS Information Corporation.

Baynton, D. (2001). Disability and the justification of inequality in American history. In Lennard J. Davis (Ed.), *The disability studies reader* (pp. 33–57). New York, NY: Routledge.

Becker, G. S. (1993). *Human capital: A theoretical and empirical analysis with special reference to education* (3rd ed.). Chicago, IL: University of Chicago Press.

Beghetto, R. A. (2010). Creativity in the classroom. In J. C. Kaufman & R. J. Sternberg (Eds.), *The Cambridge handbook of creativity* (pp. 447–463). New York: Cambridge University Press.

Berliner, D. C. (1993). The 100-year journey of educational psychology. In T. K. Fagan & G. R. Vanden-Bos (Eds.), *Exploring applied psychology: Origins and critical analyses* (pp. 37–78). Washington, DC: American Psychological Association.

Biggam, S.C. & Hyson, M.C. (2014) The Common Core State Standards and developmentally appropriate practices: Creating a relationship. Washington, DC: National Association for the Education of Young Children.

Billington, T. (2014). Towards a critical relational educational (School) psychology. In T. Corcoran (Ed.), *Psychology in education: Critical theory-practice* (pp. 113–128). Rotterdam, NL: Springer.

Bloom, B. S. (1956). *Taxonomy of educational objectives: The classification of education goals.* New York, NY: Longman.

Boden, M. A. (1996). What is creativity? In M. A. Boden (Ed.), *Dimensions of creativity* (pp. 75–118). Cambridge, MA: MIT Press.

Boekaerts, M., & Cascallar, E. (2006). How far have we moved toward the integration of theory and practice in self-regulation? *Educational Psychology Review, 18,* 199–210. http://doi.org/10.1007/s10648-006-9013-4

Boekaerts, M., Maes, S., & Karoly, P. (2005). Self-regulation across domains of applied psychology: Is there an emerging consensus? *Applied Psychology, 54,* 149–154. http://doi.org/10.1111/j.1464-0597.2005.00201.x

Boksem, M. A., Meijman, T. F., & Lorist, M. M. (2005). Effects of mental fatigue on attention: An ERP study. *Cognitive Brain Research*, *25*, 107–116.

Bonal, X. (2003). The neoliberal educational agenda and the legitimation crisis: Old and new state strategies. *British Journal of Sociology of Education*, 24, 159–175.

Bondy, E., Ross, D. D., Gallingane, C., & Hambacher, E. (2007). Creating environments of success and resilience: Culturally responsive classroom management and more. *Urban Education*, 42, 326–348.

Bornstein, M., & Lamb, M. (2011). *Developmental science: An advanced textbook* (6th ed.). New York, NY: Psychology Press.

Brainerd, C. J., & Reyna, V. F. (1990). Gist is the grist: Fuzzy-Trace theory and new intuitionism. *Developmental Review*, *10*, 3–47.

Bredekamp, S. (1987). *Developmentally appropriate practice in early childhood programs serving children from birth through age 8*. Washington, DC: National Association for the Education of Young Children.

———. (2013). *Effective practices in early childhood education: Building a foundation* (2nd ed.). Newark, NJ: Pearson Education.

Briggs, G. E. (1954). Acquisition, extinction, and recovery functions in retroactive inhibition. *Journal of Experimental Psychology*, 47, 285–293.

Bronfenbrenner, U. (2009). *The ecology of human development: Experiments by nature and design*. Cambridge, MA: Harvard University Press.

Brookfield, S. (2007). Diversifying curriculum as the practice of repressive tolerance. *Teaching in Higher Education*, *12*, 557–568.

Broom, C. (2007). Social efficiency and public schooling in British Columbia. *British Columbia History*, 40, 8–12.

Brophy, J. (1983). Conceptualizing student motivation. *Educational Psychologist*, *18*, 200–215.

———. (2006). History of research on classroom management. In E. Emmer, E. Sabornie, C. M. Evertson, & C. S. Weinstein (Eds.), *Handbook of classroom management: Research, practice, and contemporary issues* (pp. 17–43). Mahwah, NJ: Routledge.

Brown, W. (2003). Neo-liberalism and the end of liberal democracy. *Theory & Event*, 7. Retrieved from http://muse.jhu.edu/journals/theory_and_event/v007/7.1brown.html. doi.org/10.1353/tae.2003.0020

Bruner, J. S. (1996). *The culture of education*. Cambridge, MA: Harvard University Press.

Bullough, R. V. (1994). Digging at the root: Discipline, management, and metaphor. *Action in Teacher Education*, *16*, 1–10.

Burbules, N. C., & Berk, R. (1999). Critical thinking and critical pedagogy: Relations, differences, and limits. In T. S. Popkewitz & L. Fendler (Eds.), *Critical theories in education: Changing terrains of knowledge and politics* (pp. 45–65). New York, NY: Routledge.

Burman, E. (2008). *Deconstructing developmental psychology* (2nd ed.). New York, NY: Routledge.

Butler, S. M., & McMunn, N. D. (2006). *A teacher's guide to classroom assessment: Understanding and using assessment to improve student learning.* Indianapolis, IN: Jossey-Bass.

Carta, J. (1995). Developmentally appropriate practice: A critical analysis as applied to young children with disabilities. *Focus on Exceptional Children, 27,* 1–15.

Carver, C. S., & Scheier, M. F. (2000). Autonomy and self-regulation. *Psychological Inquiry, 11,* 284–291.

Casey, Z. A., Lozenski, B. D., & McManimon, S. K. (2013). From neoliberal policy to neoliberal pedagogy: Racializing and historicizing classroom management. *Journal of Pedagogy, 4,* 36–58.

Chomsky, N. (1965). *Aspects of the theory of syntax.* Cambridge, MA: MIT Press.

Chong, W. H. (2006). *Personal agency beliefs in self-regulation: The exercise of personal responsibility, choice and control in learning.* New York, NY: Cavendish Square Publishing.

Claiborne, L. (1999). Towards a more critical educational psychology. *Annual Review of Critical Psychology, 1,* 21–33.

———. (2014). The potential of critical educational psychology beyond its meritocratic past. In T. Corcoran (Ed.), *Psychology in Education: Critical theory-practice* (pp. 1–16). Rotterdam, NL: Springer.

Clarke, J. (2005). New Labour's citizens: Activated, empowered, responsibilized, abandoned? *Critical Social Policy, 25,* 447–463. http://doi.org/10.1177/0261018305057024

Cleary, T., & Zimmerman, B. J. (2004). Self-regulation empowerment program: A school-based program to enhance self-regulated and self-motivated cycles of student learning. *Psychology in the Schools, 41,* 537–550. http://doi.org/10.1002/pits.10177

Cobb, P. (1990). A constructivist perspective on information-processing theories of mathematical activity. *International Journal of Educational Research, 14,* 67–92.

Cohen, K. (2012). Let's solve our math and science challenges. Retrieved from http://www.exxonmobilperspectives.com/2012/04/08/lets-solve-our-math-and-science-challenges-3/

Cole, M. (1998). *Cultural psychology: A once and future discipline.* Cambridge, MA: Harvard University Press.

Cooke, B. (2003). The denial of slavery in management studies. *Journal of Management Studies, 408,* 1895–1918.

Corcoran, T. (2014). *Psychology in education: Critical theory-practice.* Rotterdam, NL: Springer.

Cothran, D. J., Kulinna, P. H., & Garrahy, D. A. (2003). "This is kind of giving a secret away": Students' perspectives of effective class management. *Teaching and Teacher Education, 19,* 435–444.

Council of Chief State School Officers (CCSSO) (2010). Frequently asked questions. Retrieved from http://www.ccsso.org/Documents/2010/InTASC_FAQ_2010 .pdf

———. (2011). The InTASC standards at a glance. Retrieved from http://www .ccsso.org/Documents/2011/InTASC%202011%20Standards %20At%20A% 20Glance.pdf

———. (2013). The interstate teacher assessment and support consortium. Retrieved from http://www.ccsso.org/Resources/ Programs/Interstate_Teacher _Assessment_Consortium_%28InTASC%29.html

Covin, T. M. (1974). *Readings in human development: A humanistic approach.* New York, NY: MSS Information Corporation.

Cowan, N. (1988). Evolving conceptions of memory storage, selective attention, and their mutual constraints within the human information-processing system. *Psychological Bulletin, 104,* 163–191.

Crary, J. (2001). *Suspensions of perception: Attention, spectacle, and modern culture.* Cambridge, MA: MIT Press.

Cresswell, J. (2011). Being faithful: Bakhtin and a potential postmodern psychology of self. *Culture & Psychology, 17,* 473–490.

Cruikshank, B. (1999). *The will to empower: Democratic citizens and other subjects.* Ithaca, NY: Cornell University Press.

Csikszentmihalyi, M. (1999). Implications of a systems perspective for the study of creativity. In R. J. Sternberg (Ed.), *Handbook of Creativity* (pp. 313–338). Cambridge, UK: Cambridge University Press.

Cushman, P. (1990). Why the self is empty: Toward a historically situated psychology. *American Psychologist, 45,* 599–611. http://doi.org/10.1037/0003 -066X.45.5.599

Danziger, K. (1990). *Constructing the subject: Historical origins of psychological research.* Cambridge, UK: Cambridge University Press.

Darling-Hammond, L. (1994). Performance-based assessment and educational equity. *Harvard Educational Review, 64,* 5–31.

Davies, B., & Bansel, P. (2007). Neoliberalism and education. *International Journal of Qualitative Studies in Education, 20,* 247–259. http://doi.org/10.1080 /09518390701281751

De Lissovoy, N. (2013). Pedagogy of the Impossible: Neoliberalism and the Ideology of Accountability. *Policy Futures in Education, 11,* 423–435.

De Stobbeleir, K. E. M., Ashford, S. J., & Buyens, D. (2011). Self-regulation of creativity at work: the role of feedback-seeking behavior in creative performance. *Academy of Management Journal, 54,* 811–831.

Deci, E., & Ryan, R. (2000). The "what" and "why" of goal pursuits: Human needs and the self-determination of behavior. *Psychological Inquiry, 11,* 227–268.

Deci, E. L. (1971). Effects of externally mediated rewards on intrinsic motivation. *Journal of Personality and Social Psychology, 18,* 105–115.

Deci, E. L., & Ryan, R. M. (2008). Facilitating optimal motivation and psychological well-being across life's domains. *Canadian Psychology/Psychologie Canadienne, 49*, 14–23.

Deutsch, J., & Deutsch, D. (1963). Attention: Some theoretical considerations. *Psychology Review*, 80–90.

Dewey, J. (1910/1997). *How we think*. Mineola, NY: Courier Corporation.

———. (1916/2004). *Democracy and Education*. Mineola, NY: Courier Dover Publications.

Dilts, A. (2011). From "entrepreneur of the self" to "care of the self": Neo-liberal governmentality and Foucault's ethics. *Foucault Studies, 12*, 130–146.

Doran, S. M., Van Dongen, H. P. A., & Dinges, D. F (2001). Sustained attention performance during sleep deprivation: Evidence of state instability. *Archives Italiennes de Biologie: A Journal of Neuroscience, 139*, 253–267.

Doyle, O., Harmon, C. P., Heckman, J. J., & Tremblay, R. E. (2009). Investing in early human development: timing and economic efficiency. *Economics & Human Biology, 7*, 1–6.

Du Bois, N. F., & Staley, R. K. (1997). A self-regulated learning approach to teaching educational psychology. *Educational Psychology Review, 9*, 171–197. http://doi.org/10.1023/A:1024792529797

Duckworth, A. L., Peterson, C., Matthews, M. D., & Kelly, D. R. (2007). Grit: perseverance and passion for long-term goals. *Journal of Personality and Social Psychology, 92*, 1087–1101.

Duckworth, A. L., & Quinn, P. D. (2009). Development and validation of the Short Grit Scale (GRIT-S). *Journal of Personality Assessment, 91*, 166–174.

Duckworth, A. L., & Yeager, D. S. (2015). Measurement matters assessing personal qualities other than cognitive ability for educational purposes. *Educational Researcher, 44*, 237–251.

Duncan, A. (2010). Beyond the bubble tests: The next generation of assessments. Speech presented at Achieve's American diploma project leadership team meeting, Alexandria, VA. Retrieved from http://www.ed.gov/news/speeches/beyond-bubble-tests-next-generation-assessments-secretary-arne-duncans-remarks-state-leaders-achieves-american-diploma-project-leadership-team-meeting on September 30, 2016.

Dweck, C. (2006). *Mindset: The new psychology of success*. New York, NY: Ballantine Books.

Eccles, J. S., Midgley, C., Wigfield, A., Buchanan, C. M., Reuman, D., Flanagan, C., & Mac Iver, D. (1993). Development during adolescence: the impact of stage-environment fit on young adolescents' experiences in schools and in families. *American Psychologist, 48*, 90–101.

Eckert, P. (1989). *Jocks and burnouts: Social categories and identity in the high school*. New York, NY: Teachers College Press.

Eisner, E. (2005). Back to whole. *Educational Leadership, 63*, 14–18.

Elias, M. J. (2009). Social-emotional and character development and academics as a dual focus of educational policy. *Educational Policy, 23,* 831–846.

Elkind, D. (2007). *The hurried child: Growing up too fast too soon.* Da Capo Press: Cambridge, MA.

Emmer, E. T., & Stough, L. M. (2001). Classroom management: A critical part of educational psychology, with implications for teacher education. *Educational Psychologist, 36,* 103–112.

Esch, E., & Roediger, D. (2009). One symptom of originality: Race and the management of labour in the history of the United States. *Historical Materialism, 17,* 3–43.

Etherington, M. B. (2011). Investigative primary science: A problem-based learning approach. *Australian Journal of Teacher Education, 36,* 53–74.

Evertson, C. M., & Weinstein, C. S. (2006). *Handbook of classroom management: Research, practice, and contemporary issues.* Mahwah, NJ: Lawrence Erlbaum Associates.

Fabricant, M., & Fine, M. (2012). *Charter schools and the corporate makeover of public education: What's at stake?* New York, NY: Teachers College Press.

Feistritzer, E. C. (2011). *Profile of teachers in the United States.* National Center for Education Information. Retrieved from http://www.edweek.org/media/pot2011final-blog.pdf

Felkin, H.M., & Felkin, E. (1895). *An introduction to Herbart's science and practice of education.* Boston, MA: D.C. Heath and Co.

Fendler, L. (1999). Making trouble: Prediction, agency, and critical intellectuals. In T. S. Popkewitz & L. Fendler (Eds.), *Critical theories in education: Changing terrains of knowledge and politics* (pp. 169–189). New York, NY: Routledge.

———. (2001). Educating flexible souls: The construction of subjectivity through developmentality and interaction. In K. Hultqvist & G. Dahlberg (Eds.), *Governing the child in the new millennium* (pp. 119–142). New York, NY: RoutledgeFalmer.

———. (2008). The history of the bell curve: Sorting and the idea of normal. *Educational Theory, 58,* 63–92.

———. (2013). Psychology in teacher education: Efficacy, professionalization, management, and habit. In Paul Smeyers & Marc Depaepe (Eds.), *Educational research: The attraction of psychology* (pp. 53–71). New York, NY: Springer.

Fenwick, D. (1998). Managing space, energy, and self: Junior high teachers' experiences of classroom management. *Teaching and Teacher Education, 14,* 619–631.

Fitzsimons, P. (2011). *Governing the self: A Foucauldian critique of managerialism in education.* New York, NY: Peter Lang.

Fivush, R. (2011). The development of autobiographical memory. *Annual Review of Psychology, 62,* 559–582.

Foucault, M. (1977). *Discipline and punish: The birth of the prison.* (A. Sheridan, Trans.). New York, NY: Vintage.

———. (1988). Practicing criticism (A. Sheridan et al., Trans.). In L.D. Kritzman (Ed.), *Politics, philosophy, culture: Interviews and other writings, 1977–1984* (pp. 152–158). New York, NY: Routledge.

Freiberg, H., & Lamb, S. (2009). Dimensions of person-centered classroom management. *Theory into Practice, 48,* 99–105.

Freire, P. (2000). The banking concept of education. In *Educational foundations: An anthology of critical readings* (pp. 99–111). Thousand Oaks, CA: Sage Publications.

———. (1968/2000). *Pedagogy of the oppressed.* New York, NY: Continuum.

Furnham, A., Batey, M., Booth, T. W., Patel, V., & Lozinskaya, D. (2011). Individual difference predictors of creativity in art and science students. *Thinking Skills and Creativity, 6,* 114–121.

Gallagher, S. (2003). *Educational psychology: Disrupting the dominant discourse.* New York, NY: Peter Lang.

Galotti, K. M. (2004). *Cognitive psychology: In and out of the laboratory* (3rd ed.). Belmont, CA: Wadsworth.

Gardner, D. P. (1983). *A nation at risk.* Washington, DC: The National Commission on Excellence in Education, US Department of Education.

Gaut, B. (2010). The philosophy of creativity. *Philosophy Compass, 5,* 1034–1046.

Gay, G. (2002). Preparing for culturally responsive teaching. *Journal of Teacher Education, 53,* 106–116.

Gergen, K. (1992). *The saturated self: Dilemmas of identity in contemporary life.* New York, NY: Basic Books.

Gewertz, C. (2008). States press ahead on 21st century skills. *Education Week, 28,* 21–23.

Giroux, H. A. (2009). Critical theory and educational practice. In A. Darder, M. P. Baltodano, & R. D. Torres (Eds.), *The critical pedagogy reader* (2nd ed., pp. 27–51). New York, NY: Routledge.

Giroux, H., & McLaren, P. (1986). Teacher education and the politics of engagement: The case for democratic schooling. *Harvard Educational Review, 56,* 213–239.

Giroux, H. A., & Saltman, K. (2009). Obama's betrayal of public education? Arne Duncan and the corporate model of schooling. *Cultural Studies↔Critical Methodologies, 9,* 772–779.

Gladwell, M. (2007). *Blink: The power of thinking without thinking.* New York, NY: Back Bay Books.

Glăveanu, V. P. (2010). Paradigms in the study of creativity: Introducing the perspective of cultural psychology. *New Ideas in Psychology, 28,* 79–93.

———. (2011). Children and creativity: A most (un) likely pair? *Thinking Skills and Creativity 6,* 122–131.

————. (2013). Rewriting the language of Creativity: The five A's framework. *Review of General Psychology, 17*, 69–81.

Godden, D. R., & Baddeley, A. D. (1980). When does context influence recognition memory? *British Journal of Psychology*, 99–104.

Gollwitzer, P. M., & Oettingen, G. (2001). Motivation: History of the concept. In N. J. Smelser & P. B. Baltes (Eds.), *International encyclopedia of the social and behavioral sciences* (pp. 10109–10112). Amsterdam, NL: Elsevier.

Goleman, D. (2013). *Focus: The hidden driver of excellence.* London, UK: Bloomsbury.

Goodman, G. S. (Ed.). (2008). *Educational psychology: An application of critical constructivism.* New York, NY: Peter Lang.

————. (2014). School sucks: Deconstructing Taylorist obsessions. In T. Corcoran (Ed.), *Psychology in education: Critical theory-practice* (pp. 71–82). Rotterdam, NL: Springer.

Goodnough, K., & Nolan, B. (2008). Engaging elementary teachers' pedagogical content knowledge: Adopting problem-based learning in the context of science teaching and learning. *Canadian Journal of Science, Mathematics, and Technology Education, 8*, 197–216.

Gorlewski, J. (2011). *Power, resistance, and literacy: Writing for social justice.* Charlotte, NC: Information Age Publishing.

Gough, B., McFadden, M., & McDonald, M. (2013). *Critical social psychology: An introduction.* London, UK: Palgrave Macmillan.

Gould, S. J. (1996). *The mismeasure of man.* New York, NY: W. W. Norton & Company.

Graham, S., & Weiner, B. (1996). Theories and principles of motivation. In D. C. Berliner & R. Calfee (Eds.), *Handbook of educational psychology* (Vol. 4, pp. 63–84). New York, NY: Macmillan.

Greene, M. (1988). *The dialectic of freedom.* New York, NY: Teachers College Press.

Hacking, I. (1995). The looping effects of human kinds. In D. Sperber (Ed.), *Causal cognition* (pp. 351–383). New York, NY: Oxford University Press.

————. (2002). *Historical ontology.* Cambridge, MA: Harvard University Press.

Hadwin, A., & Oshige, M. (2011). Self-regulation, coregulation, and socially shared regulation: Exploring perspectives of social in self-regulated learning theory. *Teachers College Record, 113*, 240–264.

Hadwin, A. (2012). Response to Vassallo's claims from a historically situated view of self-regulated learning as adaptation in the face of challenge. *New Ideas in Psychology.* http://doi.org/http://dx.doi.org/10.1016/j.newideapsych .2012.05.001

Hallinan, M. (2000). *Handbook of the sociology of education.* New York, NY: Springer.

Hanushek, E., Jamison, D., Woessman, L., & Jamison, E. (2008). Education and economic growth: It's not just going to school by learning that matters. *Education Next, 8*, 62–70.

Harackiewicz, J. M. (1979). The effects of reward contingency and performance feedback on intrinsic motivation. *Journal of Personality and Social Psychology, 37*, 1352–1363.

Hardcastle, V. G. (1998). The puzzle of attention, the importance of metaphors. *Philosophical Psychology, 11*, 331–351.

Hardcastle, V. G. (2003). Attention versus consciousness: A distinction with a difference. In N. Osaka (Ed.), *Neural basis of consciousness* (pp. 105–122). Amsterdam, NL: John Benjamins Publishing.

Harré, R. (2002). *Cognitive science: A philosophical introduction.* London, UK: Sage.

Harvey, D. (2007). *A brief history of neoliberalism.* Oxford, UK: Oxford University Press.

Hennessey, B. A., & Amabile, M. A. (2010). Creativity. *Annual Review of Psychology, 61*, 569–598.

Henson, K. (2009). Making the most of INTASC standards. *SRATE Journal, 18*, 34–40.

Hickey, D. T., & Zuiker, S. J. (2005). Engaged participation: A sociocultural model of motivation with implications for educational assessment. *Educational Assessment, 10*, 277–305.

Higgins, A. T., & Turnure, J. E. (1984). Distractibility and concentration of attention in children's development. *Child Development,* 1799–1810.

Hilgers, M. (2013). Embodying neoliberalism: thoughts and responses to critics. *Social Anthropology, 21*, 75–89.

Hodges, B. D. (2010). A tea-steeping or i-Doc model for medical education? *Academic Medicine, 85*, S34–S44.

Horkheimer, M., & Adorno, T. W. (2002). *Dialectic of enlightenment: Philosophical fragments.* (G. S. Noerr, Ed., E. Jephcott, Trans.). Redwood City, CA: Stanford University Press.

Hoy, W. K., Tarter, C. J., & Hoy, A. W. (2006). Academic optimism of schools: A force for student achievement. *American Educational Research Journal, 43*, 425–446.

Hsue, Y., & Aldridge, J. (1995). Developmentally appropriate practice and traditional Taiwanese culture. *Journal of Instructional Psychology, 22*, 320–324.

Huba, M. E., & Freed, J. E. (2000). Learner centered assessment on college campuses: Shifting the focus from teaching to learning. *Community College Journal of Research and Practice, 24*, 759–766.

Hull, C. L. (1943). *Principles of behavior: An introduction to behavior theory.* Oxford, UK: Appleton Century Crofts.

Hurn, C. J. (1993). *The limits and possibilities of schooling: An introduction to the sociology of schooling.* Needham Heights, MA: Allyn & Bacon.

Hursh, D. (2000). Neoliberalism and the control of teachers, students, and learning: The rise of standards, standardization, and accountability. *Cultural Logic, 4.*

———. (2007). Assessing No Child Left Behind and the rise of neoliberal education policies. *American Educational Research Journal, 44,* 493–518.

Hursh, D., & Martina, C. A. (2003). Neoliberalism and schooling in the US: How state and federal government education policies perpetuate inequality. *Journal for Critical Education Policy Studies, 1,* 1–13.

Ibáñez, T., & Íñiguez, L. (Eds.). (1997). *Critical social psychology.* London, UK: Sage.

Isen, A., & Reeve, J. (2005). The influence of positive affect on intrinsic and extrinsic motivation: Facilitating enjoyment of play, responsible work behavior, and self-control. *Motivation and Emotion, 29,* 297–324.

James, W. (1890). *The principles of psychology* (Vol. 1). New York, NY: Holt.

———. (1895). The knowing of things together. *Psychological Review, 2,* 105–124.

Järvelä, S. (2011). How does help seeking help? New prospects in a variety of contexts. *Learning and Instruction, 21,* 297–299. http://doi.org/10.1016/j.learninstruc.2010.07.006

Johnson, E. J. (2015). Reprint of Mapping the field of the whole human: Toward a form psychology. *New Ideas in Psychology, 38,* 4–24.

Johnson, W. A., & Heinz, S. P. (1978). Flexibility and capacity demands of attention. *Journal of Experimental Psychology,* 420–435.

Kaščák, O., & Pupala, B. (2013). Buttoning up the gold collar: The child in neoliberal visions of early education and care. *Human Affairs, 23,* 319–337.

Kazdin, A. (1978). *History of behavior modification: Experimental foundations of contemporary research.* Baltimore, MD: University Park Press.

Kilroy, D. A. (2004). Problem based learning. *Emergency Medicine Journal, 21,* 411–413.

Kim, J. S., & Sunderman, G. L. (2005). Measuring academic proficiency under the No Child Left Behind Act: Implications for educational equity. *Educational Researcher, 34,* 3–13.

Kincheloe, J. L. (1999). The foundations of a democratic educational psychology. In J. L. Kincheloe, S. R. Steinberg, & L. Villarde (Eds.), *Rethinking intelligence: Confronting psychological assumptions about teaching and learning* (pp. 1–26). New York, NY: Routledge.

———. (2000). Making critical thinking critical. *Counterpoints,* 23–40.

Kindermann, T. A., & Skinner, E. A. (1992). Modeling environmental development: Individual and contextual trajectories. In J. B. Asendorpf & J. Valsiner (Eds.), *Framing stability and change: An investigation into methodological issues* (pp. 155–190). Newbury Park, CA: Sage.

Kirkham, N. Z., Slemmer, J. A., & Johnson, S. P. (2002). Visual statistical learning in infancy: Evidence for a domain general learning mechanism. *Cognition, 83,* 35–42.

Kitsantis, A., & Zimmerman, B. J. (2006). Enhancing self-regulation of practice: The influence of graphing and self-evaluative standards. *Metacognition and Learning, 1*, 201–212. http://doi.org/10.1007/s11409-006-6893-0

Klein, R. M., & Lawrence, M. A. (2012). On the modes and domains of attention. *Cognitive Neuroscience of Attention, 11*–28.

Klem, A., & Connell, J. (2004). Relationships matter: Linking teacher support to student engagement and achievement. *Journal of School Health, 74*, 262–273.

Kliebard, H. M. (2004). *The struggle for the American curriculum: 1893–1958.* New York, NY: RoutledgeFalmer.

Kohn, A. (1996). *Beyond discipline: From compliance to community.* Alexandria, VA: Association for Supervision and Curriculum Development.

———. (1999). *Punished by rewards: The trouble with gold stars, incentive plans, A's, praise, and other bribes.* Boston, MA: Houghton Mifflin Company.

———. (2008). Kohn, A. (2008). Why self-discipline is overrated: The (troubling) theory and practice of control from within. *Phi Delta Kappan, 90*, 168–176.

———. (2014). *The myth of the spoiled child: Challenging the conventional wisdom about children and parenting.* Philadelphia, PA: Da Capo Press.

Kounin, J. S. (1970). *Discipline and group management in classrooms.* New York, NY: Holt, Rinehart, & Winston.

Kumashiro, K. (2009). *Against common sense: Teaching and learning toward social justice.* New York, NY: Routledge.

Kurland, J. (2011). The role that attention plays in language processing. *Perspectives on Neurophysiology and Neurogenic Speech and Language Disorders, 21*, 47–54.

Kusserow, A. (2004). *American individualisms: Child rearing and social class in three neighborhoods.* New York, NY: Palgrave Macmillan.

Kwan, A. (2009). Problem-based learning. In M. Tight, K. H. Mok, J. Huisman, & C. Morphew (Eds.), *The Routledge international handbook of higher education* (pp. 91–107). New York, NY: Routledge.

Ladson-Billings, G. (1995a). But that's just good teaching! The case for culturally relevant pedagogy. *Theory into Practice, 34*, 159–165.

———. (1995b). Toward a theory of culturally relevant pedagogy. *American Educational Research Journal, 32*, 465–491.

———. (1998). Just what is critical race theory and what's it doing in a nice field like education? *International Journal of Qualitative Studies in Education, 11*, 7–24.

Lakoff, G., & Johnson, M. (1999). *Philosophy in the flesh: The embodied mind and its challenge to Western thought.* New York, NY: Basic books.

Lave, J., & Wenger, E. (1991). *Situated learning: Legitimate peripheral participation.* Cambridge, UK: Cambridge University Press.

Leonard, P., & McLaren, P. (2002). *Paulo Freire: A critical encounter.* New York, NY: Routledge.

Lesko, N. (2001). *Act your age!: A cultural construction of adolescence.* New York, NY: Routledge.

Lewin, K. (1946). Behavior and development as a function of the total situation. In L. Carmichael (Ed.), *Manual of child psychology* (pp. 791–844). Hoboken, NJ: John Wiley & Sons, Inc.

Lindquist, E. F. (1951). *Educational measurement.* Washington, DC: American Council on Education.

Linnenbrink, E. A., & Pintrich, P. R. (2002). Motivation as an enabler for academic success. *School Psychology Review, 31,* 313.

Lipman, M. (2003). *Thinking in education* (2nd ed.). Cambridge, UK: Cambridge University Press.

Lipman, P. (2011). Neoliberal education restructuring dangers and opportunities of the present crisis. *Monthly Review, 63,* 114.

Lobel, T. (2014). *Sensation: The new science of physical intelligence.* New York, NY: Atria Books.

Lotan, R. A. (2006). Managing groupwork in the heterogeneous classroom. In E. Emmer, E. Sabornie, C. M. Evertson, & C. S. Weinstein (Eds.), *Handbook of classroom management: Research, practice, and contemporary issues* (pp. 525–539). Mahwah, NJ: Routledge.

Lubeck, S. (1994). The politics of developmentally appropriate practice: Exploring issues of culture, class, and curriculum. In B. Mallory & R. New (Eds.), *Diversity and developmentally appropriate practices: Challenges for early childhood education* (pp. 17–43). New York: Teachers College Press.

Mallory, B., & New, R. (1994). *Diversity and developmentally appropriate practices: Challenges for early childhood education.* New York, NY: Teachers College Press.

Marcuse, H. (1964/1991). *One-dimensional man: Studies in the ideology of advanced industrial society.* New York, NY: Routledge.

Martin, J. (2003). Emergent persons. *New Ideas in Psychology, 21,* 85–99.

———. (2004). The educational inadequacy of conceptions of self in educational psychology. *Interchange, 35,* 185–208. http://doi.org/10.1007/s10780-011-9143-6

———. (2007). The selves of educational psychology: Conceptions, contexts, and critical considerations. *Educational Psychologist, 42,* 79–89.

———. (2014). Psychologism, individualism and the limiting of the social context in educational psychology. In T. Corcoran (Ed.), *Psychology in education: Critical theory-practice* (pp. 167–180). Rotterdam, NL: Springer.

———. (2015). A unified psychology of the person? *New Ideas in Psychology, 38,* 31–36.

Martin, J., & McLellan, A. (2008). The educational psychology of self-regulation: A conceptual and critical analysis. *Studies in Philosophy and Education, 27,* 433–448.

Martin, J., & McLellan, A. (2013). *The education of selves: How psychology transformed students*. New York, NY: Oxford University Press.

Martin, J., & Sugarman, J. (1999). *The psychology of human possibility and constraint*. Albany, NY: SUNY Press.

Martin, J., Sugarman, J., & McNamara, J. (2000). *Models of classroom management: Principles, practices and critical considerations*. Calgary, CAN: Detselig Enterprises.

Marx, K. (2010). *Capital: A critique of political economy*. Lexington, KY: Pacific Publishing Studio.

Marzano, R. J., & Heflebower, T. (2012). *Teaching & assessing 21st century Skills. The classroom strategies series*. Bloomington, IN: Marzano Research Laboratory.

Maslow, A. (1943). A theory of human motivation. *Psychological Review, 50*, 370–396.

———. (1968). Some educational implications of the humanistic psychologies. *Harvard Educational Review, 38*, 685–696.

Mathison, S. (2008). What is the difference between evaluation and research—and why do we care. In N. L. Smith & P. R. Brandon (Eds.), *Fundamental issues in evaluation* (pp. 183–196). New York, NY: The Guilford Press.

———. (2009). Serving the public interest through Educational evaluation: Salvaging democracy by rejecting neoliberalism. In Katherine Ryan & J. Bradley Cousins (Eds.), *The SAGE international handbook of educational evaluation* (pp. 527–564). Thousand Oaks, CA: Sage.

———. (2012). Working toward a different narrative of accountability: A report from British Columbia. *Workplace: A Journal for Academic Labor, 20*. Retrieved from http://ices.library.ubc.ca/index.php/workplace/article/view/182439

Maturana, H. R., & Varela, F. J. (1987). *The tree of knowledge: The biological roots of human understanding*. Boston, MA: Shambhala Publications.

Matusov, E., & Hayes, R. (2000). Sociocultural critique of Piaget and Vygotsky. *New Ideas in Psychology*, 215–239.

McCaslin, M., Bozack, A. R., Napolean, L., Thomas, A., Vasquez, V., Wayman, V., & Zhang, J. (2006). Self-regulated learning and classroom management: Theory, research and considerations for classroom practice. In C. M. Evertson & C. S. Weinstein (Eds.), *Handbook of classroom management: Research, practice, and contemporary issues* (pp. 232–252). Mahwah, NJ: Lawrence Erlbaum.

McCoy, B. (2016). Digital distractions in the classroom phase II: Student classroom use of digital devices for non-class related purposes. *Journal of Media Education, 7*, 5–32.

McGeoch, J. A. (1932). Forgetting and the law of disuse. *Psychology Review*, 352–370.

McInerney, D. M. (2011). Culture and self-regulation in educational contexts: Assessing the relationship of cultural group to self-regulation. In B. J. Zimmerman

& D. H. Schunk (Eds.), *Handbook of self-regulation of learning and performance* (pp. 442–464). New York, NY: Routledge.

McLaren, P. (2007). *Life in schools. An introduction to critical pedagogy in the foundations of education* (5th ed.). Reading, MA: Addison Wesley Longman, Inc.

McLaren, P., & Farahmandpur, R. (2001). Teaching against globalization and the new imperialism: Toward a revolutionary pedagogy. *Journal of Teacher Education, 52,* 136–150.

McLaughlin, H. J. (1994). From negation to negotiation: Moving away from the management metaphor. *Action in Teacher Education, 16,* 75–84.

McNerney, S. (2011). A brief guide to embodied cognition: Why you are not your brain. *Scientific American.* Retrieved from http://blogs.scientificamerican.com /guest-blog/2011/11/04/a-brief-guide-to-embodied-cognition-why-you-are -not-your-brain/

Mead, G. H. (1934). *Mind, self and society.* Chicago, IL: University of Chicago Press.

Menon, U., & Shweder, R. A. (2001). The return of the "White Man's Burden": The encounter between the moral discourse of anthropology and the domestic life of Oriya women. In M. J. Packer & M. B. Tappan (Eds.), *Cultural and critical perspectives on human development* (pp. 67–112). New York, NY: SUNY Press.

Molina, S. (2012). Romanticizing culture: The role of teachers' cultural intelligence in working with diversity. *The Catesol Journal, 24,* 220–244.

Montessori, M. (1946). *Education for a new world.* Santa Barbara, CA: ABC-CLIO.

———. (1948). *The discovery of the child.* (M. A. Johnstone, Trans.). New York, NY: Aakar Books.

———. (1964/2014). *The Montessori method.* New Brunswick, NJ: Transaction Publishers.

———. (1967). *The absorbent mind* (C. Claremont, Trans.). New York, NY: Henry Holt.

Moran, S., & John-Steiner, V. (2003). Creativity in the making: Vygotsky's contemporary contribution to the dialectic of development and creativity. In R. K. Sawyer, V. John-Steiner, S. Moran, R. J. Sternberg, D. H. Feldman, J. Nakamura, & M. Csikszentmihalyi (Eds.), *Creativity and development* (pp. 61–90). Oxford, UK: Oxford University Press.

Myers, D. G. (2007). *Psychology* (8th ed.). Holland, MI: Worth Publishers.

National Association for the Education of Young Children (NAEYC) (2009a). DAP frequently asked questions. Retrieved from http://www.naeyc.org/dap /faq

———. (2009b). Developmentally appropriate practice. Retrieved from http:// www.naeyc.org/dap

————. (2009c). Developmentally appropriate practice in early childhood programs serving children from birth through age 8. Retrieved from http://www.naeyc.org/files/naeyc/file/positions/PSDAP.pdf

National Board of Professional Teaching Standards (NBPTS) (2012). Early childhood generalist standards. Retrieved from http://www.nbpts.org/sites/default/files/documents/certificates/NB-Standards/nbpts-certificate-ec-gen-standards_09.23.13.pdf

Neely, J. H. (1990). Semantic priming effects in visual word recognition: A selective review of current findings and theories. In D. Besner & G. Humphrey (Eds.), *Basic processes in reading: Visual word recognition* (pp. 264–336). Hillsdale, NJ: Lawrence Erlbaum Associates.

Neisser, U. (1976). *Cognitive and reality: Principles and implications of cognitive psychology*. San Francisco, CA: W. H. Freeman.

Neufeld, P., & Foy, M. (2006). Historical reflections on the ascendancy of ADHD in North America, c. 1980–c. 2005. *British Journal of Educational Studies, 54,* 449–470.

Niemiec, C., & Ryan, R. (2009). Autonomy, competence, and relatedness in the classroom Applying self-determination theory to educational practice. *Theory and Research in Education, 7,* 133–144.

Noddings, N. (2005). What does it mean to educate the whole child? *Educational Leadership, 63,* 3–11.

————. (2006). Educational leaders as caring teachers. *School Leadership and Management, 26,* 339–345.

Nolen, A. L. (2009). The content of educational psychology: An analysis of top ranked journals from 2003 through 2007. *Educational Psychology Review, 21,* 279–289. http://doi.org/10.1007/s10648-009-9110-2

Norman, D. A. (1968). Toward a theory of memory and attention. *Psychology Review, 75,* 522–536.

Norris, N. (1990). *Understanding educational evaluation*. London, UK: Kogan Page. Retrieved from http://library.wur.nl/WebQuery/clc/589969

O'Bannon, B. W., & Thomas, K. M. (2015). Mobile phones in the classroom: Preservice teachers answer the call. *Computers & Education, 85,* 110–122.

Ogbu, J. U., & Simons, H. D. (1998). Voluntary and involuntary minorities: A cultural-ecological theory of school performance with some implications for education. *Anthropology & Education Quarterly, 29,* 155–188.

Organization for Economic Development (2005). *The definition and selection of key competencies: Executive summary*. Paris, FRA. Retrieved from http://www.oecd.org/pisa/35070367.pdf

Ormrod, J. (2008). *Educational psychology: Developing learners* (6th ed.). Upper Saddle River, NJ: Pearson.

Ormrod, J. E. (2003). *Educational psychology: Developing learners* (4th ed.). Boston, MA: Pearson.

————. (2009). *Essentials of educational psychology* (2nd ed.). Upper Saddle River, NJ: Pearson Education, Inc.

————. (2011). *Educational psychology: Developing learners* (7th ed.). Boston, MA: Pearson.

Packer, M. (2001). The problem of transfer, and the sociocultural critique of schooling. *The Journal of the Learning Sciences, 10*, 493–514.

Packer, M. J., & Tappan, M. B. (2001). *Cultural and critical perspectives on human development.* Albany, NY: SUNY Press.

Palomba, C. A., & Banta, T. W. (1999). *Assessment essentials: Planning, implementing, and improving assessment in higher education.* San Francisco, CA: Jossey-Bass.

Parker, I. (1999). Critical psychology: Critical links. *Annual Review of Critical Psychology, 3*–18.

————. (2007). *Revolution in psychology: Alienation to emancipation.* Ann Arbor, MI: Pluto Press.

Pashler, H. E. (1998). *The psychology of attention.* Cambridge, MA: MIT Press.

Paul, R., & Elder, L. (2005). Critical thinking . . . and the art of substantive writing, Part I. *Journal of Developmental Education, 29*, 40–41.

Pellegrino, J. W. Chudowsky, N., & Glaser, R., (2001). *Knowing what students know: The science and design of educational assessment.* Washington, DC: National Academies Press.

Perkins-Gough, D. (2013). The significance of grit: A conversation with Angela Lee Duckworth. *Educational Leadership, 71*, 14–21.

Perry, N. (2002). Introduction: Using qualitative methods to enrich understandings of self-regulated learning. *Educational Psychologist, 37*, 1–3. http://doi.org/10.1207/S15326985EP3701_1

Phan, P., Zhou, J., & Abrahamson, E. (2010). Creativity, innovation, and entrepreneurship in China. *Management and Organization Review, 6*, 175–194.

Piaget, J. (1952). *The origins of intelligence in children* (M. T. Cook, Trans.). New York, NY: W. W. Norton & Co.

Piaget, J., & Inhelder, B. (1969). *The psychology of the child.* New York, NY: Basic Books.

Pink, D. H. (2011). *Drive: The surprising truth about what motivates us.* New York, NY: Riverhead Books.

Pino-Pasternak, D., & Whitebread, D. (2010). The role of parenting in children's self-regulated learning. *Educational Research Review, 5*, 220–242. http://doi.org/10.1016/j.edurev.2010.07.001

Pinquart, M., Juang, L. P., & Silbereisen, R. K. (2003). Self-efficacy and successful school-to-work transition: A longitudinal study. *Journal of Vocational Behavior, 63*, 329–346.

Pintrich, P. R. (2003). A motivational science perspective on the role of student motivation in learning and teaching contexts. *Journal of Educational Psychology, 95*, 667–686.

————. (2004). A conceptual framework for assessing motivation and self-regulated learning in college students. *Educational Psychology Review, 16*, 385–407.

Piontkowski, D., & Calfee, R. (1979). Attention in the classroom. In G. A. Hale & M. Lewis (Eds.), *Attention and cognitive development* (pp. 297–329). New York, NY: Springer.

Pithers, R. T., & Soden, R. (2000). Critical thinking in education: A review. *Educational Research, 42*, 237–249.

Pope, R. (2005). *Creativity: Theory, history, practice.* London, UK: Routledge.

Post, Y., Boyer, W., & Brett, L. (2006). A historical examination of self-regulation: helping children now and in the future. *Early Childhood Education Journal, 34*, 5–14.

Postman, L., & Stark, K. (1969). Role of response availability in transfer and interference. *Journal of Experimental Psychology, 79*, 168–177.

Powell, K. C., & Kalina, C. J. (2009). Cognitive and social constructivism: Developing tools for an effective classroom. *Education, 130*, 241–250.

Powell, W., & Kusuma-Powell, O. (2011). *How to teach now: Five keys to personalized learning in the global classroom.* Alexandria, VA: ASCD.

Reich, S., & Albarran, A. (2014). Developmental psychology, overview. In T. Teo (Ed.), *Encyclopedia of Critical Psychology* (pp. 404–410). New York, NY: Springer.

Render, G., Padilla, J., & Krank, H. (1989). Assertive discipline: A critical review and analysis. *The Teachers College Record, 90*, 607–630.

Richards, H. V., Brown, A. F., & Forde, T. B. (2007). Addressing diversity in schools: Culturally responsive pedagogy. *Teaching Exceptional Children, 39*, 64–68.

Rizzolatti, G., Riggio, L., Dascola, I., & Umiltá, C. (1987). Reorienting attention across the horizontal and vertical meridians: evidence in favor of a premotor theory of attention. *Neuropsychologia, 25*, 31–40.

Robinson, K. (2011). *Out of our minds: Learning to be creative.* West Sussex, UK: Capstone Publishing Ltd.

————. (2013). Why we need to reform education now. Retrieved from http://www.huffingtonpost.com/sir-ken-robinson/reform-american-education-now_b_3203949.html

Roediger III, H. L., & Guynn, M. J. (1996). Retrieval processes. In R. A. Bjork & E. L. Bjork (Eds.), *Memory* (pp. 197–236). San Diego, CA: Academic Press.

Rogoff, B. (2003). *The cultural nature of human development.* New York, NY: Oxford University Press.

Rose, C., & Nicholl, M. J. (1997). *Accelerated learning for the 21st century: The six-step plan to unlock your master-mind.* New York, NY: Dell Publishing.

Rose, N. (1998). *Inventing our selves: Psychology, power, and personhood.* Cambridge, UK: Cambridge University Press.

————. (1999). *Governing the soul: The shaping of the private self.* London, UK: Free Associations Books.

Rousseau, J. J. (1762/1913). *The social contract* (G. D. H. Cole, Trans.). New York, NY: E. P. Dutton & Co.

————. (1979). *Emile, or on education* (A. Bloom, Trans.). New York, NY: Basic Books.

Rueda, R., & Dembo, M. H. (1995). Motivational processes in learning: A comparative analysis of cognitive and sociocultural frameworks. *Advances in Motivation and Achievement, 9,* 255–289.

Rueda, R., & Moll, L. C. (2012). A sociocultural perspective on motivation. In H. O'Neil & M. Drillings (Eds.), *Motivation: Theory and research* (pp. 117–137). New York, NY: Routledge.

Ruff, H. A., & Capozzoli, M. C. (2003). Development of attention and distractibility in the first 4 years of life. *Developmental Psychology, 39,* 877–890.

Ryan, R. M. (2012). *The Oxford handbook of human motivation.* Oxford, UK: Oxford University Press.

Ryan, R.M., & Deci, E. (2000). Intrinsic and extrinsic motivations: Classic definitions and new directions. *Contemporary Educational Psychology, 25,* 54–67. http://doi.org/doi:10.1006/ceps.1999.1020

Sacks, P. (1997). Standardized testing: Meritocracy's crooked yardstick. *Change: The Magazine of Higher Learning, 29,* 24–31.

Sadler, D. R. (1989). Formative assessment and the design of instructional systems. *Instructional Science, 18,* 119–144.

Saffran, J. R., Aslin, R. N., & Newport, E. L. (1996). Statistical learning by 8-month-old infants. *Science, 274,* 1926–1928.

Samuels, S. J., & Turnure, J. E. (1974). Attention and reading achievement in first-grade boys and girls. *Journal of Educational Psychology, 66,* 29.

Santrock, J. W. (2008). *Educational psychology* (3rd ed.). Boston, MA: McGraw-Hill.

Sawyer, R. K., John-Steiner, V., Moran, S., Sternberg, R. J., Feldman, D. H., Nakamura, J., & Csikszentmihalyi, M. (2003). Key issues in creativity and development. In R. K. Sawyer, V. John-Steiner, S. Moran, R. J. Sternberg, D. H. Feldman, J. Nakamura, & M. Csikszentmihalyi (Eds.), *Creativity and development* (pp. 217–242). Oxford, UK: Oxford University Press.

Schön, D. A. (1987). *Educating the reflective practitioner: Toward a new design for teaching and learning in the professions.* San Francisco, CA: Jossey-Bass.

Schunk, D. H., & Zimmerman, B. J. (1997). Social origins of self-regulatory competence. *Educational Psychologist, 32,* 195–208. http://doi.org/10.1207/s15326985ep3204_1

Schutz, A. (2008). Social class and social action: The middle-class bias of democratic theory in education. *The Teachers College Record, 110,* 405–442.

Schwartz, B. (2013). Attention must be paid! Schools need to teach students to maintain attention, not cater to short-attention spans. Retrieved from http://

www.slate.com/articles/life/education/2013/09/paying_attention_is_a_skill
_schools_need_to_teach_it.html

Seifert, T. (2004). Understanding student motivation. *Educational Research, 46,*
137–149.

Seligman, M. E., Maier, S. F., & Geer, J. H. (1968). Alleviation of learned helplessness in the dog. *Journal of Abnormal Psychology, 73,* 256–262.

Shaughnessy, M. F. (2004). An interview with Anita Woolfolk: The educational psychology of teacher efficacy. *Educational Psychology Review, 16,*
153–176.

Shor, I. (1992). *Empowering education: Critical teaching for social change.* Chicago, IL: University of Chicago Press.

Siegler, R., Deloache, J., & Eisenberg, N. (n.d.). *How children develop* (2nd ed.).
New York, NY: Worth Publishers.

Silva, E. (2009). Measuring skills for 21st-century learning. *The Phi Delta Kappan, 90,* 630–634.

Sizemore, B. A. (1990). The politics of curriculum, race, and class. *The Journal of
Negro Education, 59,* 77–85.

Skinner, B. F. (1938). *The behavior of organisms: An experimental analysis.* Cambridge, MA: B. F. Skinner Foundation.

Slywester, R., & Cho, J. Y. (1992). What brain research says about paying attention. *Educational Leadership, 50,* 71–75.

Smeyers, P., & Depaepe, M. (2013). Making sense of the attraction of psychology: On the strengths and weaknesses for education and educational research.
In P. Smeyers & M. Depaepe (Eds.), *Educational research: The attraction of
psychology* (pp. 1–10). New York, NY: Springer.

Smith, E. (2013). The theology of education to come. In P. Smeyers & M. Depaepe
(Eds.), *Educational research: The attraction of psychology* (pp. 147–157).
New York, NY: Springer.

Smith, G., & Sobel, D. (2010). Bring it on home: The abstract and faraway don't
always sustain the interest of the young. Place and community-based education makes learning relevant. *Educational Leadership, 9,* 38–43.

Smith, G. A., & Sobel, D. (2010). *Place-and community-based education in
schools.* London, UK: Routledge.

Smyth, J. (2001). *Critical politics of teachers' work.* New York, NY: Peter
Lang.

Snowman, J., & McCown, R. (2015). *Psychology applied to teaching* (14th ed.).
Belmont, CA: Wadsworth.

Sobe, N. W. (2004). Challenging the gaze: The subject of attention and a 1915
Montessori demonstration classroom. *Educational Theory, 54,* 281–297.

Soder, R., Goodlad, J. I., & McMannon, T. J. (2001). *Developing democratic
character in the young.* San Francisco, CA: John Wiley & Sons.

Staddon, J., & Cerutti, D. (2003). Operant conditioning. *Annual Review of Psychology, 54,* 115–144.

Sternberg, R. J., & Lubart, T. I. (1991). An investment theory of creativity and its development. *Human Development*, 34, 1–31.

Stiggins, R. J. (1995). Assessment literacy for the 21st century. *Phi Delta Kappan*, 77, 238–245.

———. (2002). Assessment crisis: The absence of assessment for learning. *Phi Delta Kappan*, 83, 758–765.

Stobart, G. (2008). *Testing times: The uses and abuses of assessment*. New York, NY: Routledge.

Stringfield, S., & Herman, R. (1997). Assessment of the state of school effectiveness research in the United States of America. *School Effectiveness and School Improvement*, 7, 159–180.

Styles, E. (2006). *The psychology of attention* (2nd ed.). New York, NY: Psychology Press.

Sugarman, J. (2009). Historical ontology and psychological description. *Journal of Theoretical and Philosophical Psychology*, 29, 5–15. http://doi.org/10.1037/a0015301

———. (2014). Neo-Foucaultian approaches to critical inquiry in the psychology of education. In T. Corcoran (Ed.), *Psychology in education: Critical theory-practice* (pp. 53–69). Rotterdam, NL: Springer.

Sugarman, J., & Martin, J. (2010). Agentive hermeneutics. In S. Kirschner & J. Martin (Eds.), *The sociocultural turn in psychology: Contemporary perspectives on the contextual emergence of mind and self* (pp. 159–179). NY: Columbia University Press.

Sylwester, R., & Cho, J. Y. (December 1992/January 1993). What brain research says about paying attention. *Educational Leadership*, 50, 71–75.

Tanggaard, L., & Glăveanu, V. P. (2013). Creativity in children's lives: An unconditional good for whom? *An International Journal on Talent Development and Creativity*, 1, 25–30.

Tangney, J. P., Baumeister, R. F., & Boone, A. L. (2004). High self-control predicts good adjustment, less pathology, better grades, and interpersonal success. *Journal of Personality*, 72, 271–324.

Tavares, H. (1996). Classroom management and subjectivity: A genealogy of educational identities. *Educational Theory*, 46, 189–201.

Taylor, F. W. (1914). *The principles of scientific management*. New York, NY: Harper & Brothers Publishers.

Thompson, J. (2010). What impact do culturally competent teachers have on the social inclusiveness of their students? (Doctoral dissertation). Retrieved from ProQuest database. (AAT 3397657)

Thomson, D. M., & Tulving, E. (1970). Associative encoding and retrieval: Weak and strong cues. *Journal of Experimental Psychology*, 255–262.

Thorndike, E. (1927). The law of effect. *The American Journal of Psychology*, 39, 212–222.

Thorndike, E. L. (1898). *Animal intelligence: An experimental study of the associative processes in animals.* Lancaster, PA: The MacMillan Company.

Tindell, D. R., & Bohlander, R. W. (2012). The use and abuse of cell phones and text messaging in the classroom: A survey of college students. *College Teaching, 60,* 1–9.

Tough, P. (2013). *How children succeed: Grit, curiosity, and the hidden power of character.* Boston, MA: Houghton Mifflin Harcourt.

Treisman, A. M. (1964). Verbal cues, language and meaning in selective attention. *Cognitive Psychology,* 206–219.

Trilling, B., & Fadel, C. (2009). *21st century skills: Learning for life in our times.* San Francisco, CA: Jossey-Bass.

Twenge, J. M. (2014). *Generation me: Why today's young Americans are more confident, assertive, entitled—and more miserable than ever before.* Rev. and updated ed. New York, NY: Simon and Schuster.

United States Commission on Excellence in Education (1983). *A nation at risk: The imperative for educational reform: A report to the nation and the Secretary of Education, United States Department of Education.* Washington, DC: U.S. Department of Education. Retrieved from http://202.120.223.158/download /b42c4210-e82c-4244-aa4f-89d2b313f44a.doc

Vagle, M. D. (2012). *Not a stage! A critical re-conception of young adolescent education.* New York, NY: Peter Lang. Retrieved from http://eric.ed.gov/?id =ED531328

Vassallo, S. (2011). Implications of institutionalizing self-regulated learning: An analysis from four sociological perspectives. *Educational Studies, 47,* 26–49. http://doi.org/10.1080/00131946.2011.540984

———. (2013a). Considering class-based values related to guardian involvement and the development of self-regulated learning. *New Ideas in Psychology, 31,* 202–211. http://doi.org/http://dx.doi.org/10.1016/j.newideapsych.2011 .12.002

———. (2013b). *Self-regulated learning: An application of critical educational psychology.* New York, NY: Peter Lang.

———. (2014). The entanglement of thinking and learning skills in neoliberal discourse. In T. Corcoran (Ed.), *Psychology in Education: Critical theory-practice* (pp. 145–165). Rotterdam, NL: Springer.

Visser, S. N., Bitsko, R. H., Danielson, M. L., Perou, R., & Blumberg, S. J. (2010). Increasing prevalence of parent-reported attention deficit/hyperactivity disorder among children—United States, 2003 and 2007. *Morbidity and Morality Weekly Report, 59,* 1439–1443.

Vygotsky, L. (1978). *Mind in society: Development of higher psychological processes.* Cambridge, MA: Harvard University Press.

Wagner, R. B. (2013). *Accountability in education: A philosophical inquiry.* New York, NY: Routledge.

Walkerdine, V. (1993). Beyond developmentalism? *Theory & Psychology, 3*, 451–469.

———. (2003). Reclassifying upward mobility: Femininity and the neo-liberal subject. *Gender and Education, 15*, 237–248. http://doi.org/10.1080/095402 50303864

Watson, J. B. (1924/2009). *Behaviorism*. New Brunswick, NJ: Transaction Publishers. Retrieved from http://psycnet.apa.org/psycinfo/1931-00040-000.

Wegerif, R. (2010). *Mind expanding: Teaching for thinking and creativity in primary education*. Berkshire, UK: Open University Press.

Weiner, B. (1986). *An attributional theory of motivation and emotion*. New York, NY: Springer-Verlag.

Weininger, E. B., & Lareau, A. (2009). Paradoxical pathways: An ethnographic extension of Kohn's findings on class and childrearing. *Journal of Marriage and Family, 71*, 680–695. http://doi.org/10.1111/j.1741-3737.2009.00626.x

Weinstein, C. S., Tomlinson-Clarke, S., & Curran, M. (2003). Culturally responsive classroom management: Awareness into action. *Theory into Practice, 42*, 269–276.

———. (2004). Toward a conception of culturally responsive classroom management. *Journal of Teacher Education, 55*, 25–38.

Wentzel, K. R., & Brophy, J. E. (2014). *Motivating students to learn*. New York, NY: Routledge.

Wigfield, A., & Eccles, J. S. (2000). Expectancy–value theory of achievement motivation. *Contemporary Educational Psychology, 25*, 68–81.

Wilson, M. (2002). Six views of embodied cognition. *Psychonomic Bulletin & Review, 9*, 625–363.

Wolfgang, C. H. (2000). Another view on "Reinforcement in developmentally appropriate early childhood classrooms." *Childhood Education, 77*, 64–67.

Wolters, C. A. (2010). *Self-regulated learning and the 21st century competencies*. The William and Flora Hewlett Foundation. Retrieved from http://www .hewlett.org/library/grantee-publication/self-regulated-learning-and-21st -century-competencies

Wood, D. F. (2003). Problem based learning. *British Medical Journal, 326*, 328–330.

Woolfolk-Hoy, A. (2000). Educational psychology in teacher education. *Educational Psychologist, 35*, 257–270. http://doi.org/10.1207/S15326985EP3504_04

Woolfolk-Hoy, A., & Spero, R. B. (2005). Changes in teacher efficacy during the early years of teaching: A comparison of four measures. *Teaching and Teacher Education, 21*, 343–356.

Woolfolk-Hoy, A., & Weinstein, C. S. (2006). Students' and teachers' knowledge and beliefs about classroom management. In E. Emmer, E. Sabornie, C. M. Evertson, & C. S. Weinstein (Eds.), *Handbook of classroom management: Research, practice, and contemporary Issues* (pp. 181–219). Mahwah, NJ: Routledge.

Yisrael, S. B. (2012). *Classroom management: A guide for urban school teachers.* Lanham, MD: Rowman & Littlefield Education.

Zeidner, M., Boekaerts, M., & Pintrich, P. R. (2000). Self-regulation: Directions and challenges for future research. In M. Boekaerts, P. R. Pintrich, & M. Zeidner (Eds.), *Handbook of self-regulation* (pp. 750–768). San Diego, CA: Academic Press.

Zhao, Y. (2012). *World class learners: Educating creative and entrepreneurial students.* Thousand Oaks, CA: Corwin.

Zimmerman, B. J. (1986). Development of self-regulated learning: Which are the key subprocesses. *Contemporary Educational Psychology, 16,* 307–313.

———. (2000). Attaining self-regulation: A social cognitive perspective. In M. E. Boekaerts, P. R. Pintrich, & M. E. Zeidner (Eds.), *Handbook of self-regulation* (pp. 13–39). San Diego, CA: Academic Press.

———. (2002). Becoming a self-regulated learner: An overview. *Theory into Practice, 41,* 64–70.

Zimmerman, B. J., Bonner, S., & Kovach, R. (1996). *Developing self-regulated learners: Beyond achievement to self-efficacy.* Washington, DC: American Psychological Association.

Zimmerman, B. J., & Schunk, D. H. (1989). *Self-regulated learning and academic achievement: Theory, research, and practice* (1st ed.). New York, NY: Springer-Verlag.

———. (2001). *Self-regulated learning and academic achievement: Theoretical perspectives* (2nd ed.). New York, NY: Routledge.

Made in United States
North Haven, CT
04 February 2024

48349903R00137